Booker T. Washington and
the Adult Education Movement

University Press of Florida
Gainesville
Tallahassee
Tampa
Boca Raton
Pensacola
Orlando
Miami
Jacksonville

BOOKER T. WASHINGTON AND THE ADULT EDUCATION MOVEMENT

Virginia Lantz Denton

The University Press of Florida is the scholarly publishing agency
for the State University System of Florida, comprised of Florida
A & M University, Florida Atlantic University, Florida International
University, Florida State University, University of Central Florida,
University of Florida, University of North Florida, University of
South Florida, and University of West Florida.

Library of Congress Cataloging in Publication data appear on the last
printed page of the book.

University Press of Florida
15 Northwest 15th Street
Gainesville, FL 32611

This study is dedicated to the memory
of Booker T. Washington, 1856–1915

> Beside our way the streams are dried,
> And famine mates us side by side.
> Discouraged and reproachful eyes
> Seek once again the frowning skies.
> Yet shall there come, 'spite storm and shock,
> A Moses who shall smite the rock,
> Call manna from the Giver's hand,
> And lead us to the promised land.
> *Paul Laurence Dunbar in* Tuskegee Student, *"To Booker T. Washington"*

and to John R. Rachal, University of Southern Mississippi

CONTENTS

ILLUSTRATIONS *following page 105*

Booker T. Washington at his desk, Tuskegee Institute
First graduating class, Tuskegee Institute
Old brickyard at Tuskegee Institute
Vehicles and Cassedy Hall, Tuskegee Institute
Washington's speech at Alcorn University, 1912
Farmers' Conference at Tuskegee Institute
The Movable School, Jesup Agricultural Wagon
The Movable School, Knapp Agricultural Wagon
Teaching rural residents from Movable School
Founding of National Negro Business League, Boston, 1900
Theodore Roosevelt at Tuskegee with Washington, 1906
Washington's burial, Tuskegee Institute, 1915

Journeys

PREFACE

History is the cumulative record of our journeys—of people, civilizations, and nations. Whether novice or scholar, we all are participants,
able to share its lessons. Booker T. Washington's journey began in
slavery in 1856 and carried him through the crucible of assimilation in a
predominantly white society to towering world influence when he died
in 1915. In this work we revisit his indelible footprints in history relating
to his contributions in adult education and social change. An innovator,
he was the first black educator to bring education to the masses of
freedmen after the Civil War, thus facilitating their acculturation into
the American mainstream. A skilled interracial interpreter as well,
Washington was uniquely honored to have an entire era named for him:
"The Age of Booker T. Washington."

During the short span of his life, a maturing nation stumbled toward
its precarious democracy and a nebulous creed of justice in the late 1800s
and early 1900s. As the national focus became more democratic, the
education of adults proliferated, bringing social change. The common
man had greater access to education through night schools, land grant
colleges, industrial training, agricultural and extension education, and
the expansion of public schools. The first public efforts to educate the
freedmen were instigated by the northern military, by philanthropic
groups such as the American Missionary Association, and by the short-
lived Freedmen's Bureau. These seeds would spread to the Americanization movement and also benefit the influx of immigrants at the turn of

the century. Even prior to the Civil War, however, there had been what Carter Woodson called the "heyday" of education for blacks in the 1700s before repressive legislation was enacted in most states. His pioneer book, *The Education of the Negro Prior to 1861*, reported many examples of adult education in a period that is generally neglected in adult education history. Washington praised the book, expressing surprise that earlier schools for industrial training had existed and that his people had tried to provide education for themselves since revolutionary times (Sept. 21, 1915, *BTW Papers*, vol. 13, p. 367).

Just when adult education emerged as a delineated, professional field of study or movement is debatable. Some argue that the national movement began with the founding of the American Association for Adult Education in 1926. Others contend that adult education is the process of adults learning, whether in random or organized activities that use a variety of settings and methods for individuals or groups. When an entire race of freedmen, including large numbers of adults, quickly filled every night school, every schoolhouse, *adult education* appears to be the only applicable term. In its broadest sense, the one I've subscribed to, adult education includes all the experiences of mature men and women in which new skills, knowledge, values, and interests are enhanced, combining the various processes of social change, culture, production, politics, and service. Malcolm S. Knowles concluded in *Modern Practice of Adult Education* that "the education of adults has been a cultural function since ancient times" (p. 25).

My discovery of Booker T. Washington as an adult educator came unexpectedly and belatedly when I happened to read his classic, *Up from Slavery*, as an older doctoral student in adult education. Reading late at night, I recall my initial excitement at being transported to another time and place, engrossed in his vivid imagery and unique phrasing that would become so familiar to me during my subsequent years of research. During a second reading, I found myself underlining his frequent references to adults, night school, and other terms of my studies, and the realization dawned that here was an adult educator of the first order. How had I missed this man in all my years of schooling, and why was there no record of him in existing histories of adult education? Reflections on these incongruities initiated my private journey to Tuskegee and the rich discoveries of the past—not as an erudite historian but as a kindred spirit in education, teaching in public secondary schools.

Driving eastward on Highway 80 on a blistering July day in 1986, I wrestled with many perplexities about Washington and history, trying to articulate a clear statement of purpose for my journey to Tuskegee Institute. A biblical phrase kept filtering through my mind as the melting tar oozed over the hot asphalt pavement and the dry farmlands of Alabama lay thirsting for rain on either side: "What went ye out for to see?" Reconciling the past with our postmodern present, where Washington seemed buried and forgotten, was like looking for a needle in a haystack, I thought.

Some months earlier, I had made a similar journey to Hampton Institute in Virginia. Why had I been surprised to find a modern, twentieth-century university sitting unruffled on the banks of the Hampton River, caught up in the trends and technology of our modern age? The few remaining traces of Samuel Armstrong or Washington or the anxious first controversial efforts to build this place were subdued, mute, resting on long shelves of the archives where I worked during warm summer days. In the cool lingering twilight I rested, with Armstrong's Mansion House behind me. Watching lights dance on water where the first few Indians had been brought in the dark hours of early morning to study with Armstrong, I searched for voices of the past to articulate their purpose. Once the vision and intensity of one man, Armstrong, had literally wrested this university from the mosquito-infested swamps and a country unsure about the educability of freedmen. One of the few to believe in their equal capacities, now he seemed to be lost in time, denigrated in some quarters as a racist along with an "Uncle Tom" Washington.

Stopping for coffee at McDonald's, another postmodern symbol, I heard the busy bustle of Selma, Alabama. Images of a less-distant past mixed with plastic coffee cups and the pungent odors of hamburgers "to go": scenes of Martin Luther King, Jr., and the long march from Selma to Montgomery, printed indelibly on modern minds through the technology of television. Comparing King with Washington, I wondered then—and even more now—how a nation could so honor its King and forget its Washington, not even honoring the hundred-year mark of his birth. Both were peaceful men: one, a preacher, the other, an educator. One had led peaceful marches, but Washington had led generations of freedmen into the mainstream of American life through education, agitating as well for their legal and social justice. I recalled a letter

Washington had written nearly a hundred years earlier, protesting to Selma officials about discrimination to blacks who were denied coffee. Is our forgetfulness or denial, in reality, only an ignorance of what has gone before us? Washington's revolution had been launched against illiteracy and economic dependency; he believed as H. M. Kallen did that "education is the first resort as well as the last, for a worldwide solution of the problem of freedom."

Characteristic of his inimitable style with words, Washington referred to the revolution he started for the education of adults at Tuskegee as "a strange and altogether new movement." Educated himself by methods of adult education, he expanded them as a young educator in Malden, West Virginia; on the staff at Hampton Institute he participated in the experimental program of Indian education and led Hampton's first night school. It was at Tuskegee, however, where significant innovations commenced, benefiting every segment of the adult population and spreading across Alabama, the nation, and world. He placed high value on the uncommon good sense of the older population, however illiterate, and his "strange new movement" involved extension education to large masses of rural adults. If they could not come to Tuskegee, then he chose to go to them. An integral part of his times, he was also ahead of them with such currently popular concepts in adult education as night school, industrial education, agriculture extension, interracial education, women's education, family and health education, mass communication, distance and international education, mentoring, social intervention, political activism, and empowerment. The philosophy and programs of Booker T. Washington in the late 1800s were in surprising harmony with modern practices of adult education.

Washington's skill as an interracial interpreter was largely responsible for his success in facilitating social change during his time and place. After his Atlanta Exposition speech in 1895, the unknown principal from Tuskegee moved from obscurity to national and international arenas. He was trusted for his common sense, realistic judgments, and spirit of cooperation, bringing Tuskegee influences to bear on presidents, politics, and international affairs. Working secretly and openly, he effected social and political improvements, giving blacks a stronger voice in education, economics, government, civil rights, and the press.

An alert and shrewd bargainer, Washington brought great philanthropy to the South to bridge the gap of unequal public funds; he extended rural education, assisted black colleges, and laid the groundwork for more equality in public education. It was Washington who helped to secure the important Jeanes Fund, Rosenwald schools, Carnegie libraries, and YMCAs. He also had a great impact on the Peabody and Slater funds because J. L. M. Curry, general agent, adhered to Washington's pragmatic methods and philosophy of education.

When Andrew Carnegie, the steel magnate and philanthropist, gave Booker T. Washington a considerable sum in 1903 to maintain his family, he viewed Washington as "the foremost of living men" because of the uniqueness of his work. To Carnegie, Washington was a "modern Moses who leads and lifts his race through Education" (*BTW Papers*, vol. 7, p. 120). Carnegie was as optimistic as Washington that the racial problems in the South would be solved by education and that America's future would be progressively democratic, and he was correct in these assessments. Washington placed great faith in the American idea and creed but, like Moses, he would be denied entrance to the promised land of full civil rights. The most he could hope for was to lay a firm and realistic foundation in education and economic improvements, largely through adult education, upon which his race could build in succeeding generations born in freedom.

Carnegie had also prophesied that history would "know two Washingtons, one white, the other black, both Fathers of their People." In this respect, Carnegie was wrong. Infighting among his fellow blacks and too many negative portrayals of Washington as a compromiser with white supremacy, an accommodationist with expediency, and a Tuskegee Machine who misused his power have, unfortunately, obscured the magnitude of his work, relegating him to mere footnotes of irrelevance. Washington has no place on our calendar of holidays, and modern students are more likely to study the literary canon of the restless intellectual W. E. B. Du Bois, who turned to communism and left the United States. A vociferous contemporary of Washington's, Du Bois was recently cited as one of a hundred outstanding men of his century, and Carnegie would have found some provocative irony in that. Even George Washington Carver, whose achievements Washington made possible, is more revered perhaps than his mentor, as indicated by current name recognition.

Washington's journey, however, was unparalleled, bringing momentous social change to the masses through adult education. On a personal level, my journey of discovery through his life and times has been rewarding. I appreciate the guidance of my doctoral committee at the University of Southern Mississippi during the early stages of this project. John Rachal's keen interest in history initially inspired it, and his encouragement helped to insure its completion. I thank also many unnamed people in many libraries. The archivists and their staffs at Hampton University and Tuskegee University, in particular, have always provided abundant assistance, and I am grateful.

All photographs are from the Tuskegee Archives and are used with permission granted by Dr. Daniel Williams, Archivist. Halftones were prepared by Silvia Simpson, Hawkins Studio, Tuskegee, Alabama.

And finally but most important, a million tender blessings to Mom Lantz, John, and Georgia at the beginning and to Pete, Lynne, and Denny at the end.

PROLOGUE
TO FREEDOM

"Early One Morning before Day"

1

I pity from the bottom of my heart any nation or body of people that is so
unfortunate as to get entangled in the net of slavery.
Booker T. Washington, Up from Slavery, *p. 16*

Educators in the 1990s, poised on the threshold of the twenty-first
century, are perhaps as precariously situated as a Booker T. Washington. Laden with old problems, escalating new social ills, and unprecedented modern technology, they nevertheless must search for an equalizing hope in the approaching century in ways analogous to slaves set
free after the Civil War.

Over a century ago, Washington approached a similar and strategic
crossroads, traversing that span from slavery to freedom. It was the
dawn of a new age, called "The Age of Booker T. Washington" on the
strength of one man's imprint on the events of history. Looking back,
Washington recalled that his awareness of enslavement and impending
freedom came "early one morning before day." The child Booker had
heard his mother's prayers, uttered in the half-light of dawn, for the
success of Lincoln's army and freedom for slaves. Like educators
moving to a new century, Washington and other freedmen were encumbered with vestiges of a lingering past, unexpected problems, and the
blessings of their precarious new freedom, searching for an equalizing
hope in emancipation.

The milieu of slavery and Reconstruction after a devastating Civil
War was the only inheritance that a nation, founded on purely American
notions of equal justice for all, had to offer Booker T. Washington and

other freedmen. It was an era of unparalleled social change, and it would take a person like Washington to funnel its Cyclopean energy into a progressive democratization for a disfranchised people through the process of adult education. A maelstrom of physical, social, economic, political, constitutional, and moral altercations was brewing at his birth in 1856 and would continue far beyond his death in 1915. Staking his claim to the American dream, Washington shouldered, as well, the responsibilities of leadership intrinsic to that dream, choosing to fight its obstacles on the terrain he knew and loved, the South. Confronting the problems, he relished the challenge, as typified by his Carnegie Hall speech in 1906: "It is good to live in an age when unfortunate and backward races are to be helped, when great and fundamental questions are to be met and solved. For my part, I would find no interest in living in an age where there were no weak members of the human family to be helped, no wrongs to be righted. Men grow strong in proportion as they reach down to help others up."[1]

Although his birth marks the start of the Washington era, it was only a prelude to the perplexing problems of slavery and its lingering aftermath. Entangled in the net, as Washington put it, a divided nation would begin its wrangling about how to free itself. President Abraham Lincoln, the U.S. Congress, and self-serving, sectional advocates would escalate their arguments over the Constitution, states' rights, and the entangling dilemma of holding people in human bondage in opposition to a professed national creed of justice. It is ironic, in retrospect, that Lincoln, often called the Great Emancipator and eulogized as such by Booker T. Washington and many blacks, was at first more predisposed to the notion of colonization, looking for countries like Haiti and Liberia where freedmen could be relocated; it was a solution that Washington himself would abhor and discourage. A southerner by birth, like Washington, but opposed to the institution of slavery, Lincoln was unable to shake off his ingrained sympathies for the South and often proposed that southern slaveholders should be justly compensated for any loss of their "property." What emerged from such bitter and sectional wrangling were the physical altercations of the Civil War, some provisional success of Lincoln's Emancipation Proclamation, and the ultimate surrender of the South's beleaguered forces and obstinate rebellion at Appomattox on April 9, 1865. Prophesied earlier by Kentucky's John C. Breckinridge, the "loosing of all bonds" was accomplished when the Thirteenth

Amendment was ratified in December 1865; under the Constitution, all slavery and involuntary servitude were abolished in the United States and its areas of jurisdiction.[2]

Neither sword nor law could arbitrate the intrinsic moral issues of slavery, however, and they would grip the nation's conscience. As Gunnar Myrdal assessed it nearly a century later, "The American Negro problem is a problem in the heart of America. It is there that the interracial tension has its focus. It is there that the decisive struggle goes on."[3] Analyzing the "American Dilemma" in 1944, Myrdal viewed the major conflict of the entangling net of slavery as a moral one, an anomaly in the very structure of American society "to the ordinary white man in the North as well as in the South."[4] Two of Myrdal's major conclusions closely paralleled frequent arguments of Booker T. Washington in the late 1800s and early 1900s: any form of slavery, "in spite of all rationalization, was irreconcilably contrary to the American Creed,"[5] and, second, the white man's burden of slavery did not rest on the South alone but was an integral part of the "whole complex of problems in the larger American civilization."[6]

Inheriting such "great and fundamental questions" to be met and solved, Washington would always view the circumstances, timing, and geography of his origins as a challenge to positive leadership rather than a curse. It was an exciting age, with weak members of the human family to be lifted up and led and many wrongs to be righted. Strengthened by his adversities, Washington was uniquely qualified to lead, with an uncommonly broad perspective of the nation's racial maladies and a prophetic vision of the implementation of the American creed. A facilitator of progressive and positive change through the process of adult education, he would bridge the gap between blacks and whites, between South and North, and between "equal" and "unequal" in such significant areas as educational opportunities and funding, the ownership of land and agriculture, problems of housing and family relationships, the justice system and its laws, and the gaping distance between the dreaming and the American dream itself.

If the South of his birth had bequeathed the challenge of obstacles, it had also been the source of Washington's unique racial vision, understanding, determination, and later skills of interracial interpretation and cooperation. His unequivocal and lifelong southern inclinations often confounded his contemporary and future critics, and some viewed his interracial efforts as "Uncle Tom" compromises to white supremacy, not cooperation. The origins of Washington's spirit of cooperation have, therefore, been ignored or obscured, and some reflection on these origins is necessary and beneficial. Unlike many of his critics, Washington had a firsthand knowledge of the South and of the complexities of slavery. More importantly, he experienced many personal and beneficial contacts with all levels of a white society, and these contacts facilitated his understanding of the realities of the South. The first of these valuable contacts was his "old Marster," James Burroughs, in Franklin County, Virginia, where the practice of slavery did not predominate.

Burroughs had little to do with the stereotypical and popular plantation myth. In reality, he was a raw-boned yeoman farmer who raised fourteen children in a small, unpretentious farmhouse with only five rooms; he was over sixty years old when Washington was born in 1856. The 1860 census listed Burroughs with some 200 acres and six slaves, including Washington's mother, Jane, older brother, John, younger sister, Amanda, and "Bowker" (later changed to Booker). Burroughs's small slaveholding of only one intact family was still an anomaly in the greater South and especially in mountainous southwestern Virginia, largely inhabited by poor whites who barely eked out their existence on hilly, sharecropped soil.[7]

Contrary to the plantation myth perpetuated by only a few large plantations and exaggerated in the fiction of literature and films, most slaves were concentrated in the hands of a relative few. *At least three-fourths of the white population in the South in 1860 did not own any slaves;* nor did they have any economic interest in the holding of slaves or the plantation system, according to historian John Hope Franklin. Of the South's eight million whites in 1860, only 384,884 owned slaves, and more than 200,000 of these had five or fewer slaves.[8] Washington's first contact with whites through the Burroughs family was therefore one of experience with the greater reality in the heart of the South—poverty, illiteracy, ingrained "rednecked" prejudices, and struggling farmers like Burroughs, all far removed from the popular plantation myth encouraged by the enormous influence and power of the relatively few large plantations with the majority of slave holdings.

All available records seem to indicate that the physical and cultural life of the Burroughs family was not much better than the status of their few slaves. From their shared labors, a family closeness developed, and Washington left them harboring no bitterness and maintained cordial relations with several family members. He recalled that the Burroughs family had worked in the fields with his family; there was no stereotypical "overseer" or cruel slavebeater on the Burroughs farm. He also reported that the house and its premises were generally in a state of disrepair and that the "big house," revisited in adulthood, was much smaller than he remembered it. Having played and worked with the Burroughs boys, Washington shared the family's grief over their losses during the Civil War, which represented the experience of all the South and nation caught up in the power and politics of the entangling net of slavery.

Beyond the yeoman Burroughs family, other contacts would expand Washington's view of the South's white society and facilitate his subsequent interracial leadership. Shortly after he was freed and working in West Virginia, Viola Ruffner became Washington's first white mentor and his lifelong friend. She was his initial introduction into that handful of the South's true gentry, characterized by inherited wealth, inbred culture, and genteel refinements lacking in the Burroughs family. Viola encouraged young Booker's first steps toward literacy and demonstrated the social expectations of her upper echelon of society, with which he would later deal. On a deeper level, General Armstrong of Hampton Institute proved to be Washington's most significant white mentor and served as the model for his Tuskegee work. From these two invaluable contacts, Washington had early access into that largess of intelligent and genuinely benevolent whites who worked unselfishly to correct the wrongs of slavery.

It was with the dark side of the popular plantation myth, however, that Washington would have continuous contacts, facilitating his understanding of southern life, its deeper pathologies, and, consequently, the South itself. I. A. Newby identified that large and multiplying segment of poor whites in the South as the "amorphous" social class; they were an integral part of history, and a greater knowledge of their story would "cast unexpected light on the nature of southern life, especially its pathologies." According to Newby, this amorphous class consisted of two groups: one, whites who were simply poor, encompassing landless farmers, agricultural workers, unskilled laborers, dependent artisans, and indentured servants; and, two, the lowest class, known as "poor whites," about whom not much is known because their story has not been fully explicated in interpretive histories of the South.[9] Poor whites were more often relegated to Tobacco Road, shorn of any mythical qualities, and shrouded in obscurity and prejudice. These groups comprised the 80 percent of the South's white population that did not own even one slave but continued to live meagerly by tilling the soil, hunting, and trapping. With four million freedmen after 1865, poor whites would clamor also for the justice and literacy and jobs that had been denied them, commanding Washington's attention and understanding.

Lillian Smith, like Newby, has addressed the deep chasm that developed between rich and poor whites in the South, growing deeper and deeper as the "sweat of more and more slaves poured in it." On one side of the chasm were the few rich planters; on the other side were the 80 percent of poorer whites who lost favor with the planter class, becoming a target of the rich in their speeches and writing. The large amorphous class of poor whites acquired labels such as "poor white trash," "crackers," "rednecks," "hillbillies," and "pecker-woods"—all as derogatory and personally offensive as the term "nigger" was to the black man. As they had done to the Negro, Smith reported, the rich planter class "wrote off the man who lived on Tobacco Road as a liability to democracy."[10]

Washington himself could not write the poor whites off so easily. In his efforts to find jobs and education and justice for his race, he had to compete with their anger and prejudice at every junction. In Hale's Ford, Virginia, poor whites had surrounded the Burroughs farm, living in poverty, illiteracy, and hardships fairly comparable to the existence of slaves. In the salt and coal mines of Malden, West Virginia, Washington's poor white neighbors clustered in dirty shacks, cursing and clamoring for poor wages and dirty jobs. They would hover, too, in the shops and fields near Hampton Institute, deriding every effort to provide education for freedmen. And in the Black Belt of Alabama, the center of Washington's work, poor whites would compete for every job and dollar, asserting their claims above the freedmen and demanding Washington's recognition of their plight, which he frequently acknowledged with perceptive empathy.

Just as his varied contacts with all levels of the South's white society and its underlying pathologies had facilitated his unique skills of interracial leadership, in equal proportion from Hale's Ford he had also learned valuable lessons of survival and independence and an ingrained appreciation for the South's natural beauty and inherent possibilities for his people. In this rural crossroads village isolated from city influences and the larger commercialization of slavery, young Booker witnessed a sturdy, hard-working people who had maintained their independence of thought and livelihood through agriculture, various shops, and small industries. Hale's Ford had a thriving tobacco industry that processed the area's main cash crop into snuff and chewing tobacco. Slave skills were utilized in the tobacco industry, blacksmith shops, sawmills, gristmills, brandy distilleries, saddle shops, tanneries, and carpentry shops, where the region's abundant timber was used for wagons, furniture, and cabinets. Such skills learned in Hale's Ford and across the South would be valuable assets to the freedmen, giving them an advantage over the mass of poor whites who were as illiterate as the slaves and also generally unskilled. A microcosm for the rest of the South, Hale's Ford served as Washington's example for the economic freedom possible for his race through agriculture, small industries, and an enterprising spirit. The people of Hale's Ford lived simply and quietly with the ebb and flow of seasons, making economic use of their abundant natural resources while also enjoying the rustic pleasures of hunting, fishing, and communal projects such as quiltings and hog-killings. The older Washington envisioned and advocated a comparable environment for his race, removed from the crime and crowds and greater competition of cities.[11]

It was in Hale's Ford, too, where Washington gained an early appreciation for the values of family and education. More fortunate than many slaves, Booker had been blessed with an intact family, with the one exception of having a white father who never contributed to his life and whose identity Washington never acknowledged publicly. From the lifelong inspiration of his mother, Jane, young Booker learned lasting lessons of courage, perseverance, resourcefulness, and positive concepts, which influenced many tenets of his later philosophy and attitudes about women and family. Brother John would prove to be a staunch coworker at Tuskegee Institute, and sister Amanda maintained close relationships with her brothers. Even though their mother "was totally ignorant, so far as mere book knowledge was concerned," Washington said, she had mastered every difficult situation with a large fund of common sense and encouraged her children's ambitions and efforts toward literacy, which was denied them in slavery. "If I had done anything in life worth attention," Washington concluded, "I feel sure that I inherited the disposition from my mother."[12]

If they were largely isolated and unsophisticated in their rustic setting, the people of Hale's Ford and surrounding Franklin County had placed an uncommon degree of importance on education, according to available records. Adult education was transpiring in the homes, the fields, the shops, and the small industries, as valuable skills were taught and passed on. Sunday schools and Bible training occurred in the churches—mostly Baptist, with some Methodist and a few Presbyterian. Children, with greater access to schooling than their parents, helped to transfer knowledge from the classroom to the home. Laura Burroughs, for example, acquired enough formal schooling to become a teacher, possibly at the "Frog Pond" school a few miles from the Burroughs farm. Washington later recalled that he had sometimes accompanied Laura to and from her school, and this early experience had inspired his initial yearning to enter the classroom, a privilege denied him that served to whet his appetite for knowledge.

Settled in 1785, Franklin County was off the main trail of exploration and slower to develop any system of education than nearby areas. By 1829, however, the Literary Fund of Virginia was distributing its moneys on the basis of population to the various localities, and Franklin County was operating some free public schools in 1832. Several private schools and "old field" schools were scattered throughout the county. Located in open fields or in improvised, inexpensive structures, the old field schools were conducted primarily for poor people by villagers with only minimal qualifications. The Hale's Ford vicinity had some twenty one-teacher common schools, and Laura Burroughs possibly attended one of them. With meager facilities, these schools were open for sessions of three or four months, and Laura's existing letters reflect the limitations of her rudimentary education, however inspiring it appeared to the eager child Booker. In one letter, she boasted incorrectly of having "learned" Washington his letters. In spite of its scattered but persistent efforts to provide schools for the more privileged whites, however, Franklin County was still largely illiterate in the late 1800s, as reported by historian Marshall Wingfield. The majority of its rural population consisted of poor whites who were generally as illiterate as the county's comparatively few slaves; illiteracy also extended to country preachers, village leaders, and yeoman farmers.[13]

It was in the environment of this obscure village that the young Booker T. Washington first formulated his vision of the world. It was a vision framed by firsthand experience with the greater realities of the South and its people. Juxtaposed, in startling contrasts, were the conflicting elements of poverty and abundance, of obstacles and opportunities, of prejudice and conciliation, and of old bondage and impending freedom.[14]

☞ Washington had spent nine years in slavery, with the last five years surrounded by the physical, political, economic, and moral maelstrom of the Civil War. It was a period crucial to his total development and later philosophy. According to such child psychologists as Arnold Gesell, many fundamental tasks are learned during the first five years of life, with more complex concepts being mastered from ages five to ten. Motor behavior is acquired before age five, with such adaptive behavior as self-initiated learning and resourcefulness in adjusting to new situations, as well as exploitative behavior and intelligence. Language behavior evolves from signs and gestures to words and comprehension. Personal-social behavior emerges to include reactions to people, response to speech, socialized learning, and habits of self-help.

From five to ten, according to Gesell, the child undergoes the complex processes of fear, sense of self, and interpersonal relations, as well as an accompanying ethical sense and philosophic outlook. While children are certainly not philosophers in an articulate sense, they spontaneously develop "notions about natural phenomena which bear striking analogy to the concepts of the early philosophers of ancient Greece," Gesell concluded. The child also acquires the sense of physical causality. "Even in infancy, long before the age of five, he thinks thoughts which once constituted major achievements in the mental evolution of the race," Gesell further contended.[15]

Defining philosophy as the systemized knowledge of general science that integrates all science, Gesell observed that "at its highest levels it is a codification of man's reflections on his relations to the universe." Children also find modes of expression for their knowable world. "They have intellectual orientations and tendencies which constitute the essence of a philosophy in the making. It is difficult to draw a line between a complete and an incomplete philosophy, because even at adult levels no final philosophy has been achieved."[16] Gesell viewed the child between the ages of five and ten as an "embryonic philosopher" having basic ideas intact often before the age of five. Without codifying concepts, children have their characteristic ways of thinking and acting.

Robert J. Havighurst followed similar lines of reasoning, and adult educators have generally subscribed to his developmental tasks. In delineating those tasks of infancy and early childhood (ages one to six) and of middle childhood (ages six to twelve), Havighurst underscored the significance of personal, physical, attitudinal, social, and ethical concepts that have their roots in the first twelve years of life.[17] Concerning democratic and social attitudes, Havighurst argued that children acquire their concepts of social groups and institutions from three sources: through imitation of people with prestige in the eyes of the learner; from the collection and combination of pleasant or unpleasant experiences associated with a given object or situation; and from a single, deeply emotional experience, pleasant or unpleasant, associated with a given object or situation.[18]

Before the age of six, according to Havighurst, the child has no clearly articulated attitudes concerning religion, race or color, politics, economic systems, social classes, or occupational groups. Before the age of twelve, however, the situation changes, as the same child completes a full complement of social attitudes picked up from his family, teachers, peer group, and community or world. "Once he has a store of social attitudes, there is little reason for him to change them. He knows how to act, what discriminations to make, what people to favor and whom to disfavor. Unless he finds these attitudes to be grossly unpopular as he grows older, or to get him into difficulties, he is likely to retain them through life."[19]

Occurring at particular periods in the child's life, various developmental tasks are used to facilitate and amplify succeeding tasks. Successful achievement at each stage helps to determine future success. "If the task is not achieved at the proper time, it will not be achieved well, and failure in this task will cause partial or complete failure in achievement of other tasks yet to come," Havighurst contended.[20] The "teachable moment" occurs when "the body is ripe, and society requires, and the self is ready to achieve a certain task," he concluded.[21]

According to Gesell and Havighurst, the nine years that Washington spent in slavery were crucial to his development, crystallizing much of his ideology and temperament. Any fair assessment of his life and work must incorporate the significance of these developmental years because their great impact initiated many tenets of the philosophy that characterized and underpinned his pioneer educational programs for black adults in the United States and other countries. Like the soil that the farmer carefully prepares in early spring for the distribution of seeds, Washington's earth bed of ideology had been roughly plowed during the years of slavery, to be smoothed and furrowed and fertilized for the subsequent germination of seeds in his articulated philosophy and pragmatic programs. With deep roots, the most significant of his ideologies were part and parcel of Washington's fiber, as solid as rocks, to be preached in his private and public pronouncements, practiced at Tuskegee, and promulgated throughout the world.

A witness and active participant in the struggles of freedmen, Washington clearly articulated the foremost tenet of his philosophy in his ground-floor concept of social change.[22] Regardless of race or color, people must initiate their journeys on the ground floor, working their way up through the slow, complex process of change. They cannot expect to enter the mainstream of established organizations or societies on the eighth floor. For his own people, suppressed in slavery through centuries of cultural lag, Washington pioneered the hierarchy-of-needs principle that Abraham H. Maslow popularized a century later in *Motivation and Personality*. In the Washington hierarchy, education was salvation, second only to freedom itself. Like Maslow, he believed that survival and safety needs must be accomplished before the more complex needs of belonging, esteem, and self-actualization can be realized. Literacy and occupational proficiency would facilitate the ownership of homes, land, and businesses; subsequently, the race's economic independence would facilitate an imperative toward social and political freedom. For a person having no job or home to study Latin and Greek was the proverbial "cart-before-the-horse" inanity, as Washington viewed it.[23] In this respect, it is an inexplicable and incongruous irony that some modern scholars have legitimized Maslow's hierarchy of needs while at the same time renouncing Washington's advocacy of the same principles a century earlier. Neither Maslow nor Washington advocated that anyone or any race should remain on the bottom rung of the ladder; self-actualization was achieved progressively, they believed, by meeting basic needs and moving to higher levels.

In the shattered postwar economy of the South still saturated with old prejudices and with legions of poor whites also clamoring for jobs, Washington's early and persistent view of economic imperatives was based on solid pragmatism. He witnessed the bleak conditions of southern blacks and poor whites. To compete, people must be trained, and the nature of this training should be determined by the availability of jobs.[24] Trained minds and skilled hands were needed in education, agriculture, business and industry, medicine, and other professions throughout the South and nation; with the scarcity of available jobs and the disproportionate numbers seeking them, however, rigorous appropriate training and quality workmanship were all the more essential for freedmen, who were barred from jobs in mines and the textile industry on the presumption of illiteracy and incompetence. Negros had been brought to America against their will and had already acclimated themselves to its culture and economy. They had, in one sense, earned the full rights of citizenship and opportunity under the Constitution, but the hard fact of the case was that they would have to carve out their niche of economic opportunities and racial independence over and over again, substantiating their ability to produce quality goods and services. While Washington maintained that economic independence through education and training would lay claim to a fair share of the American creed for his race, he certainly had no illusions about the difficulty of the passage through the great American crucible to secure it. A prophet of the possible, however, Washington fiercely opposed any suggestion of colonization for freedmen outside the United States, promoting instead a bedrock foundation of education and economic viability and an equitable share of the American dream in the country they had helped to build.[25]

A dyed-in-the-wool southerner by birth and orientation, Washington believed that a southern strategy was not only possible and plausible but preferred for the first generations of freedmen. If such a strategy often confused his northern critics, Washington's rationale was nevertheless based on his shrewd observation and interpretation of the moving tides of history, later substantiated by Gunnar Myrdal's intensive study of the racial dilemma in America. Great civilizations had been launched in successful agriculture, and a hitherto landless, homeless people must stake their claim and establish a solid agrarian independence, he urgently contended, extending his view of rural self-sufficiency from that isolated crossroads of America, Hale's Ford, Virginia.[26] Freedmen had lived in the South and were acclimated to its soil and seasons and sentiments; he staunchly maintained that initially they were better suited to and better off in the South, where land was available and natural resources were abundant. Discouraging massive migrations of freedmen from the South, Washington viewed the large cities as cesspools of temptation, offering fewer jobs and opportunities. He also saw the North not as a haven for an uprooted, landless, unskilled people but rather as an extension of old prejudices and similar exclusions in industry, social life, and politics. He often joked that he had to go North to find out how bad things were in the South and blamed newspaper headlines that harped on the bad news while ignoring the good news coming out of the region.[27] It was toward the positive progress, the good news, that Washington directed his personal, financial, and professional energies at Tuskegee: breaking the bondage of illiteracy; training minds and hands for productive occupations and professions; abolishing peonage farming with its attendant poverty and dependency; and the urgent progressing of his race toward democratization. Against the obstacles of discrimination, prejudice, and white supremacism, Washington proved that his southern strategy was viable, disputing the charges by adversaries that his objectives merely fostered a new form of slavery. During the Washington era, the ownership of land and farms by freedmen reached its peak, and the chains of illiteracy and peonage farming were broken. Opportunities toward self-sufficiency were expanded in education, industry, business, health, housing, agriculture, and civil rights.[28]

From the peculiar institution of slavery Washington had also emerged with a strong sense of self and an unshakable affirmation of his race. His optimistic faith and racial pride filtered through every tenet of his ideology and elevated his leadership to a unique realm of greatness. Unencumbered by doubt, bitterness, or apology, he viewed the past as a stepping-stone to achievement and the present as his supreme challenge. A resolute ambassador of goodwill and social change, he carried the message of possibilities not obstacles, of success not failure, and of the promise of the future not the shadows of the past. He privately and propitiously pruned the tangled undergrowth of stumbling blocks, but he publicly praised and promoted the achievements of his race to large audiences across the country from the copious statistics compiled at Tuskegee.[29] An influential writer and speaker, Washington was the first black leader to harness effectively the power of the press for informing and persuading, thus fostering improved communication among blacks and whites. Fundamental to his racial pride and lifelong persuasion toward interracial cooperation was an ardent faith that redemption from the past was possible through the cathartic winds of change.[30] If those currents were slow, painful, and erratic, ultimately blocking his full claim to the promised land of civil rights at his death in 1915, Washington could measure, however, with great pride and confidence the long distance that freedmen had traveled from their starting gate of emancipation.[31]

Although redemption from the long night of slavery had come on that spring morning in 1865, the new day of freedom, welcomed with such wild exhilaration, would soon turn to one of fear, uncertainty, frustrations, and unexpected hardships. Illiterate, disorganized, and unprepared for the responsibilities of freedom, the Washington family and some four million other newly freed slaves had thrust upon them the ageless dilemma of trying to balance their high expectations with precarious realities. For many, the sweet nectar of freedom would sour, clabbering in the head-on confrontation with what Washington called the "great questions of the Anglo-Saxon race." Without tools or literacy, the freedmen had to assume the burdens that accompanied their freedom: finding jobs; building homes, schools, churches, and communities; and launching an entire race into that nebulous dawn of freedom where white supremacy and old prejudices raced to greet them. On the new day of freedom, a hot midday sun would illuminate the harsh realities that dogged their every step on the hazardous journey to that new place: a country hardly flowing with milk and honey but to the freedmen, nevertheless, the long-promised land.

FREEDOM
The Great Questions of
the Anglo-Saxon Race

2

The poor Negro, besotted with ignorance, & so full of freedom, looking forward
to January as to some day of Jubilee approaching, with all the difficulties and
dangers of a free man's life to encounter, & none of the experience or sense
necessary to enable him successfully to battle with them.
Letter from Augustine Smythe to his mother, quoted in Joel Williamson,
"The Meaning of Freedom," p. 201

My chil'n so hungry dey can't hole up. De Guv'ment, he han't gib we nottin'.
Said dey would put we on Board Saturday. Some libs and some dies. If dey libs
dey libs, and if dey dies dey dies.
Old woman freed in South Carolina, quoted in Williamson, p. 206

Lost in the grandiloquent speeches and stormy debates, largely predisposed toward sectional expedience, was the essential question: What
would happen to the slaves once their freedom was secured? Aside from
random colonization plans, the federal government had advanced no
other central proposal. On this point, at least, there is general consensus
among historians: The great tragedy of the period from 1860 to 1866 was
the failure to ensure the slaves' legitimate passage into freedom. This
miscarriage may have resulted from the turmoil of war that clouded
national vision or from some subconscious phobia about the South's
eventual success that would obviate any settlement of the slave question,
but the cause remains unexplained. Although never prone to criticize
the federal government as liberator, Washington lashed out against this
debacle of postwar chaos in his autobiography, speaking of education
but implying other failures. As a child and even in manhood, "I had the
feeling that it was cruelly wrong in the central government, at the

beginning of our freedom, to fail to make some provision for the general education of our people" that would better prepare them "for the duties of citizenship."[1]

In the beginning, the Union army (and later officers of the Treasury Department) inherited the contraband problem. Scattered throughout the South and commissioned to conduct a victorious war, the Union forces initially lacked the authority or wherewithal to handle the mass of deserting slaves. Often castigated for their mismanagement of contra-bands, the soldiers from the North, engaged in no missionary expedition like the benevolent associations soon to come, were expected to feed, clothe, house, heal, and administer to both the work and the educational needs of their often unwelcome charges. By the thousands, the penni-less, ignorant, and often hungry and sick contrabands were turning up at Union camps long before the war ended in 1865 with barely the shirts on their backs, and the numbers multiplied after cessation, as the former slaves looked toward their emancipators for salvation. As the northern military officers struggled with conflicting personal and regional mind-sets in devising plans to alleviate the suffering of the freedmen, the northerners often welcomed the assistance offered by benevolent associ-ations like the American Missionary Association and the subsequent federally sponsored Freedmen's Bureau. For adult education, this pe-riod of flux and testing, pregnant with opportunity, proved to be one of unprecedented challenge, physical danger, and professional growth as the various philanthropic groups ministered to both the physical suffer-ing of the freedmen and their massive thirst for literacy. Without such assistance, many of the freedmen would no doubt have been forced back into their old bondage.

According to Joel Williamson, this first testing of freedom has been the most neglected story of the Civil War. It was not enough merely to tell the slave he was free, Williamson argued, because freedom was a nominal legacy of the war. Ultimately, blacks had to establish their own freedom by some conscious, deliberate act, or they would remain slaves forever.[2] In his detailed portrayal of those first steps in South Carolina, Williamson rendered an up-close view of what happened throughout the entire South as well. It was a time of tasting the sometimes bitter fruit of freedom.[3]

The patterns that evolved in South Carolina were typical of other states that had many slaves. Some violence was recorded, perpetuated by both planters and freedmen, but sensationalized atrocities were the exception rather than the rule, according to most reports. Even when allowances are made for exaggeration, mistakes, and accidents, however, Willie Lee Rose contends that the exceptions cannot be glossed over or relegated to mere footnotes to history. Confronted with loss of valuable property, white owners sometimes resorted to murder to prevent the departure of slaves; embittered by previous cruelty, some slaves murdered the despised owner or looted and destroyed valuable possessions. The destruction was generally described as "wanton," a "malicious love of mischief gratified," and the "frustrated hostilities of generations."[4] Less violent and more common, stealing often satisfied the freedmen's desire for revenge. The main patterns of behavior that slowly emerged, however, involved mass desertion, migration, periods of idleness, the breaching of small regulations of slavery, and a new candor with whites, along with a groundswell of ambition to own land and learn to read.

Mass desertion was recorded in many planters' journals and letters. Leaving without any hesitation, household slaves, mechanics, and other extractive workers set the migration in motion. Farm hands seemed more inclined to linger until the summer crops were completed. Christmas Day 1865 found many plantations almost completely deserted. David Harris recorded in his journal: "Negroes leave today, to hunt themselves a new home, while we will be left to wait upon ourselves." After visiting a relative's plantation in February 1866, Rev. John Cornish reported, "Not one of their Negroes is with them, all have left." One owner wrote, "Many of the Negroes sought employment on other places, but the least desirable stayed with us, for they could not easily find new homes and we could not deny them shelter."[5]

Often characterized as "aimless, far-flung wandering," the migration and desertion of freedmen were more often determined by economic design and necessity, Williamson concluded. Many former slaves walked only a few miles away, often to serve other whites for the promise of food and work. Agricultural workers might wander to a neighboring village to camp out and wait for employment. Confronted with the question of what they planned to do, most of these drifters, sampling the vague essence of freedom, gave the universal answer, "I don't know." Like children turned loose in a candy store, they eyed an assortment of delicious choices but found no pennies in their tattered pockets for payment. Augustine Smythe characterized them as a "swarm of bees all buzzing about and not knowing where to settle," with "considerable trouble and moving among the negroes."[6]

Having briefly tested the distant world, many freedmen were driven back to former owners by physical need. Hungry and without work, clothing, or shelter, they exchanged the new uncertainties for old securities, simply needing a roof over their heads. A former slave, Isabella, writing from Liberty, North Carolina, in July of 1865, appealed to her former owner: "I don care if I am free. I had rather live with you, I was free while with you as I wanted to be." Her circumstances had not improved: "I am cramped hear nearly to death and no one ceares for me heare, and I want you if you pleas Sir, to send for me."[7]

Aside from physical necessity and, in many cases, a sincere affection for former owners, large numbers of freedmen were drawn back to the "old range" by ancient and universal longings, a simple love for the place where they had lived and worked and the yearning for familiar surroundings. White contemporaries, obsessed with the notion that "theirs was a white man's land," Williamson contended, have never fully understood or appreciated the fact that Negroes too were devoted to the land of their labor and strongly attached to that familiar soil. "The aged freedwomen, and also of the aged freedmen had the bump of locality like old cats," a Freedmen's Bureau officer reported. Efforts to resettle the freedmen were often unsuccessful, causing one state official to conclude: "Local attachment, you know, has always been a ruling passion with the agricultural classes of people."[8] If ironic, it was not too surprising to find that many former slaves returned to the scene of their bondage after a brief sojourn from the old range. Having been promised employment in distant places, many had found only unfulfilled dreams awaiting them, and so they returned, often wiser, more cautious.

There were those, however, who continued to drift aimlessly from place to place, never settling satisfactorily. One planter noted such wandering in his journal: "Negroes generally very idle, wandering about the country enjoying their freedom, tho to my mind wonderfully civil, under the circumstances."[9] If idleness characterized some of the drifters in the first flush of freedom, it was not the general condition of the majority, who desperately needed and wanted to work, doing so gladly when proper arrangements could be made. One migrant in Charleston, South Carolina, stated the case for many: "We wants to git

away to work on our own hook. It's not a good time at all here. We does
nothing but suffer from smoke and ketch cold. We want to begin de
planting business."[10]

The possibility of owning a piece of land became the primary concern
for most freedmen, second only to education after immediate physical
needs were met. In Booker T. Washington's later work with adults,
landownership was a central tenet, closely paralleling education. As the
Civil War slowly concluded, a fervent and widespread expectation
developed among the slaves that they would inherit a parcel of land and
tools with which to farm—the proverbial "forty acres and a mule."
Without such land, agrarian freedom was impossible. One freedman
expressed the sentiments of the other rural Negroes to a Union officer:
"Gib us our land and we take care of ourselves, but widout land, de ole
massas can hire us or starve us, as dey please." This general expectation
was not without foundation. Mary Chestnut, a cotton heiress and the
wife of a Confederate senator and general, reported that the "Negroes
declare that they are to be given lands and mules by those blessed
Yankees."[11] Northern reporters, soldiers, and speculators often encouraged the idea that the confiscated lands rightfully belonged to the
Negroes. Some military leaders had temporarily dispersed some of this
land to the congested throngs of contrabands to scatter them and provide
work for those who had flocked to their camps. Enterprising northerners
had instituted schemes to take over southern plantations, divide the
acreage into plots for Negroes, and conduct the plantations as a business
proposition, often showing more profit motive than philanthropy. In
addition to military necessity and profit schemes, there were other
genuinely humane efforts to secure land for the freedmen.

The American Missionary Association, the most entrenched and
lasting of the relief agencies that flourished during and after the Civil
War, added to its relief and educational work a considerable lobbying
force toward securing land for the freedmen. The association's land
effort, still mixed with evangelism, hoped to prove to the world that
freedmen were industrious and capable in matters of home and land
management. If the association could persuade the government to allow
blacks to settle on abandoned plantations, "all our educational and
missionary aspirations generally will go forward and our efforts will,
under the providence of God abundantly satisfy the incredulous as well
as friends," they reasoned.[12]

As early as March 1862, George Whipple represented the American Missionary Association in Washington, D.C., trying to persuade the federal government to take steps toward some land determination for the Negroes. The association argued that confiscated and abandoned lands should be distributed to the freedmen. When President Andrew Johnson later decided to return such land to the owners, the association protested strongly. As the American Missionary Association continued many varied and fervent efforts for landownership, they envisioned a productive people on small, independent farms throughout the South who could contribute to Reconstruction rather than remaining landless, wandering contrabands. "Everyday's experience increases with me the conviction that the next step to be taken in reconstruction is to break up the immense landed estates, and secure homesteads to the landless," Samuel Ashely argued, with many in agreement.[13] Ironically, the American Missionary Association's early vision of productive, independent small farmers incorporated a good portion of Washington's subsequent vision for his race, although he was impelled by economics rather than evangelism.

In pursuit of its vision, the American Missionary Association took more concrete steps when the federal government failed to act. In Providence, Virginia, in 1865, the association formed a freedmen's group that encouraged saving for the purchase of homesteads. In 1867, the group bought 175 acres near Hampton, Virginia, divided the land, and sold it cheaply to about forty families. In North Carolina, the association purchased more than a thousand acres in 1869, selling the land to freedmen on five-year contracts, with payment money going into the purchase of more land. Each settlement had a church and school, forming the nucleus for permanent communities. Similar efforts were attempted in Alabama, Florida, and other states with some initial success until poor returns caused the association to lose money. Generally, such efforts benefited only a small percentage of the southern black population, but the association continued to encourage participation in the Homestead Act of 1866, urging the importance of landownership to insure independence.[14]

The Freedmen's Bureau was no more successful in its efforts to secure land for the freedmen than was the American Missionary Association. Established in March 1865, after two years of congressional conflict, with subsequent modifications and amendments, the bureau, under the leadership of General Oliver O. Howard, was charged by the federal government with all things great and small relating to the freedmen: relief, education, finances, labor policies, justice, and the administration of Reconstruction acts and land policies. The bureau's work extended through June 1872, with many notable successes on behalf of the freedmen as well as failures caused by disorganization, poor management, and political temptations for its officers. Chief among its failures was the crucial issue of land for the freedmen.

Shortly after the bureau was organized, Treasury agents and military commanders had transferred to the bureau's land division all abandoned and confiscated lands not needed for military purposes. With the rights of ownership except the right to sell, the bureau was charged with the administration of an aggregate of about 800,000 acres. Most of this land lay in Virginia, Georgia, South Carolina, Louisiana, North Carolina, Kentucky, and Tennessee, with little in Alabama and Florida and none in Texas.[15]

In his pioneer study of the Freedmen's Bureau, Paul Skeels Peirce concluded that the bureau's initial intention had been to divide this land up and distribute it to the freedmen as homesteads. Unfortunately, several things prevented the consummation of this plan. Leases existed on some lands and had to be honored. According to Peirce, the actual amount of land under the bureau's control was small, amounting to $2/10$ of 1 percent of all land in the southern states, and "it would have been impossible to give even one acre to each family of freedmen."[16] Some lands were not suitable for homesteads; others were needed by the bureau for its hospitals, teachers, and officers. All of these factors became irrelevant, however, because President Johnson soon declared that all such property that had not already been sold should be restored to the southern owners; the bureau was then charged with administering the restoration. Having long cherished the hope that these lands would be theirs, the former slaves were sorely disappointed, as were the American Missionary Association and many northerners who had agitated for the land rights of the freedmen.

In June 1866, Congress approved an act which opened for entry by black men and white without distinction all the public lands in the states of Alabama, Mississippi, Missouri, Arkansas, and Florida. The Freedmen's Bureau published information about these lands, gave assistance and transportation to families who wished to move there, and in general promoted such moves, as did the American Missionary Association. The response was tepid, however, with only about 4,000 families taking advantage of the opportunity. Possibly the lack of mule teams and farming implements, as well as overt opposition by whites, contributed to the poor response, but probably the freedmen's affinity for the old range previously noted had even more influence on their decision not to migrate.[17]

Exploring both the mythical and real expectations of the freedmen regarding the land issue, Claude F. Oubre concluded in *Forty Acres and a Mule* (1978) that the myth still remains unexplained. Although some historians have argued that Congress never really promised land to the freedmen, reported circumstances and rumors had fostered the expectation of securing some acreage. Unfortunately, land redistribution did not happen, and the "Negro who owned his own land in the South was the exception rather than the rule when Reconstruction ended."[18] Oubre cited several reasons for the failure of freedmen to acquire land during the first crucial years of freedom. Congress had initially failed to pass legislation for freedmen's land, and President Johnson had restored southern land to former owners. Neither the military nor the Freedmen's Bureau had taken the appropriate action. Some land schemes of northerners and opposition by southerners to Negro landownership were also crucial factors. These failures often obscured the positive gains made during Reconstruction, Oubre concluded.[19]

In a fervid analysis that echoed the intensity and themes of a Booker T. Washington speech, Gunnar Myrdal also viewed the failure to secure land during Reconstruction as a crucial deterrent to the freedmen's progress. "The story of the Negro in agriculture would have been a rather different one if the Negro farmer had had the opportunity to establish himself as an independent farmer," Myrdal contended.[20] With their own land, blacks would have been firmly attached to the soil, knowing that they worked for their own benefit and could improve their level of living by their own efforts. Of greater importance, however, would have been the immediate relief from suffering, the elimination of devastating peonage problems, and a groundswell of racial pride. Slavery, Myrdal argued, had already conditioned the freedmen toward ignorance and the inability to take advantage of the few available opportunities. Such conditioning, coupled with the depressed economic conditions in the South, made the chain of peonage and tenant farming a hard one to break. According to Myrdal, specific actions should have been implemented for freedmen to alleviate the trial of homelessness, illiteracy, and inertia—conditions that Washington inherited and worked to abolish. Large plantations should have been redistributed, with fair payment going to owners for loss of slaves and land. These plantations should have been divided into small plots which the poor might have purchased with yearly payments over a long period of time. The freedmen should have been provided much closer supervision in their adjustment to freedom and effective vocational education that was imperative for farming and other job skills. Some scheme of general taxation could have been formulated to reimburse plantation owners, to allow for land purchases by the poor, and to train freedmen for production work. To help relieve the large population of freedmen in the South, some plan should have been devised to encourage blacks to participate in westward, rural migration.[21]

Because the freedmen did not get land and because there was no remuneration to former owners, a great bitterness festered on both sides. Whites often violently opposed any constructive programs aimed at raising the Negro to economic, social, or mental independence, directing their anger toward those individuals and groups who attempted such programs. On the other side, blacks were caught in a web of their own bitterness. Without land and adequate education, they walked the treadmill of peonage farming, not far removed from slavery, and many were never able to get off. The trap that so hindered Reconstruction for both blacks and whites was the inadequate planning on the part of the federal government concerning the land issue.

In spite of the great failures, there were some positive gains by 1900. In the South Atlantic area, the average landownership was 27 acres; in the south central region, the average was 48 acres.[22] Significantly, it was during the era of Washington's leadership that the greatest increase in landownership was evidenced among the blacks. In 1900, at the peak of his influence, 25 percent of all blacks (193,000) owned land and farm homes. The increase continued until 1910, with a maximum of 222,000 black farm owners. After 1920, the number started to decline, reaching a low of 174,000 by 1940, according to Myrdal.[23] In a speech in Memphis in 1914, Washington stated that blacks then owned 20 million acres of land. From 1900 to 1910, the total value of farm property owned by the black farmers of the South increased from $177,404,688 to

$492,898,218, or 177 percent.[24] Delivered about a year before his death, this speech typified the careful research undertaken at Tuskegee about the smallest gains among blacks and Washington's persistent efforts to keep such information fresh in the minds of his audience.

☞ Even before Emancipation, the slaves had friends who lobbied and worked on their behalf, whether for immediate freedom or the later needs of relief, housing, land, jobs, and education. Representatives from various religious and benevolent organizations from the North worked side by side with military and federal officials, trying to relieve suffering and insure the former slaves' safe passage into freedom. Throughout the war and afterward, a host of such organizations supported volunteer workers in the South, combining their efforts with those of military commanders and Treasury agents to encompass the two broad areas of logistics and justice. These workers assisted in regulation of the sale, leasing, and cultivation of lands; the employment of Negroes by planters on plantations, by the government on plantations, and by the government in camps, colonies, and infirmary farms; the distribution of rations, medicine, and supplies; and the transportation of freedmen, refugees, and teachers. The relief agents also pursued intellectual, moral, and religious education, the promotion of justice, the care of freedmen's savings, and the collection of claims of freedmen against the government.[25]

With some degree of success, these combined efforts had provided timely relief to the sick and helpless in camps and plantations, made tentative beginnings in education, and helped to regulate fair practices in labor. Unfortunately, these agencies reached only a small portion of the freedmen who needed help. The various agencies often overlapped, with arguments about jurisdiction and methods resulting. There was no systematic approach even in the federal government, with both military and Treasury agents vying for control and administration. In such confusion, corruption and incompetence found fertile ground, and the benevolent societies gradually consolidated their efforts toward efficiency and economy. As Peirce viewed this period of disorganization, it laid the groundwork for the Freedmen's Bureau, demonstrating the urgent need for central, unified leadership. The American Missionary Association, in conjunction with the Freedmen's Bureau, continued to expand its work, hailing the period 1861–90 as a glorious opportunity for missionary work and Christian reconstruction.

The American Missionary Association had begun its antislavery work much earlier, supporting parent societies in Jamaica, Hawaii, Egypt, Siam, the Sandwich Islands, and Africa. By the late 1840s, its work had expanded to include helping slaves who fled to Canada by providing clothes, teachers, and preachers for schools, churches, and relief; such work continued after the Emancipation Proclamation. By the mid-1850s, however, the association's main work was in the United States, preaching a gospel discrediting slavery and caste, with more than 100 missionaries in the Northwest and in the slave states of Missouri, North Carolina, and Kentucky.[26] In September 1861, the work commenced in earnest, when the association first sent missionaries to Fortress Monroe, Virginia, where the trickle of contrabands had become a flood.

The problems the association encountered at Fortress Monroe were typical of other military posts throughout the South for the duration of the war. Slaves threw themselves on the mercy of Yankee soldiers, clamoring for food, clothing, shelter, medical care, work, and the promised freedom. Many former slaves were sick, with rampant whooping cough, dysentery, mumps, measles, and respiratory problems. Concerned about the spread of illness, military officers worried about disease control, often neglecting the other problems of their unwelcome charges. With a war to fight, without authority or facilities, the military tried to give sporadic relief, usually inadequate, and often put the freedmen to work to pay for quarters, food, clothing, and medicine. In their missionary zeal, association workers frequently criticized the military, forgetting that they were, after all, fighting soldiers. While it was not "Jubilee" time for either confused soldier or sick contraband, there were unwarranted cases of brutality and inhumanity. In 1862 at Fortress Monroe alone there were, on the average, seven daily deaths reported. The first task of the missionaries, therefore, was to give immediate relief from physical suffering. Corresponding Secretary Simeon S. Jocelyn made a two-week tour, noted the needs of the contrabands, wrote to President Abraham Lincoln on their behalf, and finally persuaded the president to assign a medical surgeon to the refugees. As conflicts between the missionaries and the military persisted, the military was often branded as "old Pharaoh slavery under the Stars and Stripes," an unfair label when consideration is given to the military's mission, their many efforts to help, and the general failure of the federal government to provide for the contrabands.[27]

The patterns of work established at Fortress Monroe and at Port Royal extended throughout the South and continued into the postwar period. As immediate physical needs were met, the American Missionary Association then launched into land, education, and social issues, all liberally coated with the association's moral and religious instruction. By mid-1865, the association had 250 missionaries and teachers in the field; the number reached 353 in 1866, 451 in 1867, and about 532 in 1868.[28] Ultimately, the association would be more effective in the area of education, although the immediate relief it brought to thousands of destitute freedmen cannot be calculated.

With all of its good intentions, the American Missionary Association was not without imperfections. Often too paternalistic, these zealous missionaries came to the South enmeshed in northern white culture and were naive about the depth of prejudice in the South. They never fully understood black people's core—their background, emotional make-up, religious fervor, or desire to be in charge of their own destiny. Often self-sacrificing, straitlaced, and strict, the missionaries were quick to censor attitudes and habits spawned in slavery and not quickly shed, trying to instill in the freedmen their own moral codes. The missionaries' own prejudices affected their attitudes and methods, and they tried to change the world into their image. The American Missionary Association zealously guarded its control, carved from hard work and sacrifice, with the expressed motive of preparing more qualified blacks to lead their race.

Criticized by the majority of whites and a large number of blacks, the American Missionary Association nevertheless proved its strength, its staying power, making the most notable contributions of any organization toward the transition of blacks into freedom. It saved hundreds of lives with relief, helped many blacks acquire land, and organized orphanages, schools, and colleges, remaining a great force in the betterment of freedmen. For the hard years of lynching, disfranchisement, and discrimination ahead, the organization's work had trained many strong black leaders.[29] The association continued its major work with freedmen until 1890, pursuing its fight for their integration into society up through the 1900s, unlike its short-lived coworker, the Freedmen's Bureau.

Representing the federal government's main efforts to help the freedmen from March 1865 through June 1872, the Freedmen's Bureau worked closely with the American Missionary Association and other philanthropic organizations. So closely, in fact, did their work complement each other during the bureau's existence that conflicting credits exist: for instance, one author lists Hampton Institute as a bureau school, while another cites it as an association school. The bureau, like the American Missionary Association, actively worked to provide relief for the freedmen in the areas of caring for the sick, feeding, clothing, and sheltering the destitute, and transporting both black and white refugees to their homes or to better fields of work.[30] With the authorized power and funding of Congress, the bureau could do more while supporting the association's work.

Although the act of March 3, 1865, had made no provisions for medical or hospital care—a strange oversight—General Howard made medical care an integral part of the bureau's work. Supplies and surgeons were dispersed, and Dr. C. W. Horner, a surgeon, became the chief medical officer of the bureau. Fourteen surgeons and three assistants were installed as local bureau officers during the summer of 1865.[31] Their duties were to help the armies in caring for sick refugees and freedmen, set up new hospitals, and maintain adequate medical personnel for the care of the sick. The general surgeon provided medical supplies. Private physicians were paid by voluntary contributions or by the general fund of the bureau. After 1866, Congress corrected its error and made appropriations to the medical division, facilitating the bureau's work with the sick.

The bureau helped to maintain and enlarge existing asylums, hospitals, and colonies. These colonies existed where large numbers of freedmen congregated, providing cabins and infirmaries for the orphaned, helpless, and transient. The bureau gradually combined medical facilities, trying to turn over to state and local governments, who were not anxious to assume them, many of these responsibilities. By September 1867, the bureau reached its zenith, with forty-five hospitals and 5,292 beds. After mid-1868, the bureau phased out quickly; by June 1869, only two hospitals and one asylum remained in bureau custody. The hospitals and medical services generally were unevenly distributed in the southern states, with Virginia having the most, followed by Georgia, Alabama, North Carolina, Mississippi, Arkansas, South Carolina, and the District of Columbia in order. Florida, Louisiana, Texas, Kentucky, and Tennessee received fewer medical services, and Texas and Florida never had more than one hospital at a time.[32]

Peirce estimated that the federal government spent as much as two million dollars on medical expenses alone for the freedmen. Was the money well spent? A total of 452,519 cases were treated by bureau physicians. The death rate dropped from 30 percent to 13 percent in 1865, to 4.6 percent in 1866, to 3.4 percent in 1867, to 2.5 percent in 1868, and to 2.03 percent in 1869. White refugee death rates dropped to a low of 1.42 percent. In the large towns, both poor whites and blacks had been treated by bureau services. In general, the bureau had inspected and improved sanitation wherever it operated. Without the bureau's work, the orphaned, the aged, and the helpless would have had no assistance. The bureau tried to find permanent arrangements for these unfortunates. By cooperating with other benevolent associations, governments, and medical facilities, the bureau had provided money, supplies, and personnel and had coordinated supervision.[33] If there had been some waste, certainly the medical benefits to the freedmen and poor whites far outweighed any irregularities.

The bureau helped not only the sick but also the destitute. The military commanders were already issuing rations to the refugees, dependents, and people working with the freedmen. Some able-bodied people were positioning themselves to become permanent recipients of free government food, the bureau soon discovered. After its work began, the bureau took steps to weed out such abuse so that only the truly destitute would receive the free rations. Soup houses were started, along with efforts to find work for the indolent to allow them to pay for their rations. Idleness still persisted in August 1866, however, and the order was issued to discontinue rations except for the sick in hospitals and the orphans. So great was the destitution in some areas that this order was almost impossible to follow, but people seeking assistance had to apply through some official who could vouch for their needs.

After the winter and early spring of 1867, when great distress necessitated more aid, a joint resolution was passed to provide $500,000 more for relief. Most of this money was used to buy corn and pork for destitute people in the South. Other funds were established until January 1869, providing additional rations. For food and clothing in this relief work, the bureau spent approximately 4.5 million dollars.[34]

Another relief function of the bureau involved the transportation of white refugees, freedmen, officers and agents of the bureau, and teachers. In May 1865, General Howard ordered that white, penniless refugees who sought help in getting back home should be protected and provided transportation to their former homes. More than 2,000 such refugees were helped in this way. Again, abuses occurred, restricting the order to include only the most destitute cases, but such work continued until 1869.

Twenty thousand freedmen had congregated in Washington, D.C., alone; most large cities experienced a flood of workers exceeding the job demand. Without work, these congested masses depended on charity for survival, while in other areas workers were needed. To relieve the government's expense of caring for them and to provide them with employment, the bureau offered refugees free transportation to areas of available employment. By 1870, it is estimated that the bureau had transported some 30,000 refugees, many of them returning to their old plantations.

Free government transportation had also been provided to teachers and other volunteer workers who administered to freedmen and refugees until 1869, numbering about 4,000 for a four-year period. All officers on public duty were also entitled to free transportation, with about 2,000 passes being issued for these officials alone. Additionally, store and school supplies were shipped at government expense. With large sums expended for the transportation of both people and supplies, the resultant abuses and extravagances created heavy expenses for the bureau, as well as a diminishing reputation. At a time when nobody else was in a position to provide the relief of transportation, however, this aspect of the bureau's work, though often neglected by critics, provided a valuable service to thousands of freedmen and refugees.[35]

The Freedmen's Bureau also played a vital role in labor and legal affairs that affected the freedmen, seeking to regulate relations between employers and laborers in the insurrection states. Usually ignorant of just what their new status of freedom entailed, the freedmen were hesitant to enter into labor contracts, fearing such contracts would trick them back into their old slavery. Without understanding or respecting any drawn contracts, many deserted their employers after agreements were made; others could not perform without close supervision. Returning home after the war, even the planters did not understand the free labor system; many of them, too, were reluctant to accept it. Confusion, mistrust, and belligerent maltreatment prevailed. To protect both the freedmen and the employers, General Howard quickly devised a solution. Uniform articles of agreement were drawn up, explained to both parties, and supervised by the bureau. Generally, these efforts were directed toward protecting the freedmen from violence or any form of slavery while defending their rights to hold property, maintain fair contracts, secure fair trials with the right to testify in court, and preserve family relationships.

As a bridge from slavery to freedom, the bureau helped to establish the rights of the freedmen during a period when no specific rules had been drawn up. In addition to organizing courts and boards of arbitration to protect the interests of and justice for the freedmen, the bureau also participated in many civil court cases involving the welfare of former slaves. Agents could often settle disputes without the necessity of courts. By setting up tentative scales of wages, supervising labor contracts, and interceding for the freedmen in all legal matters, the bureau brought temporary adjustments into the troubled waters of precarious freedom. Who else was there to do it? The American Missionary Association lacked the authority, the freedmen lacked the experience, and the southern planters lacked the inclination.[36]

The Freedmen's Bureau actually became an encompassing government with legislative, executive, and judicial authority. Supported by the military forces of the United States and assisted by benevolent groups, especially the American Missionary Association, the bureau exerted enormous influence throughout the South, meeting strong opposition from native southerners. While southerners vehemently opposed all of the "damned Yankee" do-gooders and their philanthropic efforts to rearrange the status quo, the bureau's political activity riled them most. As bureau officials began to regulate suffrage and elections, act as carpetbag politicians, and hold offices in the South, the bureau became a political issue in the North as well, acquiring labels of swindler, political machine, false prophet to the freedmen, and perpetuator of the Republican party. Too often, unfortunately, the bureau's image as a political machine overshadowed the great good it had already done. Even politically, the freedmen had advanced a few steps toward acculturation. The bureau had helped to fix party lines in the South, giving blacks some voice in politics, securing for them the right of suffrage guaranteed by the Fifteenth Amendment (if soon curtailed), and advancing their civil rights.[37]

☞ Washington remembered in his autobiography that the celebration of freedom lasted only a brief period in Hale's Ford. As the slaves wandered back to their cabins, their wild joy turned to somber thoughts of responsibility. "It was very much like suddenly turning a youth of ten or twelve years out into the world to provide for himself," he said. "In a few hours the great questions with which the Anglo-Saxon race had been grappling for centuries had been thrown upon these people to be solved. These were the questions of a home, a living, the rearing of children, education, citizenship, and the establishment and support of churches." In a few short hours, the wild rejoicing had ceased also as "deep gloom" pervaded the slave quarters.[38] Weak and old, some of the slaves made arrangements to stay on with "old Missus." The Washington family, if unsure about their future, had no intention of staying.

Comparing the Washington family with other former slaves of the period is instructive, portentous perhaps, of Booker's potential for future leadership. Like the other four million slaves, they had arrived at freedom in a penniless and ignorant state, flooded with uncertainty about their new responsibilities. Unlike thousands of freedmen, however, they had not sought refuge in military reservations; they had neither expected nor received local or federal assistance. They did not migrate, like so many, to languish in unemployment and charity in congested cities. Leaving the Virginia farm without bitterness, they did not burn, loot, or desecrate the place of their enslavement. When disappointments clouded their migration, the family showed no inclination to return to the old range in search of old securities. In one sense, at least, the Washingtons were lucky, or so it seemed at the moment. They had a plan, a place to go. The salt mines of Malden, West Virginia, their destination, would prove to be, paradoxically, a long way from paradise.

A few weeks after freedom, Booker's stepfather, "Wash," arranged for a two-horse wagon to take the family to West Virginia, where he already worked in the salt mines. Jane loaded their few belongings into the wagon, said goodbye to the Burroughs family, who wished her well, and set out on the arduous, 200 mile journey over the mountains to the promised land. In poor health, Jane usually rode, while the three barefoot children walked behind the wagon. Booker later recalled that the journey took several weeks, with the family sleeping in the open air and cooking over small wood fires. The route they followed was probably the one used by Franklin County slaves when they were loaned out to work in the salt mines. Moving first to the north toward Roanoke and over to Blacksburg, Virginia, the family possibly went then to the Giles, Fayette, and Kanawha Turnpike, which the Union Army had used in 1864. For Booker, who had never been far from his birthplace, the journey into another state was an adventure, "quite an event," he called it. For Jane, who had asthma and heart palpitations, the trip was tiring and worrisome, occurring as it perhaps did in the heat of August 1865 and presaging no significant improvements in her fortunes at the end of the journey. After approximately two weeks, the motley family arrived in Malden, about five miles south of Charleston. It was shortly obvious that they had missed their mark for the promised land.[39]

From Malden, in the Kanawha Valley of West Virginia, Booker got his first impression of what living in a congested city signified, and the sights, sounds, and smells never left him. The cabin that Wash had secured for them was no better, perhaps worse, than the one they had left in Hale's Ford. It was tightly clustered among other cabins, and filth surrounded them all. Accustomed to fresh mountain air in rural Hale's Ford, Booker found the filth, with no sanitary regulations, totally unbearable. He saw up close for the first time the poor whites who were no better off than the blacks; squeezed in among the black cabins were "the poorest and most ignorant and degraded white people," he called them. A shocking new world opened before him: "Drinking, gambling, quarrels, fights, and shockingly immoral practices were frequent," he recalled.[40] Soon Booker would join his life to those of his depraved neighbors in the salt mines, working much harder than he had ever worked in slavery.

Owned by Joseph Ruffner, a wealthy farmer from the Shenandoah Valley, the Kanawha Salines salt mines had been quite prosperous from 1794 into the early 1800s, supplying salt to the pork packers in Cincinnati. Improved production methods, instituted by Joseph's sons, David, Joseph, and Tobias, had aided the booming industry, and other skilled workers like tinsmiths had come to Malden, some from as far away as Europe, In the 1850s, however, the meat packing business moved westward to Chicago; salt was no longer in great demand and business declined. The Civil War brought a temporary revival, and slave labor was used as before. When the Washingtons came to Malden, the industry was slowly dying, with management looking for industries to replace meat packing. Like the rest of the South, the economic conditions in Malden were deplorable. By 1872, the salt industry was finished, replaced by coal and timber.[41]

Booker was nine years old and his brother, John, not much older when their stepfather, Wash, took them into the salt mines to do men's work, keeping their meager wages to run the household or for other purposes. They started to work at four in the morning and worked until dark, helping Wash pack the salt into barrels. After the brine was boiled out and drying had occurred, the crystallized salt had to be shoveled into barrels and pounded until each barrel had a certain weight. It was heavy, exhausting work for children. The boys had hardly known Wash when they came to Malden and had difficulty adjusting to a father-figure, resenting him personally, chafing as he forced them to work, took their wages, and dominated the family. Booker later kept in distant contact with Wash, never showing much respect for him or having anything good to say about him. Such exploitation of children, especially disadvantaged ones in low-paying labor, became a major concern for Booker, having experienced it firsthand from both his own stepfather and the mining companies that encouraged it.[42]

As bad as things were, however, in the salt mines Booker had his first experience with "book knowledge." Each salt packer was assigned a number, and Wash's number was 18. Every barrel the Washingtons packed had to be marked with that number. Booker learned to recognize the figure and to make it himself, although he had no knowledge of other figures or letters. It was his first tentative step, however small, toward the world that would dominate his life, education.[43] If there was a way out of the salt mines, that road for him and millions like him would have to be through the door of education.

Working in the coal mines sporadically, Booker dreaded the dirty and dark work there with a passion, but he was lucky to escape it to a better position offering some valuable on-the-job training. Through the help of his mother, who must have been deeply pained to see her young sons mining the salt and coal, Booker was hired as Viola Ruffner's houseboy around 1867 at five dollars per month. Mrs. Ruffner was the second wife of General Lewis Ruffner, the most prominent and wealthy citizen in Malden, who also owned the largest and finest house in town. Viola, a transplanted New Englander, was a former English teacher who became a great influence and lifelong friend to Booker. Sensitive, intelligent, and disciplined, with very strict demands, she scared most of her houseboys off; Booker himself left occasionally but returned, acquiring an enormous respect and love for her. An outsider in a southern culture, frequently lonely and sometimes bitter, Viola developed an unusual empathy with Booker, encouraging the special qualities she saw in him. They corresponded until her death. Many years later when Washington was traveling in Arlington, Vermont, Viola's birthplace, he stopped, took off his hat, and bowed his head in silence. "For me it is a shrine," he told his escort.[44]

The Ruffners seemed to complete the puzzle about white society in Booker's inquisitive mind. From the backwoods Burroughs family, Booker had observed the fair-to-middling farmer, neither stereotypi- cally wealthy nor evil, but also sorely lacking in refinement and culture. He had seen the poorest of whites, ignorant and depraved like his own people, cringing in mountain huts near Hale's Ford and crammed into filthy mining cabins in Malden. In the Ruffners, his first contact with the white elite, he witnessed that naturally inbred refinement and culture not bought with money, infused with understanding and charity. His adjusted and broadened view freed him from crippling hatred and aberrant fear of the white man, enabling him to serve as a bridge between that race and his own during the turbulent days of disfranchise- ment. His personal acceptance in the Ruffner household had prepared him to feel at ease when his future work took him among the most important and wealthy people in the world, including American presi- dents and foreign dignitaries. He had taken careful note of the Ruffner household. Above all, Mrs. Ruffner wanted cleanliness. Work had to be done promptly and systematically. "At the bottom of everything she wanted absolute honesty and frankness. Nothing must be sloven or slipshod; every door, every fence, must be kept in repair."[45]

His on-the-job training at the Ruffners, Washington often said, was as valuable as any education he had received anywhere at any time; he would incorporate the idea into Tuskegee's programs. Because of Viola Ruffner, throughout the rest of his life he could never see scattered trash without stopping to pick it up. Filthy yards, broken, unpainted fences or houses, clothes with greasy spots and missing buttons, or any sort of "sloven slipshod" remained abhorrent to him. Biographers who puzzle over Washington's astute attention to minute details as the principal of Tuskegee could possibly find their solution in the Ruffner houseboy. Washington also credited Viola's lessons of cleanliness and efficiency for helping him pass his unusual entrance test at Hampton Institute some few years later, but her greatest encouragement had been in the area of literacy. She gave him time off for school and tutored him in his lessons, generally expanding his horizons. With her support, he started his first personal "library," contained in a dry-goods box in the Ruffner home. His real struggle toward literacy, however, had just begun and would characterize the struggle of all freedmen who were thirsty for knowledge.

While Booker's varied work experiences had helped to crystallize other priorities, they had also heightened his obsession for an education. The road he took to the classroom in Malden was a crowded one, filled with four million freedmen, whether eight years old or eighty, in thousands of villages, towns, and cities throughout the entire South. All of these former slaves clamored for the right to read. Theirs was an age-old cry, stifled by years of slavery and obstruction, a hunger that made the printed word almost a sacrament. Washington expressed the depths of their yearning. "I had no schooling whatever while I was a slave, though I remember on several occasions I went as far as the schoolhouse door with one of my young mistresses to carry her books. The picture of several dozen boys and girls in a schoolroom engaged in study made a deep impression upon me, and I had the feeling that to get into a schoolhouse and study in this way would be about the same as getting into paradise."[46]

A WHOLE RACE TRYING
TO GO TO SCHOOL

3

Education is a dependent, inter-acting unit of the whole culture. Indeed,
it lies at the heart of the culture, and necessarily reflects the contending values
which there prevail.
Doxey A. Wilkerson in Woodson, The Education of the Negro Prior to 1861, *p. 1*

Booker T. Washington often quoted the literacy rate for slaves at only 3
percent in 1861. Illustrating the great surge to the classroom among
freedmen, he reported in 1914 that the literacy rate had climbed to a
possible 69 percent.[1] Gunnar Myrdal reported that 5 percent of the slaves
could read and write in 1860.[2] Carter G. Woodson contended that by
combining estimates of free blacks and literate slaves, "It is safe to say that
ten percent of the adult Negroes had the rudiments of education in 1860."[3]
Whatever the uncertain figure, some degree of literacy was accomplished
in slavery, and other valuable working skills were acquired as well.

From the introduction of slavery in America until 1835, some education for slaves seemed prudent, motivated largely by religion, benevolence, and economics. According to Woodson, the example set by early
Spanish and French missionaries had "struck the tone" for Negro
education throughout America.[4] To advance their proselyting, these
missionaries had taught the slaves and helped to elevate the freedmen to
a higher level. Shamed by the work of the Catholics, some liberal
Puritans and the Church of England also began to educate, trying to
convert the slaves to various religions. More than any sect, however, the
Quakers promoted the general welfare and education of Negroes in all
those colonies where the Friends were free to operate.

As early as 1688, the Quakers had registered the first protest against slavery in Protestant America. According to Herbert Aptheker, the institution of Negro slavery had virtually ceased to exist among accepted Quakers by the end of the eighteenth century.[5] The Quakers gradually developed a strong network to help escaping slaves, thus posing a threat to the status quo; as a result, they became the first "cast-offs" among whites, or, as George Hesslink phrased it, "the first victims of the *American Dilemma.*"[6] In slaveholding communities, the Quakers were persecuted for being subversive to "institutions of the aristocratic settlements." They continued, however, to put themselves at risk to give the Negroes the same privileges of religion and education that Quakers enjoyed because they believed in the fatherhood of God and the brotherhood of man. They taught the Negroes privately and established the earliest permanent schools for them.

Perhaps there is too little recognition in history of the role Quakers played in the early education and support of American slaves. They advanced the cause of Negro education substantially, improved living conditions, and promoted equality for American blacks. Washington frequently remembered their work and sacrifices. In a 1903 *Outlook* article, for example, he praised the work of Quakers in Cass County, Michigan. They had left the South in opposition to slavery and started a racially mixed community in Cass County.[7] In a typical pattern, these Quakers had helped runaway slaves and offered asylum to fugitives. Assisted and encouraged, many blacks remained in Cass County, purchased small farms, established schools, and developed the capacity for self-direction and government.[8] The racial independence and self-determination in Cass County were examples of what Washington often advocated for blacks.

In conjunction with the work of Quakers and other groups, there was also a nascent social philosophy emerging in the late 1700s. In recounting many interesting examples of varied and widespread—albeit obscure—educational efforts for and by Negroes prior to 1861, Woodson called this active period in the late 1700s and early 1800s "the heyday of victory for the ante-bellum Negro" in education. From such political upheavals as the French and Indian War and especially the American Revolution (Negro soldiers had participated in both), a social conscience was beginning to stir.[9] Prominent leaders like John Adams, Benjamin Franklin, and Samuel Webster espoused education as the right of all people while criticizing the hypocrisy of slavery in a country built on political freedom. "It always appeared a most iniquitous scheme to me," Abigail Adams wrote her husband in 1774, "to fight ourselves for what we are daily robbing and plundering from those who have as good a right to freedom as we have."[10]

Many muted voices favored the suppression of slave trade, the emancipation of all slaves, and some form of education for them. Even Thomas Jefferson, unsure in his own mind about the Negro's intellect, could support a cessation of the African slave trade.[11] He also admonished slaveowners to prepare their slaves for social responsibility, self-government, and suitable industry by instruction and habit. Jefferson's plan for public schools advocated the training of slaves in industrial and agricultural fields to prepare them for freedom.[12] Although most of the noble ideas never got beyond dried ink on parchment, Woodson provided ample evidence that schools, churches, and individuals were working on the Negro's behalf, that Negroes themselves were serious about securing an education, and that the nascent social philosophy emerging in the late 1700s was beginning to show some tangible results. Short-lived and almost completely squelched after 1835, when all of the slaveholding states enacted repressive legislation against the education and public meetings of slaves, the heyday did lay the groundwork for the swell toward education among freedmen during and immediately following the Civil War.

Slave education was also advocated by some northern agitators and by benevolent white masters before repressive legislation was enacted. Largely motivated by sympathy, northern abolitionists agitated for the education and freedom of slaves long before the Civil War. Proud southerners resented such northern interference, however; they considered the agitators to be misinformed about the southern region, arrogant, and ultimately dangerous to the status quo. Though well-intentioned, these northern efforts often caused more restrictions to be placed on the slaves. In the early years of slavery, white masters had provided the best opportunity for slave education. The first motivation was economics; slaves with some education were deemed more valuable and productive. Some white masters were more Christian and benevolent than others and provided Bible instruction and ethical training for their slaves. Such benevolent attitudes began to change, however, with the dynamic encroachment of the Industrial Revolution. The cotton gin changed the practice of slavery into a strict, economic system, and beneficial contacts between slaves and their masters virtually ceased to exist as slavery changed from a patriarchal to an economic system.

The noble notion that education was the right of all men never gained much ground in the states having large numbers of slaves. To reconcile education with the low position of slavery was virtually impossible for many rural southerners, who gave little priority to education for themselves. In Virginia, Washington's birthplace, Governor William Berkeley thanked God in 1671 that the state had neither printing press nor free schools. In colonial America, education was reserved for the elite members of society only and not for the common man, and the colonial South, with its large numbers of slaves and poor whites and its isolated, rural geography, ran far behind the North in education. When Philip Alexander Bruce examined the names of more than 18,000 persons in the public records of seventeenth-century Virginia, he concluded that nearly half of adult white males and three-fourths of the adult white females in the colony could not sign their names. The state was only marginally literate in the 1700s, having few schools, books, newspapers, or libraries. Virginia had no permanent printing press until 1730. William and Mary, founded in 1693 for prominent whites, was the only college established in the colonial South, compared to eight colleges in the middle and northern states.[13]

As slavery proliferated in Virginia and other southern states after the Industrial Revolution, making cotton "king" and expanding the plantation system, slave insurrections also increased. Slavery acquired a new face in the early 1800s; literate slaves, often considered more valuable in the 1700s, now were viewed as dangerous. Benevolent masters and the southern clergy who before had encouraged some Christian instruction for slaves were infected with the rising tide of fear, believing that any education would encourage more dissatisfaction among restless slaves. As conditions worsened, one slave state after another, like a chain of dominoes collapsing, enacted harsh rules to restrict the slaves. All slave instruction was stopped, and anyone conducting such efforts would be severely punished. Travel and public meetings were curtailed, and the dissemination of printed material among slaves was strictly forbidden. Slaves were limited to oral devices and memory. A speaker in the Virginia House of Delegates in 1832 summed up the general attitude for the entire South: "We have as far as possible closed every avenue by which light may enter [the slaves'] minds. If we could extinguish the capacity to see the light, our work would be completed; they would then be on a level with the beasts of the field and we should be safe!"[14]

What had prompted such a shockingly harsh outburst was the Nat Turner insurrection in Southampton County, Virginia, on August 21–22, 1831. A semiliterate slave, Turner and sixty to eighty Negro helpers had brutally murdered more than fifty-five white people, including innocent women and children.[15] Turner believed that a "voice from heaven" had directed him to stop tyranny and fight for equality, but southerners viewed such violence as hatred for whites that had been encouraged by northern abolitionists and as an example of possible animalism lurking in blacks. Still a hero to many, Turner accomplished several things with his revolt, according to Aptheker, who regarded Turner as an "accelerator" with humanistic motives. Turner gave impetus to trends such as colonization, repressive legislation, proslavery ideology, and abolitionist agitation already in progress; Turner had also accelerated movements of longer duration such as anti-Negro apprenticeship agitation and sectionalism in Virginia. Aptheker concluded that Turner had hastened the abolition of slavery, and his revolt had been the single most overt influence in the generation preceding emancipation.[16]

For the cause of education and the general welfare of the slaves themselves, however, Turner's insurrection had devastating effects. In an atmosphere of hysteria, all communication among slaves was severely stifled. In Virginia alone, according to Stephen B. Oates, "The blacks were more shackled to the rack of slavery than they had ever been."[17] By the 1840s, there were repressive slave controls, police measures, and toughened military forces, and "The old South had devised a slave system oppressive enough to make organized rebellion all but impossible," Oates reported.[18] Nor did northern public opinion show any sympathy for slave resistance or brutal rebellion like Turner's. Many northern newspapers castigated the Turner insurrection, offering military assistance if Virginia needed help to suppress such revolts.[19]

With the exception of abolitionists, northerners in general were also growing alarmed about the large influx of southern Negroes into the North and the possible negative effects on their economic, social, and cultural life. As repression intensified in the South, northern states grew less tolerant, Woodson reported, as many free blacks and southern refugees were forced to the North. Communities once friendly to Negro education actually drove out some free blacks; others discouraged education for blacks, as illustrated by the case of Prudence Crandall. When she allowed a Negro girl to enter her school in Canterbury, Connecticut, Crandall was ultimately arrested and forced to abandon the school.[20] Woodson concluded that even those states that had been sympathetic to blacks had yielded to the fears and prejudices caused by fugitives and the circumstances of their flight from the South, and the North itself erected strong obstacles to the education of Negroes.[21] The North had forgotten and the South had never learned, Woodson aptly noted, that an educated man is far more productive than an ignorant one.[22]

The quest for schooling could not be obliterated, however, and even in the repressive South, secret efforts continued by individuals and groups, resulting in a literacy rate ranging from 3 to 10 percent for slaves. Great strides had been made in the revolutionary decades of the 1700s. The stifling measures adopted by the southern states prior to the Civil War only whetted the appetite of slaves for books and schools. When the Yankees came, bearing guns and books and freedom, the fugitives rushed by the thousands to meet them.

☞ Many benevolent groups followed the federal troops to the South. While the American Missionary Association is best known, others also did important work in promoting Negro education during the turbulence and danger of the Civil War. The New England Freedmen's Aid Society, the Pennsylvania Freedmen's Relief Association, the National Freedmen's Relief Association of New York, and the Friends Association for the Aid and Education of Freedmen joined the association's work. They reported more than 3,000 pupils in Virginia alone in 1864 with fifty-two teachers; at least five of these were blacks.[23]

The benevolent associations commissioned and paid their teachers; they all generally depended on the federal government for rations, transportation, and occasional housing. Schools were established in abandoned rebel buildings, shacks, and sometimes in the open. With no central organization at first, each society chose its own location and methods of operation until the advent of the Freedmen's Bureau and the consolidation of many smaller groups with the American Missionary Association. The eastern states reaped the greatest benefits from such efforts in the beginning. These benevolent groups usually ministered to the largest groups of fugitives, who were found with Union troops.

There is no indication that the Washington family in Hale's Ford, Virginia, received any help from the societies' work, because the family lived in rural isolation, removed from Union activity. At Hampton, Virginia, however, significant beginnings would have a great bearing on Booker's future.

With its relief work already begun at Hampton in 1861, the American Missionary Association followed in quick succession with its education work for the contrabands under federal control. When General Benjamin F. Butler gave his approval, the association sent Rev. L. C. Lockwood to Hampton in September 1861. By September 15, Lockwood had opened a Sunday school for Negroes in the home of ex-President John Tyler. Two days later, the first day school for the freedmen was opened in a little brown house with Mary S. Peake, a mulatto, as its first teacher. In a few months, other schools followed at Fortress Monroe, Washington, D.C., Norfolk, Portsmouth, Newport News, and nearby plantations.[24] Other societies joined the work of the American Missionary Association in Virginia from 1862 through 1864, and patterns of administering relief and education jointly were established that would spread to other areas.

In North Carolina, chaplains of northern regiments who served under General Ambrose E. Burnside's command opened evening schools for contrabands near their military camps. As early as the spring of 1862, chaplains of the Twenty-Fifth Massachusetts Regiment gave instruction to freedmen at Plymouth, North Carolina. The first day schools in North Carolina were opened in two Negro churches in July 1863, after Rev. Horace Jones was appointed superintendent of Negro affairs. Other schools, taught by "cultured females from the North," were opened in Morehead, Beaufort, Washington, and Plymouth, with an aggregate attendance reaching nearly 3,000 under sixty-six teachers from various societies in July 1864. Evening classes for adults were also provided. Epidemics of smallpox and yellow fever slowed the progress of 1864; thousands of Negroes and some of the teachers were victims.[25]

General Butler, who had authorized the first school at Hampton, continued to promote the education of freedmen throughout North Carolina and Virginia when he assumed command of the military in these states in 1863. A year earlier in New Orleans, he had tried to create order out of chaos: Negroes equalled or outnumbered the whites in most parishes under his command; moreover, Butler lacked the authority to drive away or free the swarms of blacks congested around the military camps. With the backing of the War Department, Butler recruited colored regiments, organized the fugitives into colonies, administered relief, and regulated the employment of blacks and whites by contract.

When he took command in 1863, Butler extended his policy of trying to centralize and unify the affairs of freedmen in Virginia and North Carolina, laying down definite rules. Butler encouraged the Negroes to buy land, build cabins, and establish settlements, and he systematized the educational facilities. Dividing large areas into districts with a superintendent, Butler appointed teachers in the manner of the New England free school system. In Hampton, where Butler had first used the phrase "contrabands of war," taken from international law, he erected a large schoolhouse to accommodate nearly 800 freedmen. Strict but fair, Butler was not always popular, especially in the South. His order directing that any woman who publicly insulted an officer of the United States should be regarded as a "woman of the street" created great bitterness in the South. Jefferson Davis, president of the Confederacy, issued a counterorder: General Butler, if captured, should be hanged as a felon. Relieved of his command, Butler worked under General Grant in the operations against Petersburg and Richmond in 1864. It was Butler, however, and other generals like Nathaniel P. Banks, William Tecumseh Sherman, Ulysses S. Grant, and John E. Wool who developed ingenious and practical plans to promote education and the general welfare of freedmen, laying the foundation for the Freedmen's Bureau.[26]

In South Carolina, the freedmen's education was first begun by the New England Freedmen's Aid Society, but General Sherman put authority and organization into the educational work. He issued a general order in 1862 that divided the federal areas of South Carolina into districts and authorized one or more instructors for each division whose duty would be "to teach both old and young the rudiments of civilization and Christianity."[27] In response to this order, the first party of New England teachers, comprised of twenty-seven men and four women, set out for South Carolina. As schools were established on the large plantations, the National Freedmen's Relief Association, the Pennsylvania Freedmen's Relief Association, the American Missionary Association, and other agencies sent more workers to the area. By June 1863, the town schools were reported to have an enrollment of 600, with plantation schools having 1,311; because this report was incomplete, the aggregate enrollment was estimated at 5,000. Plantation schools were the main source of instruction throughout the war; they started at noon and closed at three o'clock so plantation work could be done. Evening schools were also available and well attended by black adults in South Carolina. The Port Royal Experiment off the coast of South Carolina made a significant contribution to black literacy; more than 10,000 adults, soldiers, and children received instruction in day and night classes provided by zealous Gideonites from 1862 to 1865.[28]

General Banks gave the first real impetus to Negro education in the gulf region. Appalled as General Butler had been before him at the suffering of 150,000 Negroes within his jurisdiction, Banks put into effect several strict regulations, not always popular, concerning the relief, work, and education of Negroes.[29] Entirely self-taught himself, having worked his way from a bobbin boy in a cotton factory through the ranks of law, politics, and the military, Banks possibly made a better record in his work with Negro affairs than he did in the military; although later vindicated by General Grant in his *Memoirs* (1886) for his failed command in the Red River expedition in 1864, Banks as a military tactician never achieved the distinction accorded him in the work with Negroes in the gulf region. White opposition to freedmen education was strong, and benevolent societies had hesitated to initiate it, with the exception of some private individuals. General Banks moved successfully to break down this bastion of opposition to education for all persons of color in the gulf region.

In the late summer of 1863, General Banks set up a Commission of Enrollment to supervise the advancement of education in New Orleans and adjoining areas.[30] Under his orders, a system of public Negro education was instituted in February 1864 that would insure at least one school in each district. A month later Banks established a Board of Education for Freedmen, and this three-member board was delegated a multiplicity of duties, some of them precedent-setting. To establish the one or more schools in each district, these board members initially had to find and secure suitable land, erect adequate buildings, and hire the teachers, with preference being given to loyal citizens of Louisiana. In addition to purchasing and maintaining all school supplies and equipment, the board had also to regulate and supervise all courses and methods of instruction for children attending the weekday classes and for adults who attended on Sundays. Within a year, the board members levied a school tax on real and personal property, including the crops grown on plantations, to pay the costs of educational expansion. According to A. D. Mayo and Paul S. Peirce, this Louisiana taxation was one of the first regular attempts to tax the southern people en masse for the support of free public education. With the election of Lieutenant W. B. Stickney as superintendent of the public schools, board members also tried to stimulate a spirit of cooperation among all citizens. The board would gradually assume even more responsibility toward outlying schools; by the end of 1864, it reported some ninety-five schools with 162 teachers, mostly southern and a few black. In addition to day students, more than 2,000 adults were also taught. By February 1865, more than half of the school-age children were enrolled. Education in the rural areas of the state, however, did not advance as rapidly or uniformly as it did in the vicinity of New Orleans.[31]

In the areas along the Mississippi River, several benevolent groups operated generally under the leadership of Colonel John Eaton, appointed by General Grant in 1862 as superintendent of Negro affairs.[32] Having rendered organized relief to the freedmen, Eaton actively encouraged the teachers working in the Mississippi Valley, representing, at first, the American Missionary Association, the Western Freedmen's Aid Commission, the Western Sanitary Commission, and the Society of Friends. Other groups also sent workers after Vicksburg surrendered, including the Northwestern Freedmen's Aid Commission, the National Freedmen's Relief Association, the Board of Missions of the United Presbyterian Church, the Reformed Presbyterians, and the United Brethren in Christ. By government orders, teachers were generally provided with quarters, rations, transportation, and school sites. There was general disorganization, with each group working independently, until Adjutant General Lorenzo Thomas placed all educational activities under Eaton's supervision in September 1864. Superintendents were then appointed for Memphis, Vicksburg, Arkansas, Kentucky, and western Tennessee. Many rural areas, especially in Tennessee and Arkansas, were neglected because of apathy or opposition from planters and war activities, but several groups aided the work of Major G. L. Stearns in the Nashville region. In middle and eastern Tennessee and northern Georgia and Alabama, the Pennsylvania Freedmen's Relief Association worked actively through W. F. Mitchells, its representative for establishing Negro schools.[33]

All efforts to educate Negroes in wartime conditions within federal lines experienced great difficulties. Buildings for schools and equipment were nonexistent or inadequate. Churches were often used, with no provision for separating age groups or desks; teachers holding classes outside or in leaky sheds, however, would have welcomed even a church. Bibles and testaments were often the only means of teaching reading, with occasional books and pamphlets from religious organizations. Every class, day or night or Sunday, was too crowded, and students had to sit around the wall or in the aisles on the floor.

The greatest obstacle facing northern teachers, however, was southern prejudice. Bitterly opposed to the uplifting of blacks, many southerners resented the mere presence of "damned Yankee schoolteachers," calling them scum or nigger lovers and frequently resorting to violence against them. Schools were often defaced and burned; teachers were denied a place to board or a store to buy supplies. Special orders from federal officials frequently had to be issued requiring planters to provide accommodations to teachers. Black students themselves were often attacked, and several teachers were forced by threats to leave town.[34] In Brookhaven, Mississippi, for example, the white population made it a practice in 1865 to deny employment to any blacks who attended school, trying to force them away from the classroom.[35] In other towns, a general policy was to keep money out of black hands in order to starve out the schools.

In 1866, Mary Close went to Brandon, Mississippi, to teach for the American Missionary Association. Her story illustrates a community's harassment and the determination of most of the northern teachers. At first, the whites refused to acknowledge or board her, so she went to live with a mulatto woman and proceeded to open day and night schools. When white students threw rocks through the windows and Close was unable to punish the miscreants, she went to the mayor. The rock-throwing stopped, but white animosity increased. The editor of the local newspaper warned her to close her night school or suffer the consequences; she refused, inviting the editor to "bring on his consequences." The editor responded that no "person of any refinement" would stay in a community where everybody looked upon her "with loathing and disgust"; if she went to church, he said, nobody would sit close to her. Close replied that well-bred Christians would not act that way, but the editor promised to send a parent "right up to see her about that." "Send that 'Christian' parent," Close answered, hinting that Union troops in Jackson might be sent to Brandon in case of trouble.[36] Unlike Close, some teachers were frightened away by such tactics, but the majority stayed, growing stronger through their difficulties. Many of the teachers lived with the Negroes in the dilapidated huts and learned to improvise, unable to purchase supplies.

Prejudice was not the exclusive right of southerners. Having leased plantations in the South as purely speculative ventures, some northerners were reluctant to provide education for the workers, being "fatally opposed to these plans for the culture and elevation of the laborer." In New Orleans, General W. H. Emory warned against speaking publicly of black schools because it was too dangerous. Some military officers opposed the education of Negroes and refused to cooperate with teachers. In Louisiana, a provost marshal balked at assisting a teacher; he did not believe in "nigger teachers" and had not enlisted to help them, he said. In 1862, the military governor of North Carolina, Edwin Stanley, was representative of many others in his opposition to the opening of Negro schools.[37]

In all areas the shortage of teachers was another crucial problem; the supply was always insufficient for the need. Bearing the vast physical, mental, and spiritual needs of the contrabands on so few shoulders proved a heavy load for the benevolent societies. In some areas the assistance of older blacks was utilized with the younger students, and occasionally some blacks began to undertake their own education. Three black women in Natchez, Mississippi, opened three black schools and charged tuition, about two dollars per month. Waiting for white teachers, two black men taught about 150 students in 1862 at St. Helena Island; one of the black teachers was seventy years old. During this period Savannah, Georgia, had a black school board and two Negro-controlled schools that received help from the American Missionary Association and the New England Freedmen's Aid Society.[38] Subsequent consolidation of many societies alleviated some organizational problems, and the Freedmen's Bureau supplemented the work of benevolent groups during its existence from 1865 to 1872.

Irregular attendance hampered the freedmen's progress and created

another problem for teachers. During the planting and harvesting seasons, adults and children alike had to be in the fields. Frequent moves,
following jobs or military camps, were common. Attempts at keeping
attendance records were haphazard, with no uniform policies at first.
Frequent name changes among the students confounded record keeping
even more. One school in Alexandria, Virginia, for example, had 275
names on the roll but an average daily attendance of only 160 in 1864.
Attendance was erratic, with small numbers in the day classes and
greater numbers in the evening. To solve the problem of irregular
attendance, many teachers took education to the pupils on the plantations, carrying books, block letters, slates, and clothing. Two sisters in
Portsmouth, Virginia, riding in a tumbledown carriage, served eighteen
plantations in this way, administering to young and old alike and
encouraging their studies.[39]

Students who flocked to established schools were a motley mixture of
ages, sizes, hues, and conditions, requiring great ingenuity on the part
of teachers. Mother, children, and grandchildren often walked hand in
hand to the schoolroom. A school in New Bern, North Carolina, was
typical in 1863: Of 160 pupils, fifty were between six and twelve years of
age, ninety-five between twelve and forty-five, and fifteen over forty-
five. Dressed in every kind of garb, often hungry and dirty, all ages
flocked to any available school, united in their eagerness to learn to read
and firm in their belief that schools were the symbol of freedom and a
guarantee against returning to slavery. Both young and old were zealous
students, preferring school to holidays and play. Adults were reported to
take their spellers and readers to their fields of work, seeking help from
their labor supervisors. When their work was finished, they headed tired
and dirty for their night classes. One South Carolina labor supervisor
reported that the field workers studied more than they worked, and he
threatened to take their books away. Steeped in illiteracy, many adults
found the schoolwork too difficult, especially after a hard day's labor; if
they lost enthusiasm for their own education, they never lost it for their
children.[40]

The subjects receiving the most attention in these early schools were
reading, arithmetic, spelling, and writing. Geography and history were
offered to more advanced students. The New Testament was commonly
used for reading and spelling, as well as lessons in Christianity. Commonly used textbooks for both children and adults included Hilliard's

First Reader and *Second Reader,* the *Bible Reader,* Cowley's *Speller,* and the *New York Speller.* Sewing and cooking were sometimes taught to the women. The students learned the alphabet and multiplication tables by turning them into songs. In Richmond, Virginia, one school even offered "graceful gymnastics," while another on St. Helena Island taught elocution. In all schools there was strong emphasis on military and patriotic themes, especially Abraham Lincoln, the American flag, and any activities promoting freedom. The students sang spirituals and patriotic songs, including popular ones like "America," "Heaven Shall Be My Home," and "Tell My Jesus Huddy Oh." In Arlington, Virginia, a favorite verse admonished: "So come bring your books and slate, and don't be a fool, for Uncle Sam is rich enough to send us all to school."[41]

In the American Missionary Association schools, some common textbooks included Wilson's *Primary Speller,* Fetter's *Primary Arithmetic,* Goodrich's *Pictorial History of the United States,* Montieth's *United States History,* McGuffey's *Reader,* Greenleaf's *Arithmetic,* and Webster's *Speller.* Stressing morals and good citizenship, the American Tract Society published books directed toward freedmen: *The Freedmen's Primer, The Freedmen's Spelling Book, The Lincoln Primer,* and the *Freedmen's Reader,* on three levels. Slavery and rebellion were condemned in these publications, while the virtues of thrift, hard work, and loyalty were stressed, with the aim of producing "a safe working class for the South and a pious and moral membership for their churches." Manners, truthfulness, punctuality, and industry were constantly hammered into the students by zealous teachers who were also capable of putting religious instruction before all else. One teacher in Hampton, Virginia, sometimes suspended his evening classes to hold religious services. Many teachers reported that revival fervor often replaced teaching activities. Evening classes could become "prolonged prayer meetings."[42] Most of the activities, many of the textbooks, and some of the songs frequently angered southern whites. When a Charleston woman heard songs like "We'll Hang Jeff Davis to a Sour Apple Tree" or "John Brown's Body" being sung with gusto, she spoke for the majority of the whites by exclaiming, "Oh, I wish I could put a torch to that building; the niggers."[43]

Already saturated with the notions of obedience and respect for white people and property, black students in these first schools presented no enormous discipline problems to their teachers. With no previous school experience, however, they were not always the model students, quiet and attentive, that the pious teachers expected. Some teachers reported excellent deportment, while others labeled their charges as rambunctious, rowdy, and wild. They were uncommonly restless, never having been so closely contained before; some invented illnesses to escape class. With large classes and crowded conditions, many were prone to move and talk too much; others engaged in fighting, cursing, and eating. Most of the students lacked the ability to concentrate for very long, a disconcerting discovery to their strict, northern teachers, who could not begin to comprehend their background of slavery, expecting them to respond like northern whites.

Just how to mete out punishment to the wayward and obstinate students in these schools was a sticky problem; many were accustomed to brute force and probably expected such punishment, but teachers in the American Missionary Association generally tried to avoid such reminders of slavery and appealed to the students' religious nature. The threat of expulsion was widely used with success. Other teachers used kindness and perseverance to counteract "spirits of mischief." On occasions, however, the rod, the rawhide, and the switch proved "more potent incentive to duty than any appeal to the affections or reason." Parents did not seem to object to the teachers' use of physical punishment when it was necessary. One mother brought her children to a school in Hempstead, Texas, charging the teacher to "whip them 'powerful' for *they were used to it and wouldn't mind the stick.*" For this reason alone, most association teachers refrained from using harsh physical punishment. It was difficult to beat a student who had perhaps walked barefoot over frozen ground to get to school or another who had eaten nothing but wild blackberries for two days.[44]

With little notion of time, the newly freed students, young or old, lacked any common knowledge of government beyond President Lincoln, Yankee soldiers, and local military generals. A Virginia teacher asked her pupils to explain the difference between rational and irrational, and a student answered: "Why it's rational when we draw rations and irrational when we don't." In South Carolina, a teacher asked the students where the Savior was born; the quick reply was "Boston." Who wrote the Ten Commandments? "General Saxby," the name the blacks commonly used for General Rufus Saxton, was the response. In a Sea

Island school, the question was posed, "Children, who is Jesus Christ?" A student quickly yelled, "General Saxby, Sar." An old student jumped up and exclaimed, "Not so . . . Him's Massa Linkum."[45] Steeped in their own peculiar beliefs and superstitions, the students brought them to the schoolroom, often confounding their Yankee teachers.[46]

Colored by conflicting reports, the progress of the early Negro students is difficult to ascertain. Northern teachers were prone to exaggerate their reports to impress their backers in the North or because they had no specific progress to relate. Quick-witted and imitative, black students could also fool people, often pretending to read with the book upside down, quoting from memory. E. L. Pierce reported that "memory is very susceptible in them, too much so, perhaps, as it is ahead of the reasoning faculty."[47] The Department of the Gulf confirmed this opinion: "They are quick-witted, excelling in those branches that exercise the perceptive and imitative powers and the memory while they are slower in arithmetic and in studies that tax the reasoning powers."[48] More progress was made in reading and spelling, therefore, and less in arithmetic; the slaves had been schooled in the repressive decades before the war to depend on memory alone for information. Clumsiness and the conditioning of slavery often hindered adult students. One teacher in South Carolina reported in 1863 of the older blacks: "They make sorry work trying to copy figures on their slates. I let them use them every day now, however, for they must learn by gradually growing familiar with the use of the pencil not to use it like a hoe. There are furrows in the slates made by their digging, in which you might plant benny-seed if not cotton."[49]

Allowing for all reservations concerning educational progress, however, there was substantial growth for Negroes under federal control from 1861 to the end of the war. Working in wartime conditions, with shortages of teachers, buildings, and supplies, general disorganization lacking uniform guidelines, and extreme southern prejudice, conscientious northern teachers, largely women, had accomplished nothing short of a miracle: The rudiments of an educational system had begun in the South, and an entire race had started going to school. With subsequent official assistance from the Freedmen's Bureau and the consolidated benevolence of the American Missionary Association, the work of northern teachers multiplied like mushrooms throughout the South, preparing the Negro race for freedom and citizenship. Booker T.

Washington paid tribute to their work: "The part that the Yankee teachers played in the education of the Negroes immediately after the war will make one of the most thrilling parts of the history of this country. The time is not far distant when the whole South will appreciate this service in a way that it has not yet been able to do."[50]

☞ One of the first and strongest organizations in educational work for Negroes, the American Missionary Association rapidly increased its efforts when the war ended in 1865. At that time, there were already 250 teachers and missionaries in the field; by 1868, the number had more than doubled. Operating in every southern and border state, these teachers reported nearly 40,000 pupils in day and night classes in June 1867, with an additional 18,010 in Sabbath schools. Strongest in Virginia, the American Missionary Association was also the largest benevolent group in Georgia, Tennessee, Alabama, and Louisiana. Of the eighty-four benevolent schools in Georgia, for example, seventy-six of them were established by the association.[51]

In the first flush of freedom, grandparents and grandchildren alike crowded into all available schools. When the Storrs School opened in Atlanta in 1872, it could not accommodate all who tried to enter. One teacher reported: "It was a riot for an education; starved minds were claiming and fighting for food." Students who could not get in wept bitterly. When a schoolhouse in Virginia was burned, forty-five black men begged the teacher to stay, promising to build her a better building "of timber so green that it could not burn" and to keep her "supplied with green schoolhouses as long as she would stay." A white military commander in South Carolina reported that black soldiers had a "perfectly inexhaustible" love of the spelling book.[52]

Gray-haired and dim-sighted adults pored over the spelling books with younger students. A stooped, half-blind, nearly eighty-year-old man in Nashville like so many other adults went to school with the expressed purpose of reading the Bible before he died, and he made good progress. An Arkansas teacher wrote that it was often gray heads bent over the books in tents, hovels, shops, and kitchens. Other adults were motivated by improving their general conditions and learning to become better citizens. Night school students in Florida wanted to learn how to read the names on the ballot box. Some were anxious to study the Constitution. As early as 1869, a night school in the District of Columbia had 232 people enrolled, men who worked all day in the boiling sun, hurried home for a bite of supper, and got to their night classes. In Jacksonville, Florida, masons and carpenters over fifty years of age also attended reading classes at night. In Savannah, the night classes contained cooks, laundresses, ironers, cigar makers, cotton pickers, nurses, and milk carriers. These examples typified what was happening all over the South.[53]

Anxious to make up for lost time, some adults attended both day and night classes. "The war has set us free," they said, "but as yet, we are without the means of making this freedom a blessing to us. In order to use our freedom for our own good, and for the good of society, we must be educated."[54] When some adults were unable to attend school, they insisted that their children be educated, often giving of their scanty means to establish and support local schools. When Richard R. Wright sent his message through General Oliver O. Howard, he spoke for the struggles of most Negroes. "Tell them we are rising, sir."[55] In spite of the obstacles, the greatest of which were poverty and the lack of opportunity, thousands of blacks received, while not the best of education, at least enough to establish a pattern of literacy in their families and to teach others in the country districts. Many others advanced to the secondary and normal school levels, preparing themselves for black leadership in the crucial decades ahead.

With prophetic consideration for this future leadership, the American Missionary Association made its most significant and enduring contribution to black education through its system of colleges pioneered after the Civil War.[56] From 1866 to 1869, the association established seven colleges or normal schools throughout the South and assisted the funding of Howard University. Until blacks had access to all levels of education, the association contended, the task of black education would not be complete. Adopting a long-range plan, the American Missionary Association set its course to provide higher education that was denied blacks in white colleges. By 1869, having encountered and overcome many obstacles, the association had realized its dream.[57]

Berea College in Kentucky, the first of the association colleges, was founded in 1855 by John G. Fee and John A. R. Rogers and admitted its first black students in 1866. From a stormy beginning, when the school was broken up by slaveholding sympathizers, Berea has remained unique in providing education for blacks and poor whites alike, with the exception of the first decades of the 1900s, when a 1904 Kentucky law forbade integration in state schools. Fee was a loyal friend to the blacks and all underprivileged, providing them opportunities not found elsewhere. Both academic and manual training were offered at Berea, and all students worked several hours per week to earn their tuition and board. Its vast forests, varied industries, gardens, and farms have provided work for educational opportunities through many decades, keeping Berea in the foreground as a "practical demonstration of impartial education."[58]

Fisk University, founded as Fisk School in 1865 in Nashville, evolved into one of the outstanding black universities. Assisted by General Clinton Fisk of the Freedmen's Bureau, who helped secure the use of an abandoned Union hospital for the school, John Ogden, Rev. E. M. Cravath, and Rev. E. P. Smith of the American Missionary Association and the Western Freedmen's Aid Commission founded the school to help educate black teachers. Normal classes began in 1867 and regular college work in 1869, providing classical studies, teacher training, and religious instruction. Attaining national recognition, it was the first Negro institution to be fully accredited. Booker T. Washington's third wife, Margaret, attended Fisk, and it was there that Washington first met her; he would always maintain close ties with Fisk, providing influential help on many occasions.[59]

Atlanta University also offered classical studies and teacher training. Chartered in 1867 and opened in 1869, the school, like Fisk, had the advantage of being in a well-populated center, emerging, some think, as the best black college.[60] In contrast, Talladega College suffered the isolation and struggles of a rural area. A former slave, William Savery, convinced the Freedmen's Bureau in Alabama of the need for a college. The American Missionary Association, having operated the only black school in this rural region, then assisted the bureau in buying a vacant building; classes began in 1867. Talladega was the first college open to Negroes in Alabama; Addie Butler later characterized this school as one of three distinctive black colleges because of its mission, generational bonding, and unique accomplishments. Only normal work was offered at first, with regular college work beginning in the late 1800s; its primary mission was the training of teachers. Rev. Henry E. Brown, principal, urged churches to send their best prospects, accompanied by bacon and corn; hopeful students often walked up to thirty miles to

Talladega with food on their backs. William Savery, a former slave, was a trustee at Talladega; having sawed the first plank, he lived to see three of his children graduate from the school he had helped to start. The first bachelor's degree was granted in 1895.[61]

Hampton Institute in Virginia, a pioneer experiment in freedmen's education, started its work with contrabands in 1868 under the leadership of General Samuel Armstrong and the American Missionary Association. One of the first black schools to receive international recognition, it was chartered in 1870 as Hampton Normal and Agricultural Institute. Providing training in industries, farming, and basic studies, Hampton did not offer college work for several decades. From Hampton and General Armstrong, Booker T. Washington received his philosophy, training, and impetus for the founding of Tuskegee in Alabama. Washington's first two wives had close ties to Hampton, and it was Hampton teachers who advanced the initial success of Tuskegee as well as other educational efforts throughout the South.

In New Orleans, Straight (later Dillard) University was founded in 1869. A pioneering school in Louisiana, Straight provided industrial, normal, and religious instruction, with later emphasis on music, classical studies, law, and medicine. Night classes were offered in business, bookkeeping, accounting, and commercial law. Although it was not a school for the elite, some of the most influential blacks attended Straight; most students, however, were very poor, with many students leaving in the spring to work on plantations to earn money for education. Faced with many difficulties, Straight became the strongest school for blacks in Louisiana, "a beacon light and a benefactor" for the entire area, as one newspaper termed it.[62]

Tougaloo in Mississippi was incorporated as a university in 1871, graduating its first normal class in 1879. The school provided superior teacher training and became a great influence on black education. Successfully combining both industrial and academic training, Tougaloo demonstrated that the American Missionary Association was not intent on fostering one type of education while neglecting another.[63]

The debate about the advantages of liberal or industrial education that raged during the leadership of Washington had been thoroughly explored by the American Missionary Association long before Tuskegee was founded. It was, from the beginning, the belief of the association that blacks should have access to all levels of education, from manual through classical training, depending on inclination, opportunity, and background. Fostering all levels of education, the association discouraged concentration on one type alone but never imposed any limitations. Although Atlanta, Fisk, Talladega, and Straight leaned toward teacher training and more classical curricula, others like Berea and Tougaloo successfully combined industrial and academic training. The foremost example of industrial training, Hampton Institute also provided academics and teacher training. Generally missing in most of the debates about industrial education was a significant factor—money. Many of the large benevolent funds established for Negro education after the Civil War—the Slater Fund, for example—frequently stipulated that only those schools providing industrial education would receive assistance. Consequently, several schools tagged on industrial training as a loose appendix, desperately seeking funds to keep the schools open.[64]

On the other side of the coin, the association was caught in the "damned if you do, damned if you don't" syndrome and criticized for opening colleges before black students were ready for them. Such charges were unjustified. The histories of these schools reflect that students began where they were; many were still on an elementary level, while others had to depend on association colleges for secondary work because there were virtually no high schools for blacks for several decades. Fresh out of slavery, where education had been denied, very few of the freedmen were even ready for normal training; the evolution of the colleges, therefore, followed the evolution of the freedmen into college preparation. The normal schools slowly progressed to colleges and universities as more freedmen were ready for advanced studies. For many students, the process of education was a slow one because they alternated work and study. Sterling Brown was a typical case. Born a slave in Tennessee, he worked on a farm until 1867. Brown started at Fisk but had to drop out to earn enough to continue. Ten years later, he had attended school only twenty-six months.[65]

While grappling with broad ideologies inherent in its bold gamble on the future of black education, the American Missionary Association had also to confront the daily, mundane, irrefutable realities of staying in existence. Like all schools, the association lacked funds. Having overextended its work, the association often could not pay its bills until more collections were taken in the North. Supplies, libraries, and equipment were scarce or nonexistent. Frequent changes in personnel caused disruptions; white teachers who considered themselves missionaries generally stayed no longer than a year or two, and policy disagreements also brought changes in leadership. Decision making at the local level was hampered by dependence on the control center of the association in New York; permission had to be secured from New York for any personnel or curriculum changes, salaries, and necessary repairs. With understaffed, predominantly white faculties, tensions were prevalent and paternalism ever present toward students on the campuses; outside, the climate was frequently dangerous.[66]

White prejudice and hostility continued to plague the association schools. At Fisk students carried firearms for protection against Klan activities and other violence. Talladega lived in fear of being burned out because two schools had already been destroyed. Arson also demolished buildings at Tougaloo, Hampton, and Straight; practically no school was exempt from threats and some kind of damage. After Washington founded Tuskegee in 1881, his letters often reflected fear of his work being destroyed if white anger should be unduly aroused, a situation that many northerners could not understand having never lived in such an atmosphere of hostility. The arson cases became so numerous in the association schools that the Continental Insurance Company of New York canceled their policies, making the association's strained financial problems more severe.[67]

In spite of the opposition and multiple obstacles (or perhaps because of them), one of the most exciting, significant, and durable ventures in the history of education, especially for adults, succeeded: the training of black adults in association colleges when other facilities were closed to freedmen. With the help of the Freedmen's Bureau and northern philanthropy, the American Missionary Association had demonstrated a great American success story of vision, courage, and perseverance. By 1890, more than one-third of the blacks who graduated from southern and border-state colleges were from association schools. The graduates included teachers, ministers, doctors, lawyers, editors, bookkeepers, businessmen, government employees, politicians, farmers, druggists, housewives, and community leaders. Fanning across the United States, they changed the course of the black race forever, giving it dignity and direction. In addition to these graduates, many thousands had also been provided an elementary or secondary education; they returned to their communities to share their education, habits, and training, passing on a tradition of literacy to their children and grandchildren. As Joe M. Richardson concluded, "The early colleges dramatically demonstrated to a skeptical nation that blacks were as capable of higher education as any other people," training in every field the black leaders for the twentieth century and a possible equality.[68]

Just a month before his death, Washington made a speech before the American Missionary Association in New Haven, Connecticut. Recalling the great advances made by his race, he posed the question: "To what in a single generation are we indebted for this transformation in the direction of a higher civilization than the American Missionary Association?"[69] Citing the figures, he credited the association with great progress: in 1915, almost two million Negro children were enrolled in southern public schools; more than 100,000 adults attended normal schools and colleges; and black teachers numbered some 34,000, with 3,000 of these teaching in colleges, normal, and industrial schools. When the association started its work with black colleges, Washington said, there had been only four schools of this kind in the United States; in 1915, there were fifty colleges devoted to blacks in the South; thirteen for Negro women; twenty-six theological schools; three schools of law; four for medicine; two for dentistry; three for pharmacy; seventeen state agricultural and mechanical colleges; and more than 200 normal and industrial schools.[70] With its unquestioned accomplishments, however, the association had not been the solitary hero; many equally zealous benevolent societies had frequently worked beside the missionaries. Without the official support of the short-lived Freedmen's Bureau, moreover, some of the association's dreams for the black race would never have come to fruition.

☞ Although not established as an education agency, the Freedmen's Bureau also became an instrument for the education of freedmen. Because the March 3, 1865, bill authorizing the bureau did not provide for Negro education, the first year of its operation was not specifically devoted to school work; some initial steps were begun, however. General Oliver O. Howard, the bureau's appointed commissioner, found several schools already in existence in 1865, including some day schools for younger children and the unemployed, night schools for working children and adults, industrial schools for both men and women, and Sunday schools that taught both Christianity and literacy. General

Howard later stated that he had provided encouragement and protection to these existing schools, while setting up school officers in each state to help organize the work already being done, coordinate the scattered agencies, and start new schools. During this first year, Howard began his policy of allowing nonessential military buildings to be used as schools, providing transportation for teachers and the movement of supplies, and giving subsistence to all education work.[71]

The federal government in July 1866 gave official sanction to the work in progress, authorizing the bureau to assist existing schools, secure buildings for more schools, and provide protection for all teachers and schools. An appropriation of $521,000 was stipulated for the schools, with funds coming from the sale or lease of property belonging to the Confederate states; an additional $500,000 soon followed for schools and asylums. By June 1868, Congress voted to allow all funds not needed by General Howard for administering the law to be applied to the education of freedmen and refugees. As the funds increased, the bureau's education work grew more stable and uniform, and the consolidation of various benevolent societies to give strength and efficiency was encouraged under the American Missionary Association and the American Freedmen's Union Commission. By November 1867, Howard could boast that schools for freedmen had reached "the remotest counties of each of the confederate states."[72]

With elementary schools expanding, the bureau turned its attention to the training of competent black teachers. In October 1869, Howard reported that each state had at least one normal school. The bureau had strongly supported the American Missionary Association in founding Hampton Institute, Berea, Atlanta University, and Fisk; colleges received some support in Virginia, South and North Carolina, Alabama, Tennessee, Ohio, Kansas, West Virginia, Pennsylvania, and several other states. With no public high schools available for blacks, the bureau was concerned that industrial and normal schools should be available in each area for those blacks who were ready; it supported this movement with various degrees of financial assistance. One school that received inordinate support was Howard University. Incorporated in March 1867, Howard had normal, agricultural, academic, law, medical, and theological departments available to all former slaves and refugees of both sexes. With General Howard's influence, buildings were constructed and funds were made available for the support of the university.

Whatever the controversy regarding Howard University, the investment became a good one for the higher education of blacks and a permanent success.[73] The combined efforts of the bureau and the American Missionary Association had produced tangible results in training black teachers. After the Civil War, the elementary education of blacks had been conducted almost exclusively by white northern teachers; in 1869, black teachers comprised almost half of the total teaching force of 1,871.[74]

The Freedmen's Bureau had invested substantial funds in the education of freedmen. The annual school fund rose from $27,000 in 1865 to almost one million dollars in 1870. With benevolent groups and freedmen together contributing almost an equal amount, the bureau devoted $5,262,511.26 to the schools under its jurisdiction from June 1865 to September 1871. When congressional money was cut off in 1870, the bureau's main efforts were curtailed, but it maintained some supervision over the schools until it was abolished in 1872. When the bureau concluded its active participation in the area of education, it reported under its jurisdiction 2,677 day and night schools with nearly 150,000 students and more than 3,000 teachers and 1,562 Sabbath schools with nearly 100,000 pupils and more than 6,000 teachers, for a grand total of 4,239 schools, 9,307 teachers, and 247,333 students distributed unevenly throughout the South and border states. According to bureau reports, progress had been made in attendance, scholarship, and habits. The true extent of the bureau's success, however, has often been questioned.[75]

Dr. J. L. M. Curry, secretary of both the Peabody Education Fund and the John F. Slater Fund, was well acquainted with the education work of the bureau and the complexities of the South. Speaking of the bureau's work, he rendered a harsh conclusion: "What was done locally and individually was almost universally short-lived and in utter misapprehension of conditions and methods."[76] The central weakness was perhaps the teachers rather than the bureau, which had functioned mostly to coordinate and supervise. Northern teachers, often ignorant of southern slave conditions, had tried to introduce and impose inherited New England traditions and expectations, diverting the freedmen's attention away from the problems of survival in a white society. Washington often voiced that criticism: "Men have tried to use, with these simple people just freed from slavery and with no past, no inherited traditions of learning, the same methods of education which they have used in New England, with all its inherited traditions and desires."[77] Other critics denounced the bureau's education work as a flat failure, but the essential question must be raised: Without the work of the benevolent groups and the subsequent official support, funds, and leadership of the bureau, what would have happened to the freedmen? Would there have been any education at all?

Though its methods were imperfect and its life short, the bureau made significant contributions to the education of freedmen. By establishing and supporting institutions such as Howard, Fisk, and Hampton, it provided a lasting legacy to the American blacks. Some semblance of order, if not permanent or perfect, had been created from the scattered network of freedmen's education, with methods of grading and supervising village and city schools. By consolidating many societies under the American Missionary Association, the bureau proved more efficient in coordination and supervision. It provided funds, buildings, supplies, transportation, and encouragement, continuing to open new schools. Through bureau urging, more teachers were persuaded to work with freedmen, and because of its federal sanction, many philanthropists were inspired with confidence to support Negro education in the South. When the bureau discovered, sponsored, and sustained white educators such as General Samuel Armstrong of Hampton Institute, it provided worthy role models who influenced black education for many decades, if not permanently, having great impact on black leaders like Booker T. Washington, who was just starting on his path to literacy.

☞ Having left Hale's Ford, where all the slaves were illiterate according to every indication, the freed Washington family expected better circumstances when they got to Malden, West Virginia, in the late summer of 1865. The free blacks in Malden, however, including Baptist minister Lewis Rice, were illiterate like themselves. Crowded into filthy huts or slaving for pennies in coal and salt mines, the blacks in Malden provided a microcosmic view of the unquenchable thirst for learning characteristic of most freedmen throughout the South. Calling them "a whole race trying to go to school," Washington reminded later generations of the former slaves' intensity to learn after decades of denied opportunity. Young and old alike flocked to the schoolroom as fast as a teacher could be found and filled all the day and night schools. Anxious to read the Bible before they died, "men and women who were fifty or seventy-five years old would often be found in the night-school. Sunday-schools were formed soon after freedom, but the principal book studied in the Sunday-school was the spelling-book. Day-school, night-school, Sunday-school, were always crowded, and often many had to be turned away for want of more room."[78]

Washington's first brush with literacy fueled a fire within him. After work, he saw a large crowd gathered around a young black man who was reading a newspaper to the eager crowd; he watched the reader with envy, like the rest of the spectators. No school had yet been organized in Malden, but the newspaper incident spurred the dormant initiative among the free blacks to start their own school. Since the man who had read to them was too young, they hired as teacher a young man from Ohio, William Davis, who happened to wander into Malden. Every black family agreed to pay something toward the teacher's salary and help board him when their day came. William Davis proved a happy accident for the blacks of Malden.[79]

Born in Columbus, Ohio, Davis was only eighteen years old and lacked outstanding physical characteristics. Light-skinned, he stood about five feet seven inches tall. Though the blacks had eagerly hired him, he was not impressive in his academic achievements. Somehow between the years of 1861 and 1863 Davis had secured the rudiments of an education, but what he lacked in academics he made up for in dedication and wisdom. In spite of his limitations, he was an inspired teacher, starting the young Booker and other blacks on the first mile of their journey to literacy.[80]

Their first school, known as the Tinkersville School, was begun in the fall of 1865 in the bedroom of Lewis Rice, their illiterate but forceful leader, whose home had already been used for Wednesday and Sunday classes. His bed was dismantled to make room for slab benches, which would seat about ten people. The school received no assistance from whites, the county or township boards, or the newly established Freedmen's Bureau. Parents, under the guidance of Rev. Rice, who also boarded the new teacher, completely supported this school, the first of its kind in the Malden area. Working in the salt mines, Booker was unable at first to attend the day school; fortunately, Davis had opened a night class for workers, an event that would shape Washington's early thoughts and later leadership in that area. Even after a hard day's work at the mines, Washington often said that he learned more at night than the fortunate day students because of the great desire and effort required to do both.[81] Davis remained as teacher of the day and night classes until 1871, exerting a great influence on Washington's ideas and progress.

The Freedmen's Bureau turned its first attention to the blacks in the Malden area as early as 1867, sending General Charles H. Howard and other bureau officials to tour the region. Large crowds of Negroes surrounded them as they inspected the seven black schools now operating in the Kanawha Valley, promising the bureau officials that they would use any means possible to build and maintain school buildings. The bureau officials answered their enthusiasm, promising in turn to send "a first class man" to lead their education movement and to conduct institutes for the training of Negro teachers. The bureau's first-class man was a white New Yorker, Charles W. Sharp.[82]

Sharp became principal of the grade school in Charleston, West Virginia, and was also designated the supervisor of smaller schools in the surrounding Kanawha Valley. After a Malden meeting with the white school board members, Sharp felt confident that he had success with them, meeting all their objections about black schools. His subsequent optimistic report of this meeting back to the bureau was perhaps premature; the school board later reneged on any promises Sharp thought he had secured. Echoes of all the white school boards in the South came out of Malden; whites were complaining that they were already overtaxed in trying to build white schools. Continuing to have problems with all-white school boards, Sharp turned to the freedmen for subscriptions, reporting that they were "wide awake on the subject of schools." After many confrontations with the Malden board, he reported back to the bureau: "These School Boards are mostly ignorant, coarse-minded men; and while they are disposed to keep the letter of the law, are not willing to be at the slightest inconvenience in this matter."[83]

Begun in Rice's bedroom, the school at Tinkersville in the fall of 1867 had seventy-nine pupils. It was conducted in an old building completely owned by the freedmen and supported by a monthly forty dollars from the town and the rest from blacks themselves. Sharp reported to the bureau that the school "cannot be made comfortable in winter, and is in no way suited to a school, though it is better than anything the School Boards have yet provided." In the progress report submitted by Davis in November 1867, Davis indicated that he had approximately ten advanced readers. By January 1868, Davis reported that all but three of his pupils were advanced readers and that school funds had been enlarged, with Negroes still paying tuition. Continuing his night classes, Davis also separated his advanced students from the slower ones in the same room, giving special attention to each level but always emphasizing spelling and reading. Pessimism often crept into his reports. On one occasion, he wrote, "General apathy prevails where there is not decided prejudice and opposition" from whites. Sharp's reports went even deeper: "Some [whites] favor the education of freedmen in theory, but do not choose to encounter the violent prejudice of the community, by any positive action."[84]

The letters and reports of Davis, with misspellings and poor sentence structure, show his lack of adequate academic preparation, but he was an inspiring teacher, highly respected by his superiors and students alike.[85] A superintendent reported that Davis was courteous, kind, conscientious, and capable of establishing order and obedience; he had been a good example and influence for his students. When Davis was later the head of a Negro grade school in Charleston, he was given a "well qualified in every way" endorsement.[86] Caring and giving, Davis provided a special example to Booker of what a good teacher should be while giving him the foundations of his education. Because of Davis, Washington would be dedicated to the idea of night schools and opportunities for working adults. "The greater part of the education I secured in my boyhood was gathered from the night-school after my day's work was done," he wrote.[87] "My own experience in the night school gave me faith in the night school idea, with which, in after years, I had to do both at Hampton and Tuskegee."[88] Under discouraging circumstances, Washington's journey had begun. He had possibly learned all that Davis was able to teach, but he was determined to continue his education at any given opportunity.

In the darkness of the coal mines, Washington happened to hear two miners talking about a "great school somewhere in Virginia." Moving closer to listen, he learned that this school was for blacks and that students could work to pay their expenses. "It seemed to me that it must be the greatest place on earth, and not even Heaven presented more attractions for me at that time than did the Hampton Normal and Agricultural Institute in Virginia."[89] That any school could be better than the Tinkersville School was a great wonder to him. Without knowing where Hampton was or how many miles away, Washington quietly resolved to go, as excited as a child awaiting Christmas.

The road to Hampton had been a long one for Washington and his race. During the revolutionary spirit of the 1700s, blacks had made small gains, reaching a literacy rate of nearly 10 percent through scattered night schools, religious instruction, Sabbath schools, and some tolerant whites, but their heyday had been shortlived. Industrial developments, expanded use for cheaper cotton, growing agitation from the North that fostered insurrections among the slaves, and mounting fears among southern whites brought severe restrictions, virtually stifling slave education during several decades prior to the Civil War. Literacy rates dropped below 5 percent, leaving an entire race hungry for the printed word. With the arrival of Yankee soldiers carrying guns and benevolent societies bearing books and Bibles, an anxious people raced out to meet them. It was only through the prophetic wisdom of the American Missionary Association, assisted by the Freedmen's Bureau and other philanthropy, that Hampton was possible at all. Washington eulogized General Armstrong and all the men and women who had come into Negro schools at the close of the war "by the hundreds to assist in lifting up my race." They were a "Christlike" group, and "the history of the world fails to show a higher, purer, and more unselfish class of men and women than those who found their way into those Negro schools."[90]

The day was now at hand for Washington and thousands like him to start for Hampton. It would be a long physical journey, about 500 miles across the mountains, going by train, stagecoach, and foot. There would be perils; denied access to white sleeping facilities, Washington would sleep outside in the cold, often hungry. With his "soul bent upon reaching Hampton," however, neither white prejudice nor physical pain would stop him. Packing his few articles of clothing in a cheap satchel, he prepared for the journey that represented his entire race. He understood the significance of the journey, and the thing that touched him most was the interest the older blacks displayed. "They had spent the best days of their lives in slavery, and hardly expected to live to see the time when they would see a member of their race leave home to attend a boarding school. Some of these older people would give me a nickel, others a quarter, or a handkerchief."[91]

Washington reached Hampton in 1872. Footsore, dirty, hungry, and broke, the sixteen-year-old student presented himself as an unlikely candidate for entrance into this "Heaven." Only four years old itself, Hampton Institute would become the central influence in his life, philosophy, and subsequent leadership. With the rudiments of an education made possible by Davis and his on-the-job training in Viola Ruffner's employment, Washington passed his qualifying examination, the thorough cleaning of the recitation room. "I guess," Mary F. Mackie, the head teacher, told him, "you will do to enter this institution." The long night of suppression was over, not only for Washington but for "an entire race trying to go to school."

HAMPTON INSTITUTE

Adult Education for
Freedmen, Women, and Indians

4

It is a sorry caricature of the original impulse of Hampton to define it in the terms
of a pedagogical idea. It is rather a man incarnate—Armstrong himself,
multiplied and in action.
AMA Official, quoted in Joe M. Richardson, Christian Reconstruction, p. 135

One might have removed from Hampton all the buildings, class-rooms, teachers,
and industries, and given the men and women there the opportunity of coming
into daily contact with General Armstrong, and that alone would have been a
liberal education. Instead of studying books so constantly, how I wish that our
schools and colleges might learn to study men and things!
BTW, Up from Slavery, p. 55

Samuel Chapman Armstrong provided the positive mentoring for
Booker T. Washington's leadership in adult education. A mutual philosophy propelled and linked them, lifting both above the melee of medioc-
rity to international distinction. The one quality that possibly delineated
their greatness was what Horace Kallen called an "idea to bet one's life
on."[1] Such a philosophy is shaped by "critical events of a specific
person's experience," Kallen argued, and should not be depersonalized,
abstracted, or isolated from the dynamic contexts from which it springs.
"I know of no system of philosophy which is not first an event in a
personal history nor a resolution of its creator's personal problems,"
Kallen contended.[2] Molded by early and powerful influences, both
Armstrong and Washington entered the national arena with a clear
vision of the problems and needs of freedmen. Just as the milieu of
slavery initiated the philosophy of Washington, the missionary environment of Hawaii helped to mold Armstrong's ideas for social and educa-

tional programs. Implementing their dominant philosophy of head-hand-heart education, both men bet their lives on it at Hampton and Tuskegee.

From the gray ashes of the Civil War, General Armstrong rose like a restless phoenix, literally reborn in the impulses that moved Hampton Institute toward international distinction. Armstrong, the man, is inseparable from his work at Hampton, his lasting impact on black education, his strong influence as Washington's mentor, and his progressive ideas in adult education. A visionary leader, Armstrong formulated a successful blueprint for educating former slaves, poor whites, and Indians. At Hampton Institute he pioneered night classes, work study programs, nongraded instructional procedures, educational opportunities for women and older adults, and interracial studies. "It is seldom, in my opinion," wrote Booker T. Washington, "that one individual has had the opportunity through a single idea to revolutionize the educational thought and activity of so large a proportion of the world as has been true of the founder of Hampton."[3]

The seed of Armstrong's revolutionary idea for Hampton was sown in Hawaii, where he had lived with missionary parents until he entered Williams College in 1860. He had witnessed the mistakes of several methods of education, but he had also been impressed with the Hilo School and its success. Native Hawaiians boarded at Hilo and worked in various trades, learning valuable skills with their education. Edith Talbot, Armstrong's daughter, later reported that Hilo "was the only school where the Hawaiians were expected to work with *hands* as well as *heads*."[4] Its graduates became good teachers and productive workers who could build homes, earn a good living, and effectuate both social and economic change that reached the grass roots masses. Armstrong's experiences in the Civil War and subsequent work with the Freedmen's Bureau in the Hampton vicinity had reinforced his vision that a school like Hilo would be relevant to freedmen and that the country was ready to support such an idea.

During the Civil War, General Armstrong was favorably impressed with the "excellent qualities and capacities" of the black soldiers he had led. He had found them tidy and responsive, disciplined and daring in battle, devoted to their duties, and anxious to study their spelling books, even under fire.[5] When he founded Hampton Institute in 1868 with the backing of the American Missionary Association and philanthropy, his bold experiment was based on the pragmatic mission of Hilo School, as stated in his 1876 report: "The past of our colored population had been such that an institution devoted especially to them must provide a training more than usually comprehensive, must include both sexes and a variety of occupation, must produce moral as well as mental strength, and while making its students first-rate mechanical laborers must also make them first-rate men and women."[6] Future leaders like Booker T. Washington would be the beneficiaries of Armstrong's revolutionary idea.

When Washington graduated in June 1875, his three-year course at Hampton had included a surprisingly well-rounded program including language, ranging from sentence making through analysis, rhetoric, elocution, and debating; mathematics through algebra; history, American through universal; science through physiology and botany; miscellaneous courses, including Bible study, moral philosophy, music, and bookkeeping; agriculture, from the study of soil to crop rotation and meteorology; commerce, to include accounting, commercial law, and business contracts, with all students required to keep their personal accounts balanced; and mechanics, including printing and industrial, household, and agricultural machines. Leaving Hampton prepared for teaching, Washington, like thousands of other graduates, wanted to educate, not to further enslave his people. Exemplifying the spread of the Hampton idea, Washington would follow, almost to the letter, Armstrong's great commission: "Go ye out and do likewise."[7]

⟜ During his student days at Hampton, Washington participated in many programs of adult education. Older students had flocked to the school to learn trades, preaching, teaching, or combinations of these. One older man wrote Armstrong: "I am poor an nedy for the want of somebody to Teach me. I am called to preach the Gospel in the World. While I am therein the World and I want som more Instruction. If you ill take me in that Schoold, I Will find myself ef you ill find me a Bead to sleep in." Another told how he learned to count to a hundred in slavery, using a board and a piece of coal, "marking marks one by one" and reaching fifty counts when he was freed. "I kept up studying my books, and then began to teach school, studying also nights." Then he went to Hampton to improve his teaching.[8]

An older woman wrote Armstrong that the Lord had helped her in the

darkest hours of slavery; in freedom, He was helping her get an education. "I work a while, and then go to school a while, and now I am able
to teach, and have taught three years." Having found her calling, she
was "proud of the chance of coming to Hampton to fit myself for that
end." A man who had not been admitted because of his unpromising
appearance and poor showing on the entrance examination appeared
before Armstrong. Seeing the man's dejected face, Armstrong inquired
how he expected to get back home. The man told Armstrong his story.
He had walked most of the way from Russell County, West Virginia,
and had the fifty-two dollars he had earned in a blacksmith shop for
Hampton stolen by a pickpocket, leaving him with only fifty cents.
Armstrong could not make the man retrace his steps back home and
allowed him to stay at Hampton. "When I found the General would let
me stay," he reported, "I determined to do the very best I could, both in
working and studying." He was a faithful student, doing much of the
iron work on the roof of Virginia Hall and graduating in good standing.[9]

Concerning the caliber of his older classmates, Washington reported:

> I was among the youngest of the students who were in Hampton at that
> time. Most of the students were men and women—some as old as forty
> years of age. As I now recall the scene of my first year, I do not believe
> that one often has the opportunity of coming into contact with three or
> four hundred men and women who were so tremendously in earnest as
> these men and women were. Every hour was occupied in study or work.
> Nearly all had had enough actual contact with the world to teach them the
> need for education. Many of the older ones were, of course, too old to
> master the textbooks very thoroughly, and it was often sad to watch their
> struggles; but they made up in earnestness much of what they lacked in
> books. Many of them were as poor as I was, and, besides having to
> wrestle with their books, they had to struggle with a poverty which
> prevented their having the necessities of life. Many of them had aged
> parents who were dependent upon them, and some of them were men
> who had wives whose support in some way they had to provide for.[10]

With Hampton's early commitment to older students and Armstrong's insistence on the education of women, Washington also witnessed the growth of community programs, cooperative efforts to link
Hampton's programs of agriculture and industry with the practical
needs and education of surrounding areas. Another effort of inestimable

significance to the education of all blacks and for communication with whites was the publication of *Southern Workman* during Washington's first year at Hampton. The first of its kind for southern blacks, the paper has received little critical attention for its contributions to black education and its demonstration of the power of the press, a tool that Washington learned to use with great agility.

The first issue of *Southern Workman* was published on January 1, 1872. The official monthly journal of the college, it recorded Hampton history until July 1939, providing primary documentation of southern life, black education, and significant events such as addresses by presidents and the activities of Indians at Hampton.[11] It was initially edited by school officers and printed by black students, who paid their way while learning the printers' trade by typesetting and press work. By the journal's second year, it had a monthly circulation of 1,500 and paid subscriptions of over 1,100, achieving a "much nearer approach to the point of self-support than has ever been attained in the South before by any similar paper," as one solicitation boasted.[12] Printed on good paper and well illustrated, *Southern Workman* also won the support of influential whites, many of whom provided the one-dollar subscription fees to send the paper to poor families throughout the South.

Designed for freedmen, not politics, the paper was a teacher, and one observer wrote: "Such an itinerant teacher as a good newspaper is invaluable to those who can read. I find the *Southern Workman* in many of the cabins." It sent valuable information and news into isolated areas and, as literacy spread, became a strong link across the country for Hampton graduates and all blacks. The paper was filled with Hampton happenings, reports from teachers in the field, national or world events affecting the freedmen, and practical articles about agriculture, housekeeping, education, and science. One eager former slave wrote Hampton, showing the grass-roots enthusiasm for the paper; he wanted the paper issued twice a month rather than once a month, just for himself. "I have just bought a pece of Land and 1 Cow and one oxson, and I al so hav one Horse to make a Farm. I am now working out a Frame for my House, and to get my Head in order for bisness, it is my intrest to take your Paper. I like it so well that I would like to hav it come every 2 weeks. . . . You must let *me* have it that way if you cant no other person."[13]

In isolated areas like Malden, West Virginia, the *Southern Workman* was eagerly awaited and used by teachers like Booker T. Washington. The Tinkersville School patrons had hired Washington immediately at a salary of $31.50 per month after he secured his first permit to teach. Only twenty years old, restless and energetic like his mentor Armstrong, Washington began his day at 8:00 A.M. and continued until ten or later at night. A dedicated teacher, he opened a night school for older students and adults who worked all day; his night classes were as large as the day classes, overcrowded and demanding his best energy to keep tired bodies and minds awake. Over the weekends, he taught two Sunday schools, worked with a debating group, began to write newspaper articles, tutored promising students for Hampton, involved himself in community projects, and acted as clerk of the Mount Olivet Baptist Association. Taking literacy to all of Malden, he started a reading room, the seed of a public library, with old books and newspapers frequently begged from Hampton. With nearly 100 students in both day and night classes, Washington was hard pressed to keep all students motivated and progressing on various levels in different subjects while pursuing his other projects.[14]

Committed to the precepts of General Armstrong and Hampton, Washington had a dramatic and immediate impact on his students and community as well as long-lasting influence. He insisted on the value of military drill, the toothbrush, and all "hair-brushing, clothes-brushing, and scrub-brushing," conducting daily drills and inspection of personal hygiene. "In all my teaching I have watched carefully the influence of the tooth brush," he later wrote, "and I am convinced that there are few single agencies of civilization that are more far-reaching."[15] Of more significance, however, were those students he prepared for Hampton, several of whom became doctors, lawyers, and public officials. Samuel E. Courtney was one example. After Hampton, Courtney graduated from Harvard Medical School and became a prominent physician and member of the public school board in Boston. According to Courtney, six of Washington's students, known as "Booker's Boys," were thoroughly prepared for Hampton. Among the number tutored for Hampton were Booker's brother, John, his adopted brother, James, and one pretty girl of Shawnee Indian blood, Fanny N. Smith. With the latter, Washington had fallen in love; Fanny, a childhood friend of Booker's, became his first wife after she graduated from Hampton in 1882.[16]

The path Washington followed from his graduation in 1875 until his return to Hampton in 1879 was marked by some obscure twists and uncertain turns. "You always appeared to be looking for something in the distant future," one student, W. T. McKinney, later wrote him. "There was always seen a future look in your eyes."[17] Between short teaching terms he dabbled with the study of law and politics. A skilled debater already, Washington honed his public speaking and garnered name recognition when he spent the summer of 1877 speaking to a circuit of black communities. Prominent men in Charleston, West Virginia, had heard him speak and debate and wanted him to stump portions of the state to win votes for making Charleston the state capital. Often speaking to large audiences of both blacks and whites, Washington was reported to have given arguments in favor of Charleston in good style, "expressing his idea in a clear manner and with appropriate words, interspersing his speech with apt anecdotes, illustrating his arguments."[18] In the election on August 7, 1877, Charleston won out over Clarksburg and Martinsburg. Washington had effected large turn-outs in crucial areas, and this success stirred vague ambitions toward public office and the serious study of law under Romeo H. Freer, a white Republican in Charleston. Amounting to no more than the study and discussion of law texts, his political ambitions, however, seemed somehow contrary to Hampton's ideals, and Washington, facing serious career choices, looked to distant horizons. Labor friction and episodes of racial violence were occurring with greater frequency in the Kanawha Valley; the atmosphere was not always receptive to the idealism of Hampton.

At the age of twenty-two, Washington left Malden to attend Wayland Seminary in Washington, D.C., in the fall of 1878. A school for black Baptist ministers, Wayland offered courses in academic, normal, and theological areas. This eight-month, rather obscure period at Wayland was Booker's first contact with classical education, large cities, and theology, and he rejected all of them. Wayland was important, however, because it firmly cemented Washington's social and educational philosophy. Comparisons with Hampton were inevitable. He characterized the students at Wayland as stylishly dressed and book-smart, with more money to squander on frivolous things like expensive buggy rides on Sunday, but in his opinion they lacked the self-reliance of Hampton's students. Steeped in Latin and Greek, Wayland students graduated without the proper tools to improve the conditions of poverty and illiteracy, he concluded.[19] Viewed from his rural orientation, the city of Washington was a bad influence, crowded and somewhat replicating the biblical Sodom and Gomorrah. The city created a scenario for crime, he thought, and forced dependence on the federal government rather than the soil, "where all nations and races that have ever succeeded have gotten their start."[20] Washington saw a sickness in the crowded black community of the city, and the historian Constance M. Green saw a "withering of hope" and a "steady paring down of incentive" among the city's blacks.[21] Turning his back on the city and vague dreams of theology and politics, Washington received the fortuitous invitation from General Armstrong as a possible omen of the correctness of his course.

⇄ In February 1879, General Armstrong wrote Washington a typically terse note, inviting him to be the postgraduate speaker at Hampton's May graduation exercises. Armstrong offered free board and instructed Washington that "the idea is to bring out the facts of actual experience, to show what clear heads & common sense colored graduates of this school have attained, and to win the respect of all by a generous noble manly spirit." Armstrong told Washington to arrive early to confer.[22]

Carefully prepared by the honored graduate, Washington's "The Force that Wins" speech impressed the students, teachers, and a reporter from the *Congregationalist* in Boston, who called it "an earnest appeal to his colored hearers to believe in patient, unostentatious, consecrated labor in their efforts to help their race." Of the speaker himself, the reporter noted: "Mr. Washington is a remarkable man. There are some graduates of Yale or Harvard, of four years' standing, who can write a better address than his, but they are not many. Fewer yet are they who manifest such dignified ease upon a public platform, and hold so mixed an audience in such close attention. The Institute that can develop such a man, and send him out, may well take credit to itself for doing good work."[23]

Pleased with the results, the astute Armstrong invited Washington to join the Hampton faculty shortly after this speech. On July 1, 1879, Armstrong agreed with Washington's request for twenty-five dollars per month for "services here as teacher and assistant in study hour & other duty that may be assigned you." In a postscript, Armstrong threw in another carrot: "If you know a very capable & deserving but poor student who wishes to come he can come."[24] Washington's two-year tenure on Hampton's faculty, the last leg of his preparatory journey to Tuskegee, was of great significance in the maturation of his philosophy and leadership potential. Two unique programs in adult education would strongly influence his future years: the Indian education, already begun, and Washington's formulation of Hampton's first night school.

During his tenure, Washington directed considerable energy toward civilizing and instructing more than seventy-five Indians. It was a case study in racial relationships, expanding Washington's view of humanity beyond the previous black-white boundaries. "In the matter of learning trades and in mastering academic studies there was little difference between the coloured and Indian students," he observed. There were other forces at work also in this experiment, Washington keenly noted. Some black students resented the presence of Indians at Hampton, and whites were still enmeshed in the cult of supremacy, he reported. "No white American ever thinks that any other race is wholly civilized until he wears the white man's clothes, eats the white man's food, speaks the white man's language, and professes the white man's religion."[25] Washington himself was directly involved in the "curious workings of caste in America" during the Indian experiment. While transporting one of the sick Indians up to Washington, D.C., for his return to the reservation by the secretary of the interior, Washington had been refused service in the dining room on the steamboat and accommodations in a hotel in Washington; in both situations, the Indian had been freely admitted.[26] Important to Washington, Indian education at Hampton also had wide ramifications for adult education across the country, pioneering new ground. Hardly noted in adult education histories, the story of Hampton's Indian education, having begun in Florida, continued through several decades, successfully setting new precedents for adult education. How the Indians got to Hampton and their subsequent education there constitute an exciting and important chapter in adult education.

In the early morning hours of April 13, 1878, seventy Indians arrived at Hampton's waterfront, waking and surprising the sleeping campus. In a letter to his wife, Emma, Armstrong noted with laconic humor: "Night before last at 2 a.m. I was waked to find that 70 Indians were at the wharf. . . . We waked up everyone . . . put the Indians in two recitation rooms and went to bed again."[27] Having expected one Indian, Armstrong accepted with good graces the seventy, but three months later the number had dwindled when Armstrong reported to the Board of Trustees: "Curiously without effort on our part or expense to the school," Hampton had acquired seventeen Indians.[28] In an ironic twist of circumstances, these Indians had come, not in search of the white man's education, but as prisoners of war who had not known where or why they were going. They were accompanied by Captain R. H. Pratt, another unheralded hero in the annals of adult education, who had begun his work in Florida.

In 1875, the U.S. government had selected seventy-five Indians and chiefs after a tribal war in the Indian territory. They were separated from their friends as an example, bound hand and foot, and taken to St. Augustine, Florida, to be imprisoned at Old Fort Marion. The officer in charge was Captain Pratt, a man of Christian faith and great humanity. Pratt removed the chains from the Indians and became their friend and teacher during the three years of their confinement.[29]

During the course of their imprisonment, Pratt began a literacy program with the Indians. Some community women, filled with a missionary zeal to equal Pratt's, started coming to the fort to teach reading, counting, and knowledge of God, truth, and justice. So successful were their joint efforts that some of the Indians were incorporated into a regular school. One teacher had raised $220 for this purpose; with $40 left over, she urged Captain Pratt to use it for sending another Indian off to school. Pratt subsequently wrote to General Armstrong, asking him to accept this Indian at Hampton. Without any funds for such an experiment, Armstrong had nevertheless agreed to accept one Indian, not seventy or the reported seventeen.

Armstrong, the visionary, instinctively realized the possibilities for pioneering Indian education. The seventeen remaining Indians, however, were hardly sufficient for justifying such a program. Approaching General William T. Sherman and the secretary of the interior, Armstrong secured permission to have fifty more Indians sent to Hampton. Under instructions from the Department of Indian Affairs, Captain Pratt started combing the Dakota Territory, ultimately bringing forty-nine Indians to Hampton, including nine young women, on November 5, 1878.[30] Pratt's job of finding them had not been easy; he met some opposition to change. In a letter to Armstrong from Sioux City, Iowa, on October 10, 1878, Pratt told of riding 659 miles on wagons and stagecoaches in thirteen days; he had encountered great hostility from Indian chiefs to his recruitment project. At the end of October, he had secured only forty-nine students.[31]

Over a period of forty-five years, a total of 1,388 Indians passed through Hampton's program. Wanting to learn the "white man's road," many chiefs from the tribes also came, perhaps too old to learn the road for themselves but anxious to observe what this school could offer their heirs. Somewhat typical was Black Horse, a Comanche chief who had spent two years as a prisoner of war under Captain Pratt. "I have looked all around and seen what white man can do," he said in remarks translated by Captain Pratt to students and teachers at Hampton, "and I have found the white man is way ahead of everybody I know anything about." Said Lone Wolf, a prisoner at Ft. Marion who converted to the white man's road and religion, as translated by Captain Pratt: "It is God's road for all men. . . . The same things are for the red man as for the white man."[32]

Such mixing of cultures was controversial, raising perplexing questions. Should Indians be encouraged to keep their own culture or convert to the Christian white man's road? The primary question, raised earlier with the freedmen, was whether the Indian was educable. Would there be a "return to the blanket" when they left Hampton? With society still favoring Indians over blacks, was it a good idea to mix the two? Would the Indian lose his own culture, or was he capable of adjusting to the labor demands of a white society? In the Indian experiment, would the freedmen be pushed aside at Hampton?

The focus of the Bureau of Indian Affairs, Congress, and skeptics across the country was directed at the Indian experiment at Hampton. The outcome there would greatly affect attitudes of the government and the entire nation. Armstrong became a spokesman for Indians as he had been for freedmen. Facing each problem, he refuted negative arguments, often taking exception to many in authority, convinced that Hampton's education was the right road. According to an official report by Walton C. John, Hampton Institute set the example to be followed by all off-reservation schools in the country: "So marked was the success of the experiment at Hampton Institute that a public sentiment in favor of Indian education was created. From this small beginning has grown the present system of Government Indian education."[33] Captain Pratt established the first off-reservation school in the country at Carlisle, Pennsylvania, in 1879; his school was organized and run on the Hampton model, with Hampton Indians assisting its operations. Having brought the first Indians to Hampton, Pratt later reported: "Without the open door at Hampton, none of the advanced conditions in Indian school affairs to-day would have become established. It would be difficult to locate the critical period in the development of the movement, but certainly Hampton and Armstrong . . . can claim one of the foremost emergency positions."[34]

Armstrong's objectives for the Indians were based on two strong convictions. The Indians had lost self-respect through subjugation on reservations, just as blacks had in slavery; only through education could self-esteem be restored. The Indians, like freedmen, needed a means of self-support, independence, and properly trained teachers. Armstrong believed that Hampton had the method "in which the Indian may be educated to his own advantage, and to the country."[35] After four years of experimentation, the program that evolved included seven levels: the higher level of Indians ready for the regular classes in the normal school and the lower six divisions arranged according to ability and progress in English. Many in the lower groups had no knowledge of the language, and much of their early instruction was conducted orally. Math and English were the main academic emphasis, including speaking, writing, and reading. During the first year, teaching was accomplished by methods such as the use of pictures, toys, talking games, and short dialogues. Visual arts like large chromolithographs were employed the second year, with practice in letter writing and simple storytelling. By the fourth year, books were used, with exploration in simple science, American history, and practical application of knowledge to work skills. Students should be able then to read and follow instructions on the job, such as cooking, sewing, and agricultural or industrial tasks. With seven levels of academic competency, students entered at individual levels and moved at their own pace.[36]

The Indians responded with more enthusiasm to Armstrong's second objective, their preparation for economic independence. Several worked at the Heminway Farm to learn improved agricultural methods. Those who remained at Hampton during the summer worked at Shellbanks, a large tract of fertile farmland where students learned to farm by farming. While women learned firsthand skills in all areas of maintaining the household and family, men were involved in agricultural and industrial training that included printing, engineering, tinsmithing, blacksmithing, wheelwrighting, harnessmaking, butchering, shoemaking, brickmaking, and carpentry. These activities were on-the-job training, not busy work, and the Indians, like the freedmen, made products that were sold or used at Hampton. During the summer of 1879, Armstrong started an "outing" program that placed Indian workers with families in the North and East. Possibly the first work-study program in American education, according to William H. Robinson, these outings sometimes lasted an entire year; placed with good families, Indians of both sexes were introduced to family and farm life in white America, learning its manners, morals, and values while earning their way and improving work skills.[37] An article in *Southern Workman* expressed the philosophy that prompted the outing experience, obviously skewed toward the white man's road: Indian students had been instilled with the "great purposes of life." Whether they wished to "remain in the midst of civilization," become a part of it, or return and "take up land in severalty," Indians had been prepared to live and work out their "own destiny like the rest of mankind."[38] In 1882 Armstrong reported that the program had been a moral force and an educational success, providing discipline and experience.[39]

With all the progress of Indian education, however, some problems persisted throughout its duration at Hampton. Health questions were immediately serious but proved of easier solution than the difficult and continuing racial ones. With an alarming susceptibility to tuberculosis, 30 percent of the first group of forty-nine Indians experienced illness during the first three years; 20 percent died, either at Hampton or on their return to their homes. In his assessment of this problem, Armstrong discouraged the use of such statistics to curtail Indian education. "It is fair to say," he argued in 1881, "that this does not seem to be due so much to the change to civilized life, as to inherited weakness and diseased constitutions and to an utter disregard to all the laws of health."[40] With careful watching, a regular life-style, and better education, the health problem improved by 1883. The Indians showed greater stamina in the new climate and mode of life. By 1884 an epidemic of mumps was the only serious problem; from 1886 onward, Armstrong reported steady improvement in the health record of the Indians.[41]

The "race question" was the problem with no easy solution, contributing to Hampton's loss of government support in 1912. Recruiting was initially adversely affected by prejudice against a black institution in

Indian agencies. "I found this prejudice more or less at the several other agencies . . . and with like effort on the [Indian] girls," Armstrong reported in 1879. Several Indians, especially women, were "led to abandon their intention" of going to Hampton because of prejudice against the school.[42] Some citizens of Hampton, of the state of Virginia, and many others across the nation abhorred the very idea of mixing the education of two races. Concerning Indians themselves, there would be no meeting of the minds in educational philosophy. The cultural-absolutism school held that everything about the Indians' lives should be changed; the cultural-relativism philosophy, however, advocated a mixture of the white man's road and Indian culture. Armstrong walked a thin line between the two ideas. While maintaining that the Indians should keep their art and literature, Armstrong also encouraged many aspects of the white culture, such as an English-oriented education, the Puritan work ethic, and the Christian religion.[43]

Although controversy continued outside the school's boundaries, Armstrong took an optimistic stance on the mingling of the two races at Hampton. Other sources seem to support his optimism. Booker T. Washington acknowledged that a minority of blacks resented the presence of Indians, but the majority were eager to help the Indians "in every way possible," teaching them to "speak English and to acquire civilized habits."[44] Hollis Burke Frissell, Hampton's principal after Armstrong's death in 1893, generally reported that harmony existed with a minimum of conflict between the two races. According to Robinson, the "charge that the school institutionalized racism seems to have been largely unfounded," even though blacks and Indians were housed in separate facilities.[45] Helen W. Ludlow reported in her pioneer study of Hampton's Indian education that the separate housing arrangement was part of an agreement the school had made with the government to secure federal support and to ward off societal criticism and fears about mixed marriages. According to Ludlow, however, there was a congenial sharing at Hampton between the two races in the classroom, the workshop, the battalion, the farm work, and social activities.[46] Away from Hampton, the students contended with what Washington called "the curious workings of caste in America" during a similar experience. When traveling with a mixed quartet for fund-raising, blacks were not permitted to stay in hotels that welcomed the Indians from their group.[47] Complicating further the curious workings of caste and the sensitive racial question was the attitude of Indians themselves. According to Washington, "I knew that the average Indian felt himself above the white man, and, of course, he felt himself far above the Negro."[48]

The Indian experiment had demonstrated the "possibilities of harmonious cooperation" with no acknowledged interracial marriages, but Hollis Frissell, his successor, lacked Armstrong's vision and faith in the project. Armstrong's philosophy had embraced the education of all Indians, regardless of educational level, but Frissell wanted to accept at Hampton only those who were academically advanced and capable of becoming teachers and leaders for their people. In his 1903 Annual Report, Frissell summed up his view: "Unless it is possible to obtain Indians who are capable of meeting its [Hampton's] requirements for admission, it seems wise that the school should devote itself more to the education of the Negro and less to that of the Indian."[49] Finally yielding to public pressure about racial questions, Congress voted to cut off appropriations for Indian education in 1912. A few Indians continued to work their way through Hampton until 1923.[50]

Without any precedent to follow, Armstrong had initially planned and executed successfully the forty-five year mission for Indian education that challenged public sentiment and fears, effecting positive change. Through affirmative action, Hampton's Indian experiment embodied Armstrong's philosophy and proved to a skeptical society that Indians were educable, capable of progressive change, and successful in taking Hampton's precepts back to their people. Cora M. Folsom's follow-up study of 460 Indians who had studied at Hampton reported that 88 percent of them had been very successful in the areas measured, which included jobs, family life, and the establishment of schools.[51] With a high success rate for the 1,388 Indians who passed through Hampton over forty-five years, Hampton could be considered a center of research on Indian affairs and race relations during that period, expanding its resources and programs to meet the challenges of societal change. As with the freedmen, Armstrong viewed education for the Indians as "more than a preparation for their own support and decent living." They had a duty to their people, "a great work" to "teach by precept and example a more excellent way."[52]

Always ahead of his time and place, Armstrong pioneered many innovations in the Indian program. Accepting Indians of varied abilities, he was one of the first educators to employ the progressive, nongraded approach in the classroom, allowing students to start and progress according to ability and motivation. Hampton's on-the-job training permitted both Indians and blacks to earn while they learned, producing marketable products and skilled craftspeople. Alert to scientific progress in agriculture, Armstrong brought the best he could find to Hampton's farms, encouraging students to learn farming by farming in a better way. The outing experience was perhaps one of the first work-study programs in American education, with the resultant exchange of cultural experiences.

Believing that "there is no civilization without educated women," Armstrong pursued his plan for their education in the Indian experiment as he had for black women.[53] He took the progressive position that no race could rise above the level of its women. One of his winter campaign slogans, according to Folsom, had stressed this theme: "The condition of women is the test of progress. The family is the unit of Christian civilization. Girls make mothers. Mothers make the home." At Hampton he tried unsuccessfully to secure a fifty/fifty ratio of the Indian sexes, foreseeing an inevitable relapse should educated males "return home to mate themselves with savages."[54] By 1883, Hampton was pioneering education for married couples and their children, with the Sioux and Omaha tribes represented. "The parents attend school half a day and work the other half with the other scholars," Armstrong reported. "The husband and wife advance together with common interests. A home will be established on their return to the reservation, and their future will be comparatively secure." In the same report, Armstrong noted an interesting side effect of this project, a change in male attitudes. He was touched by the increasing tenderness displayed by fathers toward their children. Fathers previously had appeared scornful as they walked beside the women who carried heavy babies, leaving the fathers unburdened. The men were now taking pride in their children, often relieving the heavy burdens of their wives. Without coercion, men were learning the joys of fatherhood.[55]

Fundamental to all programs for Indians and freedmen, however, was Armstrong's futuristic view of individual and societal change through education. The training of teachers remained the primary objective of Armstrong's mission.[56] The future that he accurately envisioned would require each race to draw on its own resources. Trained teachers and leaders would make the difference between success or failure.

☞ In addition to his work with the Indian program at Hampton, Washington was challenged with another assignment. Armstrong had conceived the idea of a night school and wanted Washington to take charge of it. "As I look back over my life now," Washington wrote in 1901, the night school "seems to have come providentially, to help to prepare me for my work at Tuskegee later."[57] A keen observer of needs and possibilities, Armstrong had noted that many of the older students were too poor to pay any portion of their board or to supply themselves with books. With twelve promising candidates, Armstrong and Washington launched the new Hampton experiment in the midst of the Indian controversy and problems.

The basic plan for the night school was pragmatically designed for working adults. The selected students worked ten hours during the day and attended classes two hours at night; the men had jobs in sawmilling, carpentry, and brickmaking, while women worked in the laundry or performed other household chores. The students were paid more than the cost of their board for their work, with savings going into the school treasury. When their savings had accrued over a year or two, they could then move into the day school. Within a few weeks, there were twenty-five students in the night school. By 1900 the new experiment was so successful that it had grown to 400 students and had become a permanent program.[58]

Called the "Plucky Class," Washington's first night school students were serious and eager to learn, earning a printed certificate signifying their membership in this special group. Having attended and taught night classes in Malden, West Virginia, Washington understood the special problems associated with working hard all day and trying to learn at night. He kept students awake and motivated by frequent jokes, quick questions, and practical problems. During their working hours, his students could be heard discussing problems of arithmetic and grammar. One student worked arithmetic problems on a broken slate while he waited for his wheelbarrow to be emptied. To the night class they brought stored-up questions and often stayed until the lights-out bell rang, anxious for even more time.[59]

Writing in the *Southern Workman,* Washington praised two energetic students who had studied at night while learning blacksmithing and wheelwrighting, building a first-class cart. He also posed the question that would become a lifelong lament: "Why could not thousands of young men who hang around the streets of our cities imitate Murray's and Haw's example?"[60] Opportunities were now available, he believed; people could earn their educations by the sweat of their brows and by giving up a few evenings of pleasure. "Poverty can no longer be pleaded as an excuse for ignorance," Washington concluded.[61] As the night class drew more and more students, Washington was challenged to stay ahead of his energetic workers, and General Armstrong was kept busy looking for new industries in the surrounding areas that would hire the students for day work.

With the success of the Plucky Class and continued work with the Indians, Washington was making important impressions at Hampton. General James Marshall, the school treasurer, visited the night class with his wife, Maria; he was moved by their earnestness and gave a speech to praise the students. Several articles appeared in the *Southern Workman* under Washington's name generally relating to the Indian students or the night class.[62] Continuing his own studies, Washington formed an important alliance with Frissell (Hampton's chaplain at the time), who taught one of his advanced classes. Impressed with Washington, Frissell maintained close ties with him at Tuskegee, sharing advice and assistance, as would General Marshall. At the commencement in May 1881, Washington spoke on "The Negro and the Indian" and maintained General Armstrong's great favor. The period on Hampton's staff was grooming Washington professionally and personally for greater leadership. Acting on Armstrong's suggestion that he could bring one needy student with him to Hampton, Washington had brought Fanny Smith, whom he was seeing regularly at Hampton. After her graduation in 1882, they were married.

In May 1881, George W. Campbell asked General Armstrong to recommend a worthy white man who could provide leadership for a proposed school for blacks in Alabama's Black Belt at Tuskegee. In retrospect, there appears a certain inevitability in Armstrong's choice. He knew no white man capable of such a large task, but he was well acquainted with Booker T. Washington. Armstrong's reply to Campbell on May 31, 1881, with his characteristic terseness and scrawl, would propel Washington into national and international leadership and prominence: "The only man I can suggest is one Mr. Booker Washington a graduate of this institution, a very competent capable mulatto, clear headed, modest, sensible, polite and a thorough teacher and superior man. The best man we ever had here. I am satisfied he would not disappoint you." On Washington's behalf, Armstrong also questioned the circumstances of finances and established buildings. He then astutely laid out the color issue: Would there be any objection toward a black principal, with first-class black assistants? Armstrong concluded with his strongest recommendation: "I know of no white man who could do better. He has been teaching in this institution the past year & I am ready to promote him because he so richly deserves it."[63]

No buildings had been prepared for the proposed school, and Washington opened Tuskegee Institute in a leaky shanty adjoining the African Methodist Episcopal Church on July 4, 1881, with a meager $2,000 annual state appropriation. The school's physical struggle for survival, similar to Hampton's but even more difficult because of its isolation in the Black Belt, has been well documented in various texts and requires no repetition.[64] It was, however, the staff of Hampton Institute who nourished the infant school, providing guidance, teachers, money, and materials.

General Armstrong continued to act as Washington's mentor until the former's death in 1893, often in tangible form.[65] In dire economic straits on one occasion, Washington placed his situation before Armstrong. "Without hesitation he gave me his personal check for all the money he had saved for his own use," Washington revealed several years after Armstrong's death, and "this was not the only time General Armstrong helped Tuskegee in this way."[66] During an earlier period of great financial anxiety, "Something occurred which showed the greatness of General Armstrong—something which proved how far he was above the ordinary individual." Armstrong sent Washington a telegram inviting him to travel in the North with Armstrong and the Hampton singers for a month. To his surprise, Washington later learned that this trip was to important cities where both men would speak to raise money for Tuskegee, with all expenses paid by Hampton. This was Armstrong's way of introducing Washington to important money sources in the North.[67] Seemingly an insignificant gesture, the event had immediate and far-reaching results; backed by the respected reputation of Armstrong and

Hampton, this trip helped to build Alabama Hall, to establish Washington's credentials among prominent philanthropists, and to lay the groundwork for future trips and vital assistance to Tuskegee. Realizing that the funds raised on the trip were also needed at Hampton, Washington remembered Armstrong's unselfish gesture as a symbol of the solution for the "whole Southern problem."

More than a pedagogical idea, Hampton and its adult education programs reflected the philosophy that Armstrong, the "man incarnate," was willing to bet his life on—the development of the mind for old and young, the creative and productive use of the hands, and the building of strong moral character to channel the activities of minds and hands. Imbued with the same philosophy, Booker T. Washington would follow Armstrong's plan, "multiplied and in action" many times over at Tuskegee. His city on a hill, Tuskegee Institute, would embody and perpetuate the visionary missions of Hampton Institute while developing its own national and international programs in adult education.

TUSKEGEE

Washington as Administrator in
Public Relations and Fund-Raising

5

The place [Tuskegee] has a healthy and pleasant location—high and hilly—
think I shall like it.
BTW to J. F. B. Marshall, June 1881

When I settled down for my life's work near the little town of Tuskegee, Alabama,
I made up my mind to do as an individual that which I am striving to get my
race to do throughout the United States. I resolved to make myself, so far as I was
able, so useful to the community, the county, and the state that every man,
woman, and child, white and black, would respect me and want me to live among
them.
BTW, "What I Am Trying to Do," 1914

In 1977, Addie Butler selected Tuskegee Institute as a distinctive black college, along with Talladega and Morehouse. Without the qualifying liberal-arts orientation, Tuskegee was "paradoxically distinctive," according to Butler, because of its legend, the exploits of its organizer, its unique orientation, and its special mission. The legend and saga, coupled with its mission, generational bonding, and unique accomplishments, qualified Tuskegee as a distinctive black college, Butler concluded.[1] Although the school lost some of its distinctiveness after Washington's death, altering its orientation because of social changes, it still retained its excellence, Butler contended.[2]

The special mission that made Tuskegee unique was its adult education programs. Velma Blackwell viewed Tuskegee as a pioneer in the movement: "The evolution of Tuskegee Institute's adult education program is unique in that the Institution began as an adult education movement in 1881."[3] One of its first pupils was a local man who was fifty years old. Blackwell argued that the month that Washington spent surveying the area before he opened the school was an adult education method that translated the observed and felt needs of the community into the school's aims, objectives, and educational curriculum.[4]

Leo McGee, an author and educator, concluded that Washington was skilled in "diagnosing and assessing problems of the black masses of his time" in conjunction with his role as philosopher and leader of his race. Washington's role as an adult educator has been ignored, McGee wrote. Few have recognized Washington's ability to "conceptualize, develop, and successfully implement" many practical programs that were crucial to his people. "Little, if any, has been written about his strong concern for the adult population or his contributions as an adult educator."[5] While the top priority among most blacks of the period was directed toward establishing elementary and secondary schools and schools of higher learning, McGee argued that Washington differed from the majority in that he placed the greatest emphasis on the enlightenment of adults. With the improvement of intellectual and industrial skills, adults would become better parents, workers, citizens, and human beings in the general society. Washington himself had sounded this theme very early in his career:

> Soon after the Tuskegee Normal and Industrial Institute was established it was impressed upon my mind that much good might be accomplished by some movement which would interest the older people and inspire them to work for their own elevation. I think I first came to think of this when I had occasion to notice repeatedly the unusual amount of common sense displayed by what is termed the ignorant colored man of the South. In my opinion the uneducated black man of the South, especially the one living in the country districts, has more natural sense than the uneducated ignorant class of almost any other race. This led me to the conclusion that any people who could see so clearly into their own condition and describe their own condition so vividly as can the common farming class of colored people in the South, could be led to do a great deal towards their own elevation.[6]

The condition of the rural farming class, mired in poverty and peonage, had captured Washington's attention during his first summer survey in 1881. The priority that he assigned to farmers' needs, resulting in the Tuskegee Negro Conference and innovative extension programs, was justified by the conditions themselves and by the large number of farmers and families affected by them. When the Civil War started, only 4.2 percent of Alabama's slaves and 5.7 percent of its whites had lived in towns with populations over 2,500; in 1900, the state remained largely agricultural, with about 90 percent of blacks living in rural areas.[7] Alabama had begun a slight shift from cotton to steel in the mid-1800s, according to Horace Mann Bond, with the development of vast mineral resources in the northern areas and the completion of two railroad lines in the state. The industrialization and urbanization that occurred after 1900 were of little consequence, however, to black farmers immediately after the Civil War.

In the post-war period, agricultural conditions had deteriorated. When Washington arrived in Alabama, cotton production had shifted to the state's uplands because of poor agricultural methods, lack of supervision, depleted soil, and the prohibitive cost of farm supplies in the Black Belt, where blacks outnumbered whites about three to one. The Black Belt had seen immediate and harsh agricultural changes after the Civil War, as noted by Bond, and sharecropping was plagued by exploitation and control. The planting class had shrunk, and a merchant class had risen to take its place as cotton production had declined in the Black Belt, resulting in the rise of yeoman white farmers. Because the increased economic and social power of the class of yeoman farmers also translated into their greater political power, black farmers were exploited.[8]

In his first tour of the Black Belt, Washington had seen the degeneracy of intelligence and spirit—multiplied several times over for blacks—that John Milner had observed in whites twenty years after the Civil War: "White people here now all belong to the super-abundant non-producing class and will work nowhere in the fields. They are educated and born non-producers." Milner saw no signs of agriculture—no fences, hogs, cattle—nothing. Alabama soil was depleted, unable to support the state's population, he said, and large farmers had gone broke everywhere. Not one farm in a hundred could make a crop without a mortgage for a year's supplies, and he wondered to whom the lands in Alabama really belonged.[9] Blacks were even more destitute. Contributing to the degeneracy of spirit among blacks were the practice of peonage farming, depleted soil, and substandard living conditions, resulting in sheer exploitation. Poor, often illiterate farmers rented land and depended on merchants for advances to make their crops, paying from 50 to 90 percent interest, ending up with nothing for a year's work. One observer noted that he had seen black men make a large crop and not have enough money to buy a suit of clothes for the family after paying the debts incurred. "I have seen the taking of all crop by the merchant, and also, the horse or mule and other chattels which were given as collateral security for the debt in making a crop in one year."[10]

The scarcity of other job opportunities contributed further to the degeneracy of spirit, keeping the rural poor in the peonage cycle of farming. The large amorphous class of poor whites, identified by I. A. Newby, also suffered in destitution and was growing larger and more vociferous. According to Bond, they added to the pathological landscape of Alabama, competing for the best farm work, pushing blacks out of industrial and mining jobs, and directing frustrated anger against the use of public money for black education.[11] Samuel Chapman Armstrong had foreseen this problem, urging more training for poor whites. Washington himself, having lived among them in West Virginia, also frequently addressed the problem, sometimes blaming the churches for neglecting their "duty to the millions of poor whites in the South." He had consistently maintained that "When you help the poor whites, you help the Negro. So long as the poor whites are ignorant, so long there will be crime against the Negro and civilization."[12] In Alabama along the Georgia border and elsewhere across the South, the textile industry would not employ blacks in the mills, using the argument that blacks could not learn how to use the intricate machinery. Bond, however, contended that the textile industry had used its humanitarian appeal of uplifting the South's poor whites to excuse its blatant discriminatory practices. The industry had popularized the propaganda that poor whites had entered the textile mills to avoid competition with blacks in the cotton fields, and blacks had been almost totally barred from the textile industry.[13]

The practice of assigning blacks to the roughest labor in mines continued, if they were hired at all. Mechanics, foremen, and skilled operatives were white. In the 1880s the job market showed little improvement over conditions for free blacks prior to the Civil War. In 1853, Frederick Douglass replied to Harriet Beecher Stowe's question about how best to apply a sum of money she planned to use for black education. Douglass advocated that blacks should be given technical training: "Prejudice against the free colored people in the United States has shown itself nowhere so invincible as among mechanics," he wrote. He said he could more easily get his son into a law office than into a blacksmith shop. "We must build as well as live in houses," he said. "We are, in the Northern states, unknown as mechanics. We give no proof of genius or skill at the county, state or national fairs."[14]

Cheap black labor in Alabama was often utilized as insurance against labor troubles. "Industry in Alabama increasingly followed the example of Southern railroad management which frankly used Negroes to weaken white unions and depress wages," Bond said.[15] Even though blacks had been skilled as slaves, the general attitude of the state in 1900 toward the one-third-black labor force was still blatantly racist, as expressed in the Montgomery *Advertiser*, which stated the "undeniable truth" that "the Negro is not fitted to perform successfully any work which requires skill, patience, or mental capacity. There is something lacking in their brain and in their body." Their minds could not comprehend and their hands could not accomplish mechanical work.[16] Industrial promoters at a conference in 1900 voiced the opinion that "Negroes are well adapted for common labor, and in some instances can be satisfactorily used for semi-skilled capacities."[17] The training of Tuskegee and other schools was beginning to show some results, however. By 1890, there were 3,687 black mine operatives in the bituminous fields of Alabama, compared to 2,787 native whites and 1,492 foreign-born whites. By 1900, the number of black operatives had increased to 9,735. Steel mills were also using blacks as engine toppers or helpers in pipe-fitting, blast-furnace, and blacksmith work. It was not until 1907, however, that blacks were used as skilled workers and supervisors, according to Bond.[18]

Education, tied inextricably as it was to the social, economic, and political climate, was at low ebb in 1881, and the separate and unequal policy would continue to spread. The prevailing sentiment when Washington entered the Alabama scene was that education would only serve to take Negroes out of their place and keep school money from white students. Small concessions toward black education were made with bitterness, as expressed by "Old South" in the Montgomery *Advertiser:* "In our dismay . . . we turn tail and fly to education. 'Wo! Is me, Alabama!' Well, of course, let education go on. It serves our purpose: it appeases, a little, political masters and religious cranks. But it is a stupendous farce and a snare."[19] The earlier educational work of the Freedmen's Bureau and the American Missionary Association in Alabama, according to Bond, had reflected the "natural outgrowth of a social and political theory diametrically opposed to that of the conservative whites." Opposition to black education drew a clear line between two different social and economic systems, with the school logically regarded as an instrument of social control. "Prejudice against educating Negroes developed from the identification of the school with the Northern humanitarian program of social revolution in Alabama," Bond concluded.[20] In many respects, Bond blamed the wrong source for centuries of prejudice in the South and gave little credit to the educational work of the northern humanitarians.

Assessing the conditions of the rural Black Belt during the summer of 1881, Washington was appalled by the scene around him. Stated simply and with some rhetorical exaggeration, perhaps, his findings had shattered his generally unshakeable optimism. Like Armstrong in Hawaii and Hampton, Washington traveled the dusty, hot countryside with a mule and buggy for a month before Tuskegee opened in July. Like an Israelite in Egypt, he had been commissioned to "make bricks without straw," he concluded. Educators in the modern, more affluent America can only speculate on the trauma he experienced that hot summer. Twenty-five years old and separated from the familiar environment of Hampton, he was in a strange country, himself a stranger, to open a school without buildings, students, money, or supplies among people who lived in conditions not far removed from slavery itself.

The thick, dark, naturally rich soil of the Black Belt had been depleted by the repeated and unnurtured growth of cotton. Many of the poor farm families lived in crowded, one-room cabins, going daily to the cotton fields on a meager diet usually consisting of fat pork and cornbread, Washington reported after living with them during his travels.[21] Bogged down in the exploitative sharecropping system, farmers owed more to the merchants for supplies at the end of the year than they had made.[22] The majority lived on rented land in tumbledown rented cabins without medical attention, job training, education, money, or equipment. The few scattered schools in the rural districts were conducted in churches or log cabins that had no heat in winter and no books or supplies except an occasional rough blackboard. They remained in session for less than three months each year. According to

Washington, the teachers in these outlying districts were "miserably poor in preparation for their work," with some defects in their moral character.[23] Rural churches, in his estimation, were in the same condition: "What I have said concerning the character of the schoolhouses and teachers will also apply quite accurately as a description of the church buildings and the ministers."[24] His analysis of area problems and needs clearly indicated that the majority of them involved the adult population, to whom his subsequent work would be largely directed. Although he lacked straws to build, he was endowed with his mother's common-sense philosophy of substitution, and the sleepy town of Tuskegee provided an operational base from which to start the slow process of change in adult lives.

A typical Alabama town, Tuskegee was still a country village at the turn of the century. In its broad public square, around which clustered brick and wooden stores, livery stables, and law offices, the streets were often cluttered with displays of goods, whiskey barrels, and loiterers who sat on public benches on pleasant days, discussing serious and trivial affairs. According to Clifton Johnson, the town's "serene though antiquated dignity" was usually very quiet. Store proprietors often whiled away leisured recesses at their shops "with a guitar, or cornet, or fiddle," but market day on Saturday brought a flurry of activity, attracting "country people from miles around" and crowds of mules, horses, ox teams, and shoppers. Visitors could wander from the town's center across the hilltops toward the "fountainhead of knowledge and inspiration," Tuskegee Institute, passing along the way blooming dogwood, azaleas, honeysuckle, blackberry, and wild roses. Travelers might hear a "mocker in full, eloquent song" among the brooks and streams in the "loosely wooded hollow."[25]

Centrally located in the Black Belt about forty miles east of the state capital, Montgomery, Tuskegee is the seat of Macon County. Incorporated in 1843, the town had its early origin as an Indian village called Tuskigi, from Taskialgi warriors. Marching inland, the explorer Hernando De Soto found the Indian village, according to Max Bennett Thrasher.[26] Major W. W. Screws, an early editor of the Montgomery *Advertiser*, reported that Creek Indians inhabited the area in large numbers until 1836, when they started to move westward. As reported by Screws, the town was noted for its healthfulness because of its location on a high and dry ridge. Prominent settlers came and purchased rich lands on the banks of creeks and streams; they built stately homes, valued education, and established a center of "refinement, politeness and all the gentle amenities which tend to make life comfortable"— largely with the benefit of slave labor, it should be noted.[27]

When Washington arrived in Tuskegee in 1881, the town's population was around 2,000, about half black.[28] Working primarily as artisans and servants and contributing to the gentle amenities of the prosperous whites, Tuskegee's black residents had a somewhat easier life, however, than the field hands or outlying farmers, but they were still segregated socially from the local whites. They were also largely illiterate. One important exception was Lewis Adams, a former slave born in South Carolina. He was thirty-seven years old when he outbargained the politicians to secure a black school in Tuskegee. A mechanic by trade, Adams had learned shoemaking, harness-making, and tinsmithing skills in slavery, later teaching them at Tuskegee Institute. Without formal schooling, Adams had learned to read and write; his literacy enhanced his position of influence and leadership among blacks and whites. Working with George W. Campbell, a white merchant and banker, Adams helped to establish and support Tuskegee Institute.[29] Although some whites like Campbell supported the idea of a black school in their midst, many others looked with disfavor on the project. Like the majority of white southerners, the opposition voiced fears of trouble between the two races and of losing cheap farm labor and domestic servants as a result of black education. They questioned such schooling, picturing, as Washington once phrased it, "an educated Negro, with a high hat, imitation gold eye-glasses, a showy walking-stick, kid gloves, fancy boots, and what not—in a word, a man who was determined to live by his wits."[30]

Illustrative of the irony that sometimes determines the fate of people and events, forces stronger than local opposition to black education merged in Tuskegee. They were propelled by the sagacious Adams, political opportunism, and self-interest among influential whites. Adams had carved out his niche of leadership through hard work, practical skill, and benign assertiveness. He owned a hardware and leatherworking store in the town square. Working in tin, he also made kitchen utensils for Tuskegee housewives and applied roofing to the town's business buildings. Active in Republican Reconstruction politics, Adams had considerable influence with blacks and whites, and he was a shrewd bargainer with whites for black education. When two hopeful Democratic candidates for state offices approached him for help with the black vote, he traded his influence for the promise of Tuskegee Institute and delivered a large number of votes to the Democratic party in 1880.[31] The act to establish a "Normal School for colored teachers" in Tuskegee was signed by Governor Rufus W. Cobb on February 10, 1881, making all blacks the beneficiaries of Adams's shrewd political bargain.[32]

Certainly the carrot of Tuskegee Institute would be profitable in stemming the tide of black exodus from the area, some whites could argue. The self-interest of keeping cheap farm and domestic labor could hardly be served by another large exodus like that which had occurred to Kansas back in 1879. The new destinations were industrial centers like Birmingham and better farm opportunities in Kansas. The editor of the local Tuskegee *News* lamented in March 1881 that Macon County had lost more of its population in the previous ten years than any other Alabama county. Alarmed that many Tuskegee blacks were restless and ready to follow labor agents who had come to town, enticing blacks to break their sharecropping contracts, the editor had issued earlier warnings of starvation and ruin in Kansas, advising further: "It is high time that the negroes here were realizing the fact that they are doing as well here if not better, than they could do elsewhere, and the climate is better suited to outdoor work."[33]

In an atmosphere of overt white supremacy, political maneuvers, social segregation, economic depression, stagnant illiteracy, and low standards of living for most blacks, Washington correctly read the storm warnings as a clarion forecast for failure. Discouraged after his month of travel and investigation, he wondered how one person could make a difference in helping his people here. Could he accomplish anything, and was it worthwhile for him to try?[34] In later years, many people asked him how he succeeded, and his usual answer was "constant, hard, conscientious work," coupled with worthy and high aims:

Luck, as I have experienced it, is only another name for hard work. Almost any individual can succeed in any legitimate enterprise that he sets his heart upon if he is willing to pay the price, but the price, in most cases, is being willing to toil when others are resting, being willing to work while others are sleeping, being willing to put forth the severest effort when there is no one to see or applaud. It is comparatively easy to find people who are willing to work when the world is looking on and ready to give applause, but very hard to find those who are willing to work in the corner or at midnight when there is no watchful eye or anyone to give applause.[35]

As the copious documents of Washington's life attest, he did bring the aims and constant, conscientious work to Alabama that would ultimately touch every aspect of adult lives, ranging from literacy to secret political battles for civil rights. The complicated task of making bricks without straw, however, required far more than long, hard work. He brought to his enterprise at Tuskegee all the forces and training of his life, combined with a philosophy he bet his life on. To the problems and programs for adult education in Alabama, Washington also brought ingenuity, pragmatic wisdom, and a wide vision that would effect changes for adults across America and around the world.

The majority of Tuskegee's first thirty students were public-school teachers from Macon County, some nearly forty years old. With them came some of their students, who often were placed in higher levels of achievement than the teachers. Around this nucleus, Washington's work as a planner, facilitator, and administrator of adult education at Tuskegee began on July 4, 1881. Planning, initiating, implementing, and evaluating each step individually, Washington built programs in academics, agriculture, industrial arts, health, religion, and music around the community needs of Tuskegee and its environs. With a rigid Hampton type of program, boarding facilities were soon provided, and night school was implemented as attendance and needs increased. From the first, the school had as its mission the improvement of life through pragmatic changes in education, agriculture, job skills, health, and family. From the local initiative would grow many national and international programs of adult education at the turn of the century.

While conducting the daily operations, building, and expansion of the school, Washington had two other important functions as an administrator of adult education that were unique to his time and circumstances—fund-raising and public relations. Both were essential to the school's survival, demanding months of travel, constant contact with local, state, and national sources, and close scrutiny of all funding policies and legislation that affected schools like Tuskegee, education in Alabama, and blacks across the country. Maintaining close supervision of Tuskegee even when traveling, Washington worked at fund-raising that required prolific writing and public speaking. He once told the story of traveling 2,000 miles from Boston to Atlanta and starting back to Boston the same day, just for a five-minute speech.[36] Such expenditure of energy was not uncommon for Washington, and his seemingly insignificant effort brought significant results. This short speech laid the groundwork for his invitation to address the Atlanta Cotton and International Exposition in 1895, an event that catapulted Washington into national prominence and controversy.

While good public relations is an important and vulnerable area for any administrator, it was crucial to Washington's survival in Alabama during the late 1800s. Like modern administrators in some respects, he had to get along and sometimes appear to go along to accomplish his underlying mission; unlike modern administrators, he worked in a hostile environment that partially expected and would certainly welcome his failure. An exemplary organization was essential to establish public trust and respect. In an early break from the policies of Hampton, Washington maintained an all-black resident staff, hoping to demonstrate that his race could teach and administer effectively their own educational programs. The slipshod, the careless—anything that negatively affected good management—could not and would not be tolerated. Teachers and staff were required to maintain a high moral profile, the behavior of students was carefully monitored, and administrative contacts with the town, county, and state were meticulously handled to preserve the credit and character of the school. The physical grounds should reflect cleanliness, order, and efficient administration to any visitor who unexpectedly toured the school; to that end, Washington himself daily inspected the campus when he was there, making notes of small and large improvements to be quickly implemented. If Armstrong, a white man, had failed with his Hampton experiment, his efforts possibly would have been praised and his failure attributed to an impossible situation; if Washington, a black man, failed at Tuskegee, many whites would attribute his failure to their image of careless blacks, incapable of running a first-class institution.

Effective communication was also essential to good public relations. Often called an interracial interpreter, Washington became a masterful communicator with blacks and whites, largely through quiet diplomacy, public speaking, and the printed word. From his earlier public speaking success in West Virginia and at Hampton, Washington understood the power of the spoken word; from the *Southern Workman*, he knew the immediate and far-reaching impact of the printed word. Publications such as the *Southern Letter*, *Tuskegee Institute Bulletin*, *The Negro Farmer*, *Tuskegee Student*, and numerous reports from the principal and staff emanated from Tuskegee, spreading information and linking blacks and whites across the country. Beginning with local and state newspapers, Washington was soon writing editorials and articles for major newspapers and magazines throughout the nation, responding to issues affecting the educational, social, economic, and political progress of his race. Near the turn of the century, he invested funds in several newspapers, using them to great advantage. As whites had done for decades, Washington was the first black leader to recognize and capitalize on the power of the press; through this mass media he disseminated information, responded to pressing issues, and gave blacks an influential public voice. As indicated in his published *Papers*, he would also utilize other writers in newspapers to express more militant stances than he could take publicly on civil rights and politics.[37]

Washington's communication skills also included the prolific production of important books, widely read by blacks and whites around the world. These works generally reflected a simplicity of style and repetition of themes about racial pride and mastery of obstacles to inspire his race. Major books published under Washington's name included *The Future of the American Negro* (1899), *The Story of My Life and Work* (1900), *Sowing and Reaping* (1900), *Up from Slavery* (1901), *Character Building* (1902), *Working with the Hands* (1904), *Tuskegee and Its People* (1905), *Putting the Most into Life* (1906), *The Negro in Business* (1907), *Frederick Douglass* (1907), *The Story of the Negro* (2 vols., 1909), *My Larger Education* (1911), and *The Man Farthest Down*, with Robert E. Park (1912). Washington made time in his busy schedule to write, not for entertainment but for information and uplift, much like a sermon with an important message to communicate. His canon of literature helped to build an understanding of blacks, give hope and inspiration, and light the path to the future.

Representing his clearest theme and best writing, *Up from Slavery* was translated from English into other major languages, becoming an international classic and influence. Initially written to inspire the mass of struggling blacks, the book became equally popular with whites and "the man farthest down." Its theme represented the universal human struggle against obstacles to make life more than a fleeting shadow or a minuscule grain of sand; people are capable of ultimate triumph. The book also evoked the style of writing and speaking that Washington had developed into a successful formula: a simple and direct conversational tone, the cadence and phrasing that captured the music of the King James Bible, with which he was well versed, and the play of vivid, staccato images. A professor of composition at Harvard for twenty years, Barrett Wendell, wrote to Washington with great praise: "It is hard to remember when a book, casually taken up, has proven . . . so satisfactory as yours. No style could be more simple, more unobtrusive; yet, few styles I know seem to be more laden—as distinguished from over-burdened—with meaning."[38] An *Atlantic Monthly* reviewer also praised the book's message of inspiration: "to live cleanly, to work honestly, and to love one's neighbor, and to have that long patience which is another name for faith."[39] In a long review of the book and its author, William Dean Howells, the dean of American literature, was impressed by Washington's "constant activity for the good of others" and his "constant common sense." Recalling an occasion when he heard Washington speak in conjunction with several distinguished white men, Howells also noted: "When this marvelous yellow man came upon the platform, and stood for a moment, with his hands in his pockets, and with downcast eyes, and then began to *talk* at his hearers the clearest, soundest sense, he made me forget all those distinguished white speakers . . . and remember General Armstrong, from whom he had learned that excellent manner."[40]

Reflecting the book's national impact, William T. Harris, U.S. commissioner of education, called *Up from Slavery* "one of the great books of the year" and compared its influence with that of Harriet Beecher Stowe's *Uncle Tom's Cabin:* "You have written a book which I think will do more than anything else to guide us to the true road on which we may successfully solve the problems left us by that civil war."[41] Examples of its international influence came from Europe and the Far East. An Englishman wrote: "No drama of Shakespeare's is, at this moment and for the masses, of such vivid interest."[42] From Japan came the message that *Up from Slavery* was "one of the best books to encourage the spirit of young folks of the world,"[43] and proof of its inspirational uplift came from the downtrodden around the world. A good book should have a beginning that illuminates the end, "and the central idea should shine through every part."[44] *Up from Slavery* had met such rigid demands.

In his administrative duties of fund-raising and public relations, Washington's considerable skills in debating and public speaking also served to enlarge his role as communicator and interracial interpreter. From his Sunday evening talks, sincere and unmasked, with the students at Tuskegee or elsewhere in America or Europe, Washington set a precedent that few adult educators can hope to emulate. According to all written accounts (Tony Brown's "Journal" aired a rare but poor quality recording), Washington could enthrall any audience with his unique oratorical style. He was equally at home with blacks and whites, whether poor tenant farmers or the rich and powerful. His subjects were repetitive but relevant to each audience, stressing education, agricultural improvement, the acquisition of homes, land, and businesses, the uplift of family life in rural and urban areas, racial pride, and interracial cooperation. He sprinkled each speech with pertinent examples of individual and group accomplishments and wrapped serious messages in humorous anecdotes or pragmatic advice to match the individual audiences. Often asked about the secrets of his great success with audiences, he answered that he made it a rule "never to go before an audience, on any occasion, without asking the blessing of God upon what I want to say" and to make special preparation for each address because no two audiences were exactly alike. "It is my aim to reach and talk to the heart of each individual audience, taking it into my confidence very much as I would a person. . . . I care little for how what I am saying is going to sound in the newspapers, or to another audience, or to an individual. At the time, the audience before me absorbs all my sympathy, thought and energy."[45]

In a similar spirit but with heavier responsibility, Washington approached his historic and controversial address in Atlanta in 1895. He was invited to deliver one of the opening addresses at the Atlanta Cotton and International Exposition on September 18, a historic moment for Washington, the South, and the nation. This was the first time that a black man would speak from the same platform with influential white men on a national occasion in the South. His racially mixed audience was composed of former slaveholders, southern and northern whites, and members of his own race just thirty years removed from slavery. Agonizing over the speech and its potential for disaster in further divisiveness and discrimination or its possibilities for racial understanding and cooperation, Washington pondered prayerfully his several options, from peacemaker to appeaser, from harmony to revolution. One white farmer in Tuskegee jokingly depicted his precarious dilemma: "You have spoken before Northern white people, the Negroes in the South, and to us country white people in the South; but in Atlanta, tomorrow, you will have before you the Northern whites, and the Negroes all together. I am afraid you have got yourself into a tight place."[46]

Washington correctly viewed the entire exposition as a rare opportunity for the display of black progress and pride. A special building was designed and erected by skilled black artisans, and both Tuskegee and Hampton had impressive exhibitions of freedmen's progress since emancipation, another first in the South, of which Washington was justly proud. Following the dictates of his heart, his philosophy, and his fourteen years' work at Tuskegee, Washington gave, according to both southern and northern reporters, "the most notable speech ever delivered to a southern audience." Carefully crafted and concise, the text made subtle and strategic points: blacks had already made important contributions to the South; what blacks needed and wanted was "an interlacing of industrial, commercial, civil, and religious life," but "in all things that are purely social we can be as separate as the fingers, yet one as the hand in all things essential to mutual progress." Interspersed were also admonitions about racial injustice. There would be "no defense or security for any of us except in the highest intelligence and development of all." The lives of southern whites and blacks were inextricably woven together—"We march to fate abreast." Neither the oppressor nor the oppressed could escape the laws of man or God.[47]

In the ensuing critical and prolonged evaluations of the speech, largely relating to the "separate fingers" image of segregation, little, if any, attention has been given to Washington's subtle message and warnings or to the merits of the speech as a literary work.[48] Also missed in the clamor were the larger values that the exposition had for adult education. Black pride and progress were demonstrated for national view in the well-designed building and the exhibitions of skilled craftsmen from Tuskegee and Hampton.[49] Of greater significance, however, was the fairly obscure black principal of Tuskegee Institute who had rocked the nation with the quality and power of a single address. The doors of a reluctant nation would open, allowing him entrance. The equally obscure programs of adult education in the Black Belt of Alabama would find a national following through Washington after his Atlanta speech.

Less publicized but highly significant to adult education and Washington's public role in the movement were his whistle-stop education tours and speeches begun in 1905. Capturing the Chautauqua and Lyceum spirit and the Jesup wagon idea of extension, these state tours were directed at large areas of isolated adults for the purpose of teaching, informing, inspiring, and unifying them in common objectives. Funded largely by a nominal salary from the Southern Education Board, the railroads provided these tours with special rates and schedules for the entourage of influential blacks, whites, and reporters who accompanied Washington on these journeys. Arrangements were made in advance for facilities and publicity, usually through local members of the National Business League, ministers, and community leaders. Large numbers of blacks and whites were exposed to Washington's message of education, self-help, agricultural and business enterprise, and family uplift. Widely publicized in newspapers before the event and written about afterward in magazine articles, these tours became what Louis R. Harlan called Washington's "triumphal marches" for education throughout the southern states.[50]

The first of these special tours occurred in 1905 and encompassed the Oklahoma and Indian territories. In Little Rock, Arkansas, the crowd at the Opera House was so large that thousands could not get in. In a unique reversal, many whites were denied seats by blacks. Emmett Scott, Washington's secretary who did much of the planning, recorded that "in many respects it was one of the most remarkable meetings of colored and white people ever held in the South." People from the entire countryside came out to hear and see "the Sage of Tuskegee," and blacks made the occasion a public holiday. They were told, amid the holiday festivities, that "a people without food must be taught how to grow food, a people without homes must be taught how to build homes, and a people without the proper method of living must be taught how to live." Ignorance and race hatred "never solved a single problem," Washington said. Hatred only degraded and narrowed a people, but "the spirit of love, sympathy and helpfulness strengthened peace and prosperity between the races." In what Scott called a remarkable demonstration, "Whites and blacks crowded indiscriminately to the platform to press the speaker's hand, and to express their appreciation of his words."[51] Various articles on Indians, western blacks, and comparisons with southern blacks resulted from the tour of Indian territories.

The *World's Work* headlined its article on Washington's tour through racially torn Mississippi in 1908 as "A Cheerful Journey."[52] Some cheer was certainly in order, because the state's leading racial demagogue, Governor James K. Vardaman, had urged the state's whites not to attend the Washington meetings; hundreds did so, however, in Jackson and Vicksburg. While many blacks were busy denouncing Vardaman and praising Washington, some white hoodlums hanged two blacks along the railroad tracks in hopes that Washington would see them as his train passed; during this tour, a country newspaper also called Washington a "saddle-colored accident of an evening's intemperance."[53] Such incidents could not stifle, however, the message of hope that he had come to deliver: The black race in Mississippi, in spite of opposition, had made some progress in education, business and land acquisition, and financial independence. In Jackson alone, Washington pointed out, there were ninety-three businesses conducted by blacks; Mississippi also had eleven of the South's more than forty black banks. Educational institutions were springing up, such as Campbell and Jackson College for blacks in Jackson and Utica Institute in Utica.[54] These messages of cheer were delivered at stops in Holly Springs, Utica, Jackson, Natchez, Vicksburg, Greenville, and Mound Bayou. Washington proudly pointed out in Holly Springs that Marshall County had witnessed only one lynching since the Civil War and that a large number of the county's black farmers owned their own farms.[55] His most cheerful moment, however, occurred in Mound Bayou, a town founded and operated independently by blacks that Washington had praised and supported for its early promise of total financial independence, a dream that later went awry.[56]

Following the pattern of the Mississippi tour, Washington's next educational pilgrimage, as one reporter called it, covered the states of South Carolina, Virginia, West Virginia, and Tennessee.[57] The entourage traveled over the new Virginian Railroad in the summer of 1909, keeping a promise that Washington had made to Henry H. Rogers, the

Standard Oil genius who was building the railroad into the coal fields of West Virginia when he died.[58] Robert R. Moton, who succeeded Washington at Tuskegee, was a regular member of the traveling group; as thousands gathered at the numerous railroad stops, Moton often led the crowd in singing old plantation songs. It was "a weird and interesting sight to see and hear them sing these songs often late at night," Washington reported.[59]

During the fall of 1909, the pilgrimage went through the mountains of eastern and middle Tennessee, meeting large crowds of blacks and whites. In Greenville, Washington spoke to a mixed audience of 6,000. Arriving in Bristol during a driving snowstorm, the group was welcomed by hundreds at the train station. A massive crowd clamored for seats at the Opera House the next day to hear "the distinguished son of the Old Dominion," but "color lines, of course, were pretty faithfully observed, both on the stage and off," a report in the *New York Evening Post* was quick to note.[60] Rev. A. H. Burroughs came to the station to see the group's departure. He told Washington that he was from the Burroughs family in Franklin County, Virginia, Washington's former owners. Washington turned to the crowd and exclaimed, "Why, Dr. Burroughs and I belong to the same family." As the train pulled out, Dr. Burroughs exclaimed over and over: "What changes time does bring. Just to think of it. That great man once belonged to our family. I'm proud of him, sir—mighty proud of him."[61]

In Chattanooga, Knoxville, and Nashville and into Kentucky, Washington repeated his educational themes to the rich and poor, both black and white, speaking from the rear platform of the train, in churches, banquet halls, and parks. According to an editorial in the *New York Evening Post*, this tour demonstrated Washington's great usefulness to the entire country. "In this role as an interpreter of one race to another, pleading harmony, mutual respect, and justice, he is performing a patriotic service which it would be hard to overestimate."[62] On hearing the details of this Tennessee tour, a leading southern white educator exclaimed, "Now I believe there is going to be a revolution in the South in favor of the Negro."[63] Even though the "lynching barbarities still continue," an editorial in the *Boston Transcript* observed, "the ties of good will and mutual helpfulness between Southern whites and blacks are steadily growing stronger," largely as a result of educational tours of this nature.[64] On that trip alone, Washington had touched the lives of more than 50,000 adults of both races, bringing hope, understanding, and the promise of a better life. In 1910, there was a week's tour of North Carolina.[65]

By the time of Washington's Texas tour of 1911, disfranchisement and violence had grown worse in some southern areas. Extra precautions were needed to protect him from possible "barbarities."[66] In 1912, his tour went to Florida, and in 1913, Washington toured Tidewater Virginia under the sponsorship of Hampton Institute. His last educational pilgrimage occurred in Louisiana in 1915. Washington's health had so deteriorated that Emmett Scott had to request that a rostrum be provided for Washington to lean on during the Louisiana tour. Not one to lean, however, Washington spoke to packed houses and roaring crowds, seemingly sustained by the spirit of the people.[67] His educational pilgrimages had covered virtually all parts of the South, with Georgia and Alabama having been visited frequently during his work at Tuskegee.

As administrator during the strenuous building of a school with few resources, Washington spent well over half his time in the unique roles of public relations and fund-raising. He traveled thousands of miles to speak to thousands of people and communicated his message through the printed and spoken word. Tuskegee Institute prevailed as a consequence of his tireless efforts, growing from straw to a symbol of strength and a lighthouse of knowledge, like a city on a hill. These high-profile duties had come from necessity, not choice, as Washington later noted. He had neither planned nor wanted to devote so much time to talking about things, whether speaking or writing. "I have always had more of an ambition to *do* things than merely to *talk about* doing them," he said.[68] It was in the area of planning, implementing, and extending pragmatic programs of adult education at Tuskegee that he found his greatest challenge as an agent of change for the masses. Aimed at local needs, his "strange and altogether new movement" would improve every aspect of adult life, including literacy and education, agriculture, vocational and job training, housing and family life, community and economic development, health and sanitation, religion, politics, civil rights, and interracial relationships. From the Black Belt of Alabama, these programs were extended, effecting change across a wide spectrum of nations.

Booker T. Washington at his desk, Tuskegee Institute, ca. 1905. The furniture
was made by Tuskegee students.

The first graduating class at Tuskegee Institute, May 25, 1885

Old brickyard at Tuskegee Institute, 1880s

Vehicles in front of Cassedy Hall, Tuskegee Institute. Vehicles were made by
and the hall built by Tuskegee students.

BTW's speech at Alcorn University, Mississippi, 1912

Farmers' Conference at Tuskegee Institute

The Movable School, Jesup Agricultural Wagon

The Movable School, Knapp Agricultural Wagon

Teaching rural residents from Movable School, Macon County, Alabama

Founding of National Negro Business League, Boston, Massachusetts, August 22, 1900. BTW is in the front center.

President Theodore Roosevelt at Tuskegee with BTW, October 24, 1906, on the occasion of Tuskegee's twenty-fifth anniversary

BTW's burial, Tuskegee Institute, November 18, 1915. "Gone; you are gone," wrote the Harlem Renaissance poet Claude McKay, "and O! we feel so utterly alone."

SOCIAL CHANGE
THROUGH EXTENSION

Taking Adult Education to the Masses

6

According to E. J. Boone, an adult educator and agricultural extensionist, the change process commences with the mission of the adult education institution, which embraces philosophy, clientele needs, and role definition. Subsequent objectives and programs and their implementation emerge from assessed clientele needs, administered within the framework of the institutional mission, as Boone and other educational theorists like Ralph Tyler have contended.[1] Booker T. Washington always perceived the mission of Tuskegee Institute as one of social change through extension, as illustrated by his early statement of purpose.

Anxious for the influence of Tuskegee to reach the greatest number of people, Washington contended that the school's primary aim was to increase its extension activities. Initially, students leaving Tuskegee should "go forth as its representatives" to improve their communities. They should also carry the Tuskegee spirit and build up communities around them infused with that spirit. Washington cited such programs as the Negro Conference, the Teachers' and Farmers' Institutes, and the Business League as vital extensions of Tuskegee and an "essential part of the scheme of education." Such programs exposed real problems and the true mission of the school, "which is not so much to educate a few hundred or a few thousand . . . as to change conditions among the masses of the Negro people."[2]

Velma L. Blackwell viewed Tuskegee's mission as being one "to help people help themselves out of conditions imposed by historical circumstances, including birth, which hamper their fulfillment according to the American ideal of life, liberty, and the pursuit of happiness."[3] Important macro-objectives evolved from the mission, Blackwell argued. Foremost was Tuskegee's dedication to the solution of societal problems that historically had meant the disadvantaged and the Negro, although not exclusively. Strong occupation- and career-oriented programs would give economic stability to families and communities, whether through trades, sophisticated skills, or research. This represented a functional approach to problems. Personal development that aided self-realization, physical health, sound minds, and spiritual values also constituted an integral part of Tuskegee's macro-objectives. The logical extension of such programs to other states and countries occurred through the classroom, laboratory methodology, and the application of science and wisdom to practical problems. Tuskegee's open-door policy provided opportunities for individual development and fulfillment, serving as a bridge over the "chasm of ignorance which robs man of his finest possibilities to himself and his fellow man." According to Blackwell, the school also dared to be different, providing leadership in education and freedom in its approach to the improvement of social problems. The main thrust of Tuskegee's mission, however, called for teamwork, requiring the cooperation of individuals and organized groups. Such teamwork had resulted in a wide range of successful cooperative programs that made the Tuskegee story distinctive, deserving special treatment.[4]

By 1900, extension through the zealous work of over 1,000 Tuskegee students was well established in twenty-eight states, Cuba, Jamaica, Africa, Puerto Rico, and Barbados.[5] On entering the regular four-year course, each student was required to choose some occupational skill, dependent on inclination, aptitude, and available slots. Washington contended that even the regular normal-school graduates, going out to teach or preach, should have occupational skills to use for supplementary jobs and for the purpose of community training; teachers, for instance, only taught for three months of the year—often less—and needed other skills to supplement their low salaries. Occupation-track students likewise were required to have some academic training for the purpose of literacy and community leadership. Comprising about one-third of the enrollment, women worked in occupations of mattressmaking, sewing, dressmaking, millinery, cooking, laundry, and general housekeeping. Both men and women could study typesetting, tailoring, sick care, market gardening, poultry raising, beekeeping, horticulture, and floriculture.[6] The male-oriented skills included expanded agricultural work, wheelwrighting, machine work, blacksmithing, carpentry, brickmaking and masonry, saddle and harnessmaking, carriage trimming, and tinsmithing. Students following an occupational track, in mechanics, for example, were afforded several progressive levels of training; by the time they graduated, they were proficient in reading instructions, maintaining and operating a shop and machinery, and the handling of tools, well prepared to work at their trade and teach others the same skills.[7] Normal-school graduates, possibly going out to teach, were also equipped with occupational skills, prepared to use and teach them in the communities where they worked. With the economic depression in Alabama and across the South and scarcity of skilled work for blacks (often tinged with the charge that blacks were incapable of reading instructions or operating complicated machinery), Washington placed a high priority on occupational proficiency. All graduates were commissioned to carry their Tuskegee training back to their communities and extend their skills to others.

Often called the prophet of the practical, Washington wanted the total curriculum at Tuskegee—from agriculture to religion—to incorporate his pragmatic philosophy. Academic classes coordinated their work with the students' occupational training. English compositions, for example, should be written about how to shoe a horse or make a mattress, and mathematical problems should be derived from practical things like land measurements, building requirements, or soil composition. Conversely, occupational students should know how to write, speak, and read well; they were required to write monthly compositions relating to their training, take written and oral exams, and make oral presentations dealing with their occupations. Practical demonstrations were encouraged to support theory and practice. Max Bennett Thrasher related how he watched students in horseshoeing dissect a dead horse, studying the lower joints and hoofs of the hind and front legs to learn how the shoe should be nailed on for best results and to avoid careless or harmful effects.[8] Washington believed that all training, deriving its meaning and purpose from real problems, could be extended toward the elevation of individual and community life when the student left Tuskegee.

Following a natural order of extension, night school opened in the fall of 1883 based on the Hampton plan, which Washington had initiated. The campus night school opened, as Washington recalled, with just one teacher and one pupil. By 1900 the enrollment had increased to 450 students, most of them older, working during the day and attending industrial classes at night.[9] Three miles away at the Marshall Farm, from thirty to forty-five men later worked the 800-acre farm and attended night classes in the large old house once called the "mansion-house."[10] As industrial programs became established, many of them were extended to adults in the environs of Tuskegee. One example was the popular brickwork program. Washington rented training space in the heart of Tuskegee and offered this program to adults not connected with the institute. From October through March, the more advanced and skilled students in the program conducted training classes three nights a week in the areas of brickmaking and masonry. The town night school soon had eight teachers, offering classes in academics, carpentry, painting, cooking, and sewing.[11] As agricultural and industrial products became available beyond the needs of the school, local markets were developed, providing products as well as training to the economy while linking the school to the community through trade. Bricks and wagons produced at Tuskegee were popular items of barter, and the school utilized local stores for needed merchandise, maintaining some balance of trade and local cooperation.

The largest and most innovative extension of Tuskegee into rural Alabama, however, occurred in February 1892 at the Tuskegee Negro Conference. Washington called it a "day memorable in the lives and fortunes of the great bulk of the Negro population in the 'Black Belt' of the South," a "strange and altogether new movement in which the Negro was called upon to participate." Having studied closely the "weak points and the strong points, of the older people," Washington said he had been impressed with "how much common sense and wisdom these older people possessed," notwithstanding their considerable illiteracy. Consequently, during the first part of January 1892 Washington sent out invitations to seventy-five "common, hard-working farmers," mechanics, ministers, and teachers, inviting them to Tuskegee for a day of conference.[12] His purpose was twofold, he wrote. First, the conference should be a needs assessment, studying the actual industrial, moral, and educational conditions of the masses. The second challenge was to determine ways of correcting problems, elevating the standards of rural blacks, and improving the training of Tuskegee students.[13] In a surprising response, nearly "400 men and women of all kinds and conditions came," and Washington set some ground rules for the event which became an important annual adult education conference. He wanted the common people to speak for themselves, without exaggeration, complaints, or fault-finding. There would be no "cut and dried or prepared speeches," and he would not allow "people who were far above them in education and surroundings to take up time in merely giving advice to these representatives of the masses."[14]

Through honest, open discussion, assessments were made as to numbers who owned farms, rented land, lived in one-room cabins, and mortgaged their crops; attention was also directed toward educational conditions, moral and religious life, and the kind of minister and church each community had. It was determined that four-fifths of these blacks were still living in one-room cabins on rented land; they were mortgaging their crops for food, paying from 15 to 40 percent annual interest on mortgages. Schools, if they existed at all, were still being conducted in rundown buildings often for less than three months out of the year. Churches were in the same bad state, often conducted in the "brush arbor" by untrained ministers. There was a loud, clear call for action, resulting in written resolutions for general improvement in the lives of the 90 percent of blacks who lived in rural areas and received little assistance; economic guidelines were provided with encouragement to remain in the South, stop complaining, and lower the crime rate. Moral and religious training was also emphasized, especially for ministers and teachers. People were urged to buy land, cultivate it, and grow their own food. Debts and lawsuits should be avoided, and women should be treated better. Houses needed to be larger than one room, and the school year should be extended to at least three months, even if to do so required raising taxes. And finally, "nowhere is there afforded us such business opportunities as are afforded in the South. Self-respect will bring us many rights denied us. Crime among us decreases as property increases." Conferences such as this one should be conducted in every community.[15]

These resolutions served as a starting point for discussions of new problems and solutions in succeeding conferences. Nearly 800 people attended the second conference one year later, coming from all over the South. Some progress was reported: fourteen people in one community had purchased land, crop mortgaging was decreasing, living conditions had improved, and some schools had been built and the school year extended. With each succeeding year, the number of conference attendees grew larger, representing expanded sections of the country. By 1900, the resolutions were refined, with specific instructions for both men and women. Larger declarations included statements of instruction and encouragement that "should be tacked up" at home and referred to during the next year:

> As a race, we feel that we are to work out our destiny through the slow and often trying processes of natural growth rather than by any easy, sudden, or superficial method. . . .
>
> We have advised in previous years, that , while not overlooking our rights as citizens, it should still be our main concern to use our energy in continuing to secure homes, better schools, a higher degree of skill, and Christian character, and in the practice of industry and economy.
>
> We are glad to note the growing interest of the best Southern white people in our elevation, as shown by the various conferences. . . .
>
> Our people charged with crime, and in Southern prisons, have, as a rule, little or no education, and are largely without industrial and moral training. . . .
>
> The openings in the South for employment, especially in the direction of skilled labor, were never greater than now.
>
> We urge all to become tax-payers and to promptly pay their taxes, to keep out of the courts, to cease loafing on the streets and in public places; and to prepare to do well the work which the best interests of the community demand.[16]

Thomas M. Campbell, a Tuskegee graduate who operated Washington's "Movable School" and became the first black extension agent of the Department of Agriculture, recorded his assessment of Washington's successful leadership of these meetings and rural blacks. Calling Washington the "champion of black farmers," Campbell reported that nothing was more important to Washington among all the events in his busy schedule than these annual meetings with black farmers and workers. When each conference convened, Campbell noted, Washington conducted the meeting in an informal and simple manner, making each person feel welcome and at ease at Tuskegee. The meetings usually were opened with the singing of some old plantation melody, with all joining in, humming, nodding, and keeping time with their feet. Self-consciousness and fears soon dissolved, and the audience became responsive to Washington's tactful approach to many delicate subjects that closely affected their daily lives, feeling free to discuss in open forum their innermost thoughts. Washington frequently reminded the attendees that these meetings were not for politicians or politics, but for hardworking farmers, mechanics, ministers, and teachers—the "bone and sinew of the Negro race." It was possible, he further reminded them, to discuss any number of wrongs that needed correction, but "it seems to me that it is best to lay hold of the things that can be put aright, rather than those with which we can do nothing but find fault." Problems of the conference should, therefore, be confined primarily to solutions within their reach.[17]

According to Campbell, Washington continued his early practice of visiting the homes of rural people until 1914. Usually going on these rural tours on Sundays, Washington took careful note of physical conditions, listened patiently as people related their stories of disappointments, and gave suggestions for help or examples of others who had overcome. He encouraged people to clean up their yards, repair broken fences, and whitewash their houses and buildings. "Quit living out of tin cans and paper bags," he often told them, urging them to grow their own food, exhibit it on the roadside, and take some into town to sell. Once he went to a local grocer in Tuskegee and borrowed cans of blackberries, peaches, tomatoes, and syrup to take on one of these Sunday tours. He chided the farmers for buying such items when they could easily have grown the same items in their own gardens.[18] A few weeks before Washington's death, he urged Campbell in a memo to encourage all residents of Macon County to keep up their yards and fences and to paint or whitewash all buildings. In private conversations and more public conferences, Washington's two greatest concerns were acquiring land and eliminating the mortgage system of farming, Campbell concluded. Washington's advice was persistent and pragmatic: "Live at home; take a load of produce to town to exchange for those items that you cannot raise; keep a year round garden, a pig, a cow and raise some fruit; start a bank account; put aside a little money each year until you get enough to buy a piece of land, even if it is but one acre."[19]

The Farmers' Institute was organized to instruct Macon County black farmers. Meeting on campus once a month with Tuskegee's farm superintendent, this institute disseminated relevant information concerning soil maintenance, crop rotation, fertilizers, and product prices and markets throughout the county.[20] Even with this group and the increasingly successful annual Farmers' Conference, Washington realized that a better means was needed to reach the masses, especially those who did not attend the annual conference. According to Campbell, many of the poorer farmers feared the self-consciousness or imaginary discomforts they might experience among "those educated people" at Tuskegee. If they would not come, Washington reasoned, Tuskegee would go to them through the "Movable School."[21] Led by George Washington Carver, a committee met to draw up specific plans for a wagon that would have special equipment to carry farm demonstrations to the doors of the poorest farmers.[22] When the plans were completed, Morris K. Jesup, a self-made, wealthy New York businessman, provided the money to buy and equip this vehicle, named the Jesup Agricultural Wagon, or the first Movable School. It started its operations in June 1906.

Washington asked Thomas M. Campbell, a recent graduate of Tuskegee, to begin the "new and rather peculiar type of work," then known as the Farmers' Cooperative Demonstration, in Macon County. "The reason I am anxious for you to begin the work is that the farmers who need instruction most, I fear, are not getting it. We must, in a larger measure, take the information to them," he told Campbell. The idea was actual demonstration, not speechmaking or lectures: "Instead of telling the farmer what to do, show him how to do and he will never forget it," he instructed Campbell, characterizing this wagon as "A Farmers' College on Wheels."[23] Well equipped with items simple to operate, the Jesup Wagon carried a milk tester, a cream separator, a revolving hand churn, a two-horse steel-beam plow, a one-horse steel-beam plow, a diverse cultivator, a spike-toothed harrow, a middle "burster," a set of garden tools, and other portable equipment.[24]

The work of the Jesup Wagon depended on the seasons, local needs, and available resources. Campbell reported that he seldom used the cream separator or churn because so few farmers had cows. During the planting season, the vehicle was equipped with a portable garden with growing vegetables. Demonstrations were given on how to prepare the land, how to fertilize, and how to plant gardens. Plowing demonstrations were popular, showing better plows and the proper preparation of the soil. Farmers often were inspired to purchase better equipment and share information with neighboring farmers. Traveling to various parts of Macon County during the week, the Jesup Wagon also provided transportation for speakers from Tuskegee to visit rural churches on Sunday. Because Campbell often had to remain overnight with the wagon in isolated communities, he became familiar with the schools, churches, and social problems, reporting back to Tuskegee on special problems and needs. Beginning as an agricultural project, the wagon was also instrumental in other aspects of change for rural residents.[25]

After the passage of the Smith-Lever Act in 1914, the extension work begun by Tuskegee was greatly expanded with the additional funds, and Auburn University assumed responsibility for all extension work in agriculture and home economics in Alabama, working closely with Tuskegee. The Movable School expanded its operations to include home and health demonstrations, adding classes in cooking, horticulture, and health, which were conducted by doctors and nurses. The great advantage of the Movable School was its immediacy, demonstrating practical improvements on the spot and becoming the center of interest for isolated rural residents. When the medical demonstrations were added, special health problems of each community were studied and practical ways to remedy local health problems were demonstrated. One serious and common dilemma was the abundance of flies, generally aggravated by having outdoor toilets and livestock too close to the house with resultant health problems.[26]

Washington's plan to transport information to the masses through the Movable School underwent periods of experimentation. Personnel often changed, necessitating some standardization for both the demonstrator and the rural participants; processes evolved that could be repeated by the average country individual. If the black farmer and his family could not "repeat, reproduce, or re-enact the things done by the Movable School instructors, it was doubtful whether the subject introduced was practical and timely."[27] Instructors had to keep in mind that many of the farmers could not read or write; instructions had to be visual, audible, and understandable. The availability of farm supplies and equipment was another significant factor. If farmers could not afford to buy commercial fertilizer, they had to be instructed to utilize available resources for soil enrichment and to practice proper crop rotations. According to Campbell, Washington insisted that the Movable School address needs as they existed rather than introducing methods that could not be understood or applied. "We strove at all times to know more about the needs of the Negro farmer for better farming methods and the needs of the farm family for better living conditions, and sought for a better understanding of ways to remedy existing conditions. This was and is still a great problem when the isolation of Negro farmers, . . . out of touch with modern methods, is taken into account."[28] An outgrowth of the annual Farmers' Conference, the Movable School became a significant adult education movement, transporting education in agriculture, health, and family living to rural adults. By 1923, the program initiated and implemented by Washington had passed far beyond experimentation, having spread through all of rural Alabama and the adjoining counties in Mississippi and Georgia while establishing a model that was widely copied in agricultural regions across the country.

The mule-drawn Jesup Wagon, often called an agricultural classroom on wheels, had to be abandoned after years of hard use over bad roads. Shortly after Washington's death, some 30,000 Alabama farmers contributed $5,000 to purchase the Knapp Truck as the wagon's replacement, to be named the "Booker T. Washington Agricultural School on Wheels." Carrying trained workers and special equipment for farm, health, home, and recreation demonstrations, the new school on wheels continued to exemplify the ideas of Washington, "who helped to make Negro extension work possible, and who loved the country people and the great out of doors," as the memorial panels of the vehicle so stated. Henry Wallace, the secretary of the U.S. Department of Agriculture in 1936, also summed up Washington's credentials for agricultural extension leadership: "A man is not fit to work with the country people unless he has smelled the soil and can converse with them in their own 'lingo.' "[29] Combating illiteracy, indifference, and poverty, the Movable School gradually made significant improvements in farming, health, family life, and economics in the rural South, an influence that extended across the country, perpetuated by agricultural colleges and extension services.

The "Hill Taylor Project" exemplified the application of Washington's philosophy that motivated the Movable School. Hill Taylor was a black farmer who owned 518 acres of land in Macon County. He permitted the use of his home and farm as a practical demonstration of the concepts of the Movable School program. More than sixty-five rural families participated in the daily demonstrations, with an average of more than 100 people in attendance every day. The demonstration agents began with the home and extended to the farmlands after an extensive survey of existing conditions and materials readily available for use on the premises. The house itself was transformed by renovation and redecoration, including a new kitchen, dining room, bathroom, and plumbing. Bedspreads and curtains were made from unbleached muslin, and rugs were made from fertilizer sacks, corn shucks, and salvaged rags, bleached and dyed to harmonize with the decor. The lawn was transformed by replacing the old fence with a hedge, sodding with new grass, and planting flowers and shrubs. Students from Tuskegee lent their considerable talents to all aspects of the transformation, from decorating to plumbing and agricultural improvements. The farmlands were then improved by Tuskegee methods of soil enrichment, livestock husbandry, and skilled gardening techniques.[30] When completed, the entire project demonstrated the practical possibilities of improvement through the use of available resources with work and ingenuity. Robert R. Moton went to see the finished product and praised what he saw as the firsthand demonstration of Washington's Movable School in action, recalling an anecdote about the man who had inspired the project: "Dr. Washington used to tell a story of a man who was asked where he lived. He didn't live anywhere, he said, but he *stayed* over there on the hill. Lots of people don't live anywhere; they simply stay on their land."[31]

In addition to the Movable School, another important extension of the annual Farmers' Conference at Tuskegee was the Workers' Conference. Composed of white and black teachers, professionals, and business leaders, this conference met annually on the day following the Farmers' Conference. It was designed to be a practical follow-up to the farmers' meeting because Washington believed that rural farm problems affected every area of society. Teachers, ministers, and business leaders, in particular, needed to know the conditions of rural farms and to learn how to deal with the problems. In conjunction with the Farmers'

Conference, representatives from the South and other areas of the country flocked to the Workers' Conference. Using the same informal format, Washington encouraged the free discussion of problems, progress, and solutions in education, religion, and business that had flowed from farmers on the previous day. Surveys of progress from the previous year were taken, and speakers from successful enterprises brought further encouragement. Attainable objectives were established for the following year, and possible solutions to lingering problems were discussed, helping to focus, if not solve, the broad range of professional and business concerns relating to education and agriculture.[32]

Contributing to the enormous success of the Farmers' and Workers' Conferences, with increasingly large attendance and influence, was the dissemination of information. Handled with the know-how and wide contacts of Tuskegee, massive correspondence was required before and after the meetings for the purpose of notification, summary, and propagation across the nation. Initially this work required the full-time services of T. J. Jackson, whose main mission was to promote the interests of the conferences. With Tuskegee's success, local organizations sprang up across the southern states, spreading across the country. By 1900, more than 250 local conferences had spawned from the Tuskegee meetings. Jackson ably coordinated and supported these clones, attending local meetings, giving encouragement and advice, and helping organize new organizations in isolated, obscure places. Other staff members from Tuskegee also assisted these local groups by participating in their meetings and keeping information circulating among them. As Tuskegee graduates fanned across the country, many of them organized similar organizations, receiving speakers and other assistance from their alma mater. Like the Tuskegee conferences, the primary objective of the clone groups was to promote education, land- and homeownership, the establishment of businesses and banks, and the general uplift of health and family life.[33]

Washington himself kept a watchful eye on the Tuskegee conferences and their offspring. He often visited and spoke to regional organizations. In circular letters sent to all conference members, Washington typically gave information, encouragement, and some chastisement, as illustrated by one in 1899. He warned about illiteracy, waste of money on things like cheap jewelry, the varying price of cotton, the need to increase the school year to six months, and habits of thrift to insure mortgage payments. He urged more purchases of homes and land, which was "cheaper than it will ever be again," and more local self-help.[34]

Like Samuel Chapman Armstrong, Washington frequently railed at moral laxity, impatient with the squandering of time and resources and untrained rural ministers who were "called" but often incapable of moral leadership. From his first survey in 1881, Washington had put top priority on the training of ministers, inviting them to the annual conferences. With financial assistance from Caroline and Olivia Phelps Stokes, ardent supporters of Tuskegee, the Bible School opened in 1893 with the construction of Phelps Hall. Nondenominational, the school's purpose was "not so much for preachers of a high grade of mental ability" as it was "for conscientious, earnest teachers of a wholesome life." The Bible School was a separate department at Tuskegee; according to Thrasher, it was not "in any sense a theological school."[35] Washington stated, in pragmatic terms, what he wanted the Bible School to accomplish: "What we desire and aim at is to give men and women a thorough knowledge of the English Bible, and to give them ideas of doing right for right's sake—to inspire them to go out to work for the race, to help in uplifting the race and in teaching it right principles."[36] In the Washington lexicon, the right principles included also a foundation in education, agriculture, and job training. A preacher should not only preach but lead in the total life of his community, supporting schools, farming, and industry. The Bible School stressed the dignity of labor. Along with their academic training, ministers were encouraged to learn useful trades themselves, including carpentry, farming, tailoring, and brickwork.[37]

In the summer of 1893, the Bible School was extended into summer sessions. Two-week seminars were planned for August, with lectures from "the best class of ministers throughout the South," perhaps two each day. For advice and help, Washington wrote to his trusted friend, the Reverend Robert C. Bedford, asking him to give some lectures because he knew better than anyone "the condition and needs of the colored ministers." The idea was to bring together the most prominent black bishops and white teachers in the South to inspire faltering ministers toward higher morals and effective community leadership. "Of course you understand," Washington emphasized to Bedford, "that it is very necessary that everything be [s]imple and practical. . . . We think that a great deal of good will come from this movement."[38]

By 1900, the regular Bible School had eighty-three adults in attendance, and the summer seminars provided extension education for
hundreds of others unable to attend the regular term classes. Washington evaluated the new movement to train rural ministers as a successful
venture. Many hearts, he said, had been inspired with "a noble ambition
to go out into the dark and benighted districts of the South and give their
lives for the elevation and Christianizing of the South."[39]

With the established success of Washington's regional programs
throughout the South and the national prominence accorded his leadership after the Atlanta Exposition speech in 1895, the extension of his
adult education programs followed in rapid but natural succession
across the nation. Embracing the same pragmatic philosophy and repeated themes of his Tuskegee conferences and regional programs,
Washington's work and vision during the last two decades of his life
turned more and more toward national unity and progress for the entire
race. As early as 1891, he had given considerable consideration to a
suggestion made by J. H. Lewis to create a national organization for
adults who were engaged in business enterprises, and the idea became a
reality in Boston in 1900.

Before the first meeting convened in August, Washington informed
his secretary, Emmett Scott, what the mission was: "I want it understood that this organization is for the colored people who are engaged in
the most humble business as well as those engaged in what is call[ed] the
higher business or trade." He further instructed Scott to disseminate
information about many successful black people "succeeding in a quiet
way, but not often heard of." The object of the new movement, he
stated, was "to get hold of all such people, and give them such advice,
encouragement and inspiration as will enable them to do more and better
business."[40] In a subsequent interview with the Boston *Journal*, Washington also stipulated what the organization did not aim to do: "This
meeting is to be purely a business one, and not a political affair. Politics
and other general matters are dealt with in the National Afro-American
Council which meets in Indianapolis. It would be a mistake to have the
two bodies take up the same line of work."[41] In Washington's opinion,
"helping the Negro along commercial lines will assist in settling his
political status," the *Journal* reported. J. H. Lewis, who supported the
organization, was one example of self-sufficiency, enterprise, and suc-

cess that would be showcased in this new effort, to be called the National Negro Business League (NNBL).

Born in poverty in Heathsville, North Carolina, Lewis had started his own business in Boston, with $100 capital after working as a tailor in Concord during the 1870s. Operating one of the largest tailor shops in Boston, Lewis gained a reputation for his manufacture of bell-bottom trousers. His fashionable shop broke through the color barrier in business, employing and servicing both blacks and whites, an idea Washington favored but found difficult to implement in the deep South. By the mid-1890s, Lewis was doing an annual volume of business of $150,000, and by 1900 he was one of the wealthiest black men in America.[42] With Lewis's sponsorship and example, the NNBL got off to a successful start on August 23, 1900; some 300 businessmen met, having "come to Boston for a definite purpose with which politics had no connection," to attend "strictly to business," Washington reported.[43]

Washington opened this landmark initiative with a speech launched with levity but laced with serious meaning. Joking about the erudite Boston, he had heard a story, he said, that this city never allowed any bad grammar. If a stranger happened in town with some bad grammar attached to him, "when he speaks the winds very softly and gently waft his language out into the harbor and the words return to the Boston audience perfectly purified." From the humblest to the highest, all businesspeople should "speak out plainly and openly regardless of rhetoric, and regardless of mere grammatical forms," keeping all speeches and papers as short as possible. While material possessions were not the chief end of life, better business practices would promote civil rights, education, useful citizenship, and the country's highest welfare. The purposes of the NNBL, stated simply, were to gain closer personal acquaintances, to receive encouragement, inspiration, and information, and to organize local business groups across the country within the national organization. Whether in the North or South, Washington observed, "Wherever I have seen a black man who was succeeding in business, who was a tax-payer, and who possessed intelligence and high character, that individual was treated with the highest respect by the members of the white race." All people should strive to become "useful and indispensable" where they lived: "A useless, shiftless, idle class is a menace and a danger to any community." Every success was earned through "paying the price which nature demands from all": "We cannot get something for nothing." Success in business, "however humble and simple that business may be," had come from important mastered lessons of "cleanliness, promptness, system, honesty, and progressiveness." Having traveled a great distance in thirty-five years of freedom, Washington concluded, "May we ever keep in mind that the law which recognizes and rewards merit, no matter under what skin found, is universal and eternal, and can no more be nullified than we can stop the life-giving influence of the daily sun."[44]

The NNBL grew into a strong business network, with hundreds of local leagues across the nation. Washington provided active leadership for the entire organization until his death. He spoke, wrote about, planned, coordinated, and disseminated information through Tuskegee's printing facilities and newspaper contacts for local groups and the annual national meeting. The effectiveness of the organization was measured by increasing numbers of black businesses, public recognition, racial pride, cooperation, and success, as well as increased wealth—all carefully tabulated annually on the meticulous adding machine at Tuskegee and kept in public view by Washington. To be expected in such a large and diverse group, there were some maneuverings and infighting regarding administrative policies, leadership, priorities, and control, but the basic mission—to promote economic development among blacks in the business sector—remained on course. In Washington's last address as president of the NNBL in 1915, he restated the original mission he had envisioned in his first speech in 1900: Organizations like the NNBL should aid their fellow blacks in every aspect of life, including education, economic development, civil rights, politics, and family uplift across all lines. An economic foundation for the race was, however, the fundamental issue for any organization, with strong emphasis on home- and landownership and economic independence.[45] An editorial in the *New Republic* when Washington died summed up the significant contribution he had made: "If the goal of an oppressed race is political equality, economic progress is usually the only feasible road to its attainment. Booker T. Washington saw more clearly than any other American the fundamental conditions upon which the progress of his race must depend, and he created an effective technique accordingly."[46]

Serving as an advisor and board member, Washington also provided leadership for the National Urban League. Founded in 1910 by interra-

cial and civic groups, this organization was a voluntary community-service agency that promoted equal opportunities for blacks in education, employment, housing, health, and general uplift in the urban settings. Ruth S. Baldwin, wife of a Tuskegee trustee, William H. Baldwin, continued her friendship and assistance to Washington after her husband's death in 1905; she was also one of the founders of the National League for the Protection of Colored Women, which merged with other groups to establish the National Urban League.[47] As the league's first president and a lifelong supporter, she frequently consulted Washington concerning the crucial urban problems, largely in the areas of health, housing, and employment. With the great migration that started at the turn of the century, shifting large numbers of blacks to urban centers, the health crisis would be compounded in the cities, agitated by overcrowding, disease epidemics, and the sanitation problems created by substandard housing.[48] As a board member, Washington brought his considerable experience, influence, and public communication to the league's objectives, speaking, writing, and advising on its behalf.

When Robert Moton founded the Negro Organization Society of Virginia in 1914, Booker supported this group as he had the Urban League. Moton, who traveled with Washington on many of the education tours, wanted this organization to do for the rural areas what the Urban League was trying to do in the cities.[49] The Virginia objectives in the Moton initiative were, of course, what Washington had been trying to do in Alabama since 1881, and he could freely support, advise, and speak for them. Washington was, in fact, scheduled to speak before this interracial organization in Petersburg, Virginia, on November 5, 1915. Sick in New York, Washington wired Moton on November 4: "It is perfectly exasperating and heartbreaking for me not to be with you tomorrow night."[50] From the records of the Washington papers, Moton and Washington seemed to share the same pragmatic philosophy and vision; in that regard, it was fortunate that Moton was chosen to succeed Washington at Tuskegee.

Health had, from the beginning, been one of Washington's major concerns. At Tuskegee, he had insisted on healthy habits, sanitary conditions, and the improvement of campus water, toilet facilities, and swimming/bathing facilities. A training school for nurses was established early, providing practical and theoretical training through the school's hospital, with emphasis on the improvement of rural health.[51] The Movable School had instructed rural and isolated families in methods of improving family health, and Tuskegee students worked in the community to provide training and health care for the elderly. With the help of the National Tuberculosis Association's traveling exhibit and stereopticon lectures, Washington held a five-day conference at Tuskegee in 1908 on the study and prevention of tuberculosis. With increasing concern for better public health, he proposed that all clubs, organizations, and insurance companies combine their efforts through a special conference to be held in connection with the annual Tuskegee Negro Conference. His proposal received little response, but the seed of the idea remained in Washington's mind, leading toward a national movement for health improvement.[52]

Inspired by his attendance at a conference on race betterment in Battle Creek, Michigan, sponsored by John H. Kellogg and focused on health and nutrition, Washington turned one day of the annual Negro Conference at Tuskegee in 1914 into a public-health conference. Dr. John A. Kenney and his staff of nurses from the newly completed John A. Andrew Hospital at Tuskegee gave presentations on sanitation, nursing, and patent medicine frauds. George Washington Carver, the school's now-famous agricultural expert, demonstrated the difference between pure and impure water, and the school's dairy instructor showed the proper way to prepare milk, butter, and cheese. Other focal points included child care, dental care, and the harmful effects of cheap liquor.

Washington had broadened the base of this conference by having present the head of the Alabama State Board of Health and many visiting doctors. Dr. Oscar H. Dowling, president of the Louisiana State Board of Health, brought to the conference the Louisiana Health Car, a traveling exhibit designed in 1912 to travel the countryside much like the Jesup Wagon for the purpose of improving rural health. In his address to this group, Washington stressed that health was a national problem affecting both blacks and whites. "The life of the humblest black person in the South in some way touches the life of the most exalted white person in the South," he said, but the death rate among blacks was much higher than that of whites. Of the 9,000,000 southern blacks, he estimated that some 200,000 of them carried diseases that could easily have been prevented. He urged joint cooperation among whites and blacks and asked ministers, business leagues, and all organizations to join hands in the prevention of illness.[53]

With this regional beginning, Washington started early to plan for a national campaign in 1915 that would have greater system and unity. He enlisted private donations for the purpose of educating people across the nation concerning health problems. "Our people have remarkable ability to help themselves," he wrote one possible donor, "but they have got to be educated as to how to help."[54] Moton and the Negro Organization Society of Virginia immediately joined in the efforts to promote this national campaign. Washington asked the NNBL to sponsor National Negro Health Week, to be conducted March 21–27, 1915, and the National Urban League also contributed its support in the cities. The driving force behind this national promotion, however, was the major effort exerted by Washington and Emmett Scott, with the broad contacts and printing facilities of Tuskegee Institute. The week's activities, focused across the country on disease prevention, better health, and education with the help of local organizations, climaxed when Washington spoke in Baltimore, at the Bethel A.M.E. Church. Some 3,000 people crowded into the church, and thousands were turned away, testifying, according to one black journalist, "to the enthusiastic interest all are taking in [Washington's] campaign for better health conditions for the people of the entire country."[55]

Black population centers across America also witnessed an enthusiastic response during National Health Week. Large crowds gathered, receiving information and direction for health improvement. Health officials were motivated to provide "whole-souled cooperation" to national health problems. A one-week conference could not hope, however, to produce any massive, overnight solutions to serious and longstanding health problems, but Washington's objective of promoting national awareness and education was achieved, with the promise of continued education toward disease prevention and national health improvement. There was, in retrospect, an ironic postscript to Washington's drive to raise the national consciousness toward better health and disease prevention in March of 1915. Keeping his own illness carefully hidden from public knowledge and refusing to slow down long enough for medical attention, Washington died eight months later, largely from overwork, hardening of the arteries, high blood pressure, and kidney problems—possibly preventable and mostly treatable conditions.

☞ Closely connected to health problems of the rural and urban masses were the general conditions of the family, including substandard housing and the low position of women, who strongly influenced the entire family in matters of education, living conditions, and health. From his first summer in Alabama, Washington had directed considerable adult education toward the improvement of family life and the elevation of women through education in his extension work. The Movable School had demonstrated practical ways of improvement; larger organizations like the annual Negro Conference at Tuskegee, the NNBL, the National Urban League, and the Negro Organization Society of Virginia had focused national attention on family life, better housing, and the education of women. Like General Armstrong at Hampton, Washington realized that effective family uplift could never be accomplished without the education and cooperation of women. In this respect, Washington was fortunate to have three wives who embraced his philosophy and served as strong role models for black women across the country; he was, however, equally unfortunate in losing his first wife, Fanny, shortly after the birth of their daughter, Portia, and his second wife, Olivia, mother of their two sons, Booker, Jr., and Ernest Davidson. It would be left to Margaret, Washington's third wife, to continue Fanny and Olivia's example and to perpetuate Washington's philosophy of extension to families across the country. Well-educated teachers, all three wives began their work with the local needs at Tuskegee; through Olivia and Margaret, the education of women for family uplift would be extended across the nation. Their lives helped to illuminate the private man, just as their work served to perpetuate Washington's public work in adult education.

Somewhat obscured in later history, Fanny N. Smith was a longtime friend of Booker's in West Virginia, where he had tutored her in preparation for Hampton. Teaching in West Virginia, she ultimately graduated from Hampton in the spring of 1882 and married Washington in August. Besides his mother, Fanny seems to have been Washington's main female influence prior to his work at Tuskegee Institute. Having just commenced his Tuskegee work the year before, Washington took Fanny to Alabama for the new fall term; they secured a large house, which would serve as the residence for other faculty members as well.

Assuming an inconspicuous role at the school, Fanny did not even teach, probably at the preference of her husband and her own desire to establish a model home for him and the other teachers. Ironically, she was listed as "housekeeper" in some official correspondence, but Fanny made a significant contribution toward demonstration work for women in the model home she maintained.[56]

Described as "gentle and kind in disposition and quite a favorite with people," Fanny appears to have brought great comfort to Washington during his early struggle at Tuskegee; from all indications, their short marriage was a happy one. Washington's only daughter, Portia, was born in 1883. After less than two years of marriage, however, Fanny died at the age of twenty-six in the spring of 1884. The cause of her death, from available reports, is almost as obscure as her life. A Montgomery newspaper reported the cause of death as consumption of the bowels. Louis R. Harlan, however, reported that Portia indicated to him in a 1967 interview that Fanny's death may have resulted from internal injuries caused by a fall from a farm wagon at Tuskegee.[57] The tombstone at Tuskegee that marks Fanny's grave has a simple epitaph: "Our Lord is risen from the dead; our Jesus is gone up on high," perhaps from a song Fanny favored. Not one to parade his grief publicly, Washington did compose, however, an eloquent but brief eulogy for Fanny. She was able to impress others most with her life by her extreme neatness in the home and other efforts, he wrote. "Nothing was done loosely or carelessly. . . . She taught our students many valuable lessons. Her heart was set on making her home an object lesson for those about her, who were so much in need of such help."[58]

With grief, loneliness, and the care of a small child added to his heavy responsibilities of "making bricks without straw," Washington turned more and more to his great helpmate, Olivia A. Davidson. Having come to Tuskegee at Booker's request shortly after her graduation in 1881 from Framingham State Normal School near Boston, Olivia was a principal, teacher, inspirational fund-raiser, and a significant catalyst for the early success of Tuskegee. Graduating from Hampton in 1879, she had heard Washington's postgraduation speech, "The Force that Wins." He was well acquainted with her brilliance, talent, and experience as a teacher, excellent educational background, and personal qualities of tact, maturity, dedication, and beauty; three days after he opened Tuskegee, he wrote and asked her to come help him. She came eventually, after a bout with illness, bringing excellent credentials and a personal drive and dedication that outreached her physical frailness.

Olivia was born a slave in 1854 in Tazewell County, Virginia. Her light color indicated that her father, like Washington's, had been a white man. Educated initially in Ohio at the Albany Enterprise Academy, an excellent private school for blacks, Olivia had then moved to Hernando, Mississippi, to teach former slaves. She subsequently went to Hampton and Framingham, impressing people with her superior mind, grace, and personal qualities. At Framingham, she had been exposed to more sophisticated and improved teaching techniques while making influential friends who would be helpful in raising money for Tuskegee in the North.[59]

Booker and Olivia married in 1885. Her influence in his personal life was noted in his softer letters; he started to lose the brusque outward appearance as the depression caused by Fanny's death disappeared. Under the careful scrutiny of Olivia's excellent mind and literary influences, Washington's speeches and writing acquired more smoothness, unity, and sophistication, enriched with classical quotes and references. United in their efforts at Tuskegee, Booker and Olivia also shared fund-raising chores in the North, often to the point of exhaustion for both of them and frequently through Olivia's contacts.[60] Booker T. Washington, Jr., known as Brother or Baker, was born in the summer of 1887 in Boston. The second son, Ernest Davidson Washington, was born in 1889. Recovering from the birth of Davidson two days before, Olivia was forced out of the house with the baby and the other children on a cold February night at 4 A.M. by a house fire caused by a defective chimney. This shock and exposure caused a complete breakdown in Olivia's precarious health. Fund-raising in the North when this occurred, Washington quickly moved Olivia to a Boston hospital, dropped all engagements, and stayed by her side until she died in May 1889.[61] Completely devastated by grief, Washington again had to pick up the pieces of his life and work, wrestling also with the raising of three small children as a single father.

Olivia's lasting impact on Washington had been inestimable; her contributions to building Tuskegee were enormous. She had brought to the rural women of Alabama and the South a genteel example of feminine modesty, sensibility, intelligence, and leadership in the home and school. Working with Tuskegee and area women, Olivia had helped to alter many personal habits of black women, such as the dipping of snuff, the wearing of garish clothes and head wraps, "degrading home influences," and the "intellectual deformity of slavery." An effective speaker, she frequently addressed large groups like the Alabama State Association of Colored Teachers on such subjects as "How Shall We Make the Woman of Our Race Stronger?" Maintaining her family life and home, Olivia had been an effective leader at the school, in the community, and in the South, having great influence in the North as well.[62] In *The Story of My Life and Work* (1900), Washington referred to the eulogy of the Reverend R. C. Bedford as his own regarding Olivia's life and legacy. "The stamp of her influence on the higher life of the school no time can ever efface," Bedford had written. Hers had been a religion of action, not one of show, practiced by so many. Olivia administered to the poor, the blind, and the aged, often feeding them during holidays at her own table with her own hands. She visited the sick and relieved suffering. "No woman ever had a truer husband or more devoted friends," Bedford concluded, and such a legacy would rest "upon the school and upon all who loved her as long as time shall last."[63]

Margaret Murray was graduating from Fisk University in June 1889 when Washington first met her. Perhaps sensing her mental acuity, physical stamina, and potential for leadership, Washington persuaded her to come to Tuskegee; in the vacuum left by Olivia's death, the school could well be served by a woman like Margaret Murray. Determined, strong, and intelligent, reared in poverty in Macon, Mississippi, Margaret had begun teaching school when she was fourteen and had slowly worked her way through Fisk. She became "Lady Principal," teacher, and mother confessor to Tuskegee women, bringing her strength of leadership to local and national programs of adult education.[64] After a period of shared working experiences, in the summer of 1892 Margaret became Booker's third wife—albeit with many misgivings about raising his three small children. Full of self-doubt and ignorance about child care, she had finally decided to brave it. "I will learn my lessons alone," she wrote Washington while he was away, "but all that I learn improperly you may correct when you come back."[65] Typically, she did learn and manage, keeping up with school duties and family responsibilities while sharing Washington's philosophy about educational extension for women, the family, health, and housing. Vital and socially conscious, Margaret watched over the school and family during Washington's frequent absences, continued his programs, and started new ones on her own initiative. Making of their home, "The Oaks," a place of quiet dignity, beauty, and warm hospitality for students, staff, and visiting dignitaries, she demonstrated what was possible for all women with determination.

When the first annual Negro Conference met in 1892, Margaret realized that its objectives would not be successful without the training and education of women. "While there were many women present at this first conference they did not seem to realize that they had any interest in the practical affairs that were being discussed by their sons and husbands," Emmett Scott wrote in one profile of Margaret's leadership.[66] Margaret assessed the need and organized the first Mothers' Meeting in town, conducted in the upper story of an old store on main street. She vividly recalled that initial encounter. As the women shyly straggled in, she later wrote, they looked at her in some confusion and seemed to ask, "Where is it?" Her first task was putting the women at ease. "We talked it all over," she said, "the needs of our women of the country, the best way of helping each other." That was the beginning of the Mothers' Meeting, which grew to several hundred attendees by 1899.[67]

A larger meeting place was soon required. More and more women came, walking long distances on foot, children in tow. Mothers were instructed in simple lessons of home improvement, family health, proper dress and behavior, family budgeting to enable home- and land-ownership, racial pride, and the important role of women. Children were also provided with educational activities as the mothers met in serious discussions. Many of the women in attendance could not recall how old they were; Margaret created a sense of history through encouraging them to recall incidents in their lives to establish an approximate age.[68] Growing out of the observed needs of the annual Negro Conference, the Mothers' Meetings became popular throughout the region, expanding with the Negro Conference. As Washington met with blacks across the country about the NNBL and other concerns, it became an established practice for Margaret to meet with the women, extending her Mothers' Meeting idea across the nation.

Some fifteen miles from Tuskegee, Margaret started a demonstration project that affected more than thirty black families. The white owner of Russell Plantation and two other white families lived in the area; black families worked the 1,400 acres, primarily growing cotton. Margaret found these blacks living in one-room cabins, often with six or ten people in the small space, most of them illiterate. Margaret secured the permission of the plantation owner, surveyed the area of black cabins, and chose one cabin in which to begin her work. Going weekly to the cabin, where adults began to gather, Margaret won their confidence by friendly discussions, singing, prayer, and subtle house-cleaning demonstrations. Gradually she introduced classes in literacy and practical lessons in home improvement and health. Using an abandoned cabin donated by the plantation owner, a regular school was then established. A Tuskegee graduate conducted the school, making the cabin also a demonstration of cleanliness and housekeeping. Children attended during the day; parents had classes in the evening. All contributed to the cultivation of a vegetable and flower garden, and the raising of chickens was introduced. As the adults learned to read, they also acquired skills in gardening, cooking, cleaning, washing, ironing, and sewing. Family health improved, and a church was soon added to the settlement. With the success of this project, Margaret purchased ten acres of land and had a double house built there; one area was used as the school, and the other was used as a model house. A popular site, visitors from surrounding areas came to study the school, model house, and garden. Margaret and the staff of Tuskegee continued to support the project, extending the growth of literacy, better housing and health, and improved personal habits and attitudes.[69]

Max Bennett Thrasher related an example of other benefits ensuing from the Russell Plantation project. Margaret had selected one man to serve on the school committee who had favorably impressed her with his general manner and the appearance of his home. When it was reported to her that this man and the woman with whom he'd lived for several years were not married, Margaret approached them, insisting that they be married immediately for the reputation of the project. They gave various excuses, all true, to postpone the wedding: They had no money for a license or minister, and they had no suitable clothes. She instructed them to be at her home the next morning. Margaret purchased the license, secured a minister, and prepared some of Washington's clothes for the man. Faculty members prepared clothes for the woman and fixed food and gifts for the reception and shower. The couple was married in the parlor of the Washington home the next morning. Sponge cake and lemonade were served afterward, and the couple received many useful household articles as wedding gifts. Given dignity, this wedding served as an example for the entire community.[70]

Margaret expanded education for women and the family through club work, using the motto, "Lifting as We Climb." In the Tuskegee Woman's Club, joint efforts were directed toward night school and Sunday school. In 1895 this group was successful in getting three resolutions passed at the Cotton Exposition in Atlanta to condemn the sale of alcoholic beverages. The Woman's Club improved the community by decorating the local train station, distributing reading materials and food to men in jail, and funding the new reformatories for boys and girls near Montgomery, Alabama. Literacy and black history were emphasized for Sunday and night schools. Black students needed to "know and revere their own men and women of note," and the Woman's Club insisted that such history be incorporated into night classes. Any school that failed to include black history would be considered "derelict in its duties."[71]

Like her husband, Margaret extended her regional work to national influence. In 1895, she was elected president of the National Federation of Afro-American Women, a group that merged with other national movements to form the National Association of Colored Women's Clubs (NACWC). The stated purpose of this organization was to produce "harmony of action and cooperation among all women in raising to the highest plane the home, moral and civic life." Serving in various offices of this group, Margaret helped to promote women's suffrage, patriotism, education, music, and the basic ideals of her Tuskegee Mothers' Meetings; she also edited the organization's official newspaper, *National Notes*. Biennial conventions helped to coordinate local and national objectives, evaluate established goals, and formulate new direction. Concerned about political rights, the NACWC also incorporated education toward understanding the Constitution and all state and national policies that related to voting. Margaret believed that if equal justice and fair play were to serve all races, "there must be an equal chance for all women as well as men to express their preference through their vote."[72]

As president of the NACWC in 1912, Margaret, with Washington's help, cooperated with the Frederick Douglass Memorial and Historical Association and its efforts to make the twenty-room mansion of Douglass' Cedar Hill in Washington, D.C., a national shrine and landmark for the preservation of black history. During her last year as president, the NACWC presented President Woodrow Wilson with petitions that were signed by state convention members urging the president to use his influence to stop lynchings. These women had condemned lynching as early as 1901; in 1916, their telegram entreated the president to speak out against "the atrocities being committed against innocent black men, women, and children."[73]

Margaret Washington stayed active in local and national causes until her death in 1925. A. L. Jackson of the *Chicago Defender* eulogized her double role and influence, first, for her role as the helpmate of a great man and, second, for her individual leadership and personality. "In her work at Tuskegee Institute she had long been an indispensable factor," Jackson wrote, "and her position in various organizations throughout the country was recognized as strong and helpful." Perhaps her real worth would not be determined, Jackson concluded, "until biographers and students of history shall write the real story of Booker T. Washington. . . . But when it is told his wife will figure largely in the picture."[74] In 1901, Washington dedicated *Up from Slavery* to Margaret as well as to his brother John. In warm praise of Margaret's leadership at Tuskegee, in the region, and across the nation, Washington said, "Mrs. Washington is completely one with me, . . . relieving me of many burdens and perplexities."[75] Indeed, as revealed in his papers, all three wives had made significant contributions, each in her own way, toward the success of Tuskegee, regional programs of adult education, and national influence. Other women as well, from the North and South, had contributed generously in terms of money, moral support, and leadership, justifying the great faith that both Armstrong and Washington had placed in the role of women in effecting social change.

✏ Like Margaret's demonstration housing at the Russell Plantation project, Washington established Greenwood Village to provide a model black village. Greenwood was a residential extension of the institute itself. After the purchase of 200 acres north of the campus, the building and loan association of the institute laid out the village in 1904 and offered low financing. The 70-by-210-foot lots were sold for fifty or sixty dollars. A Village Improvement Association was charged with monitoring the area for cleanliness and order, and no liquor was allowed. With streets that were lighted, paved, and lined with trees, the village also had a city park and model school called the Children's House. By 1906, the village had some 2,100 residents, including local farmers, laborers, and institute personnel.[76]

Washington took inordinate pride in Greenwood Village, watching over it paternally and inspecting it carefully, as he did the campus grounds. If he chanced to see stray chickens or careless trash, he fired off immediate memos, urging prompt correction. Once he wrote a resident that wrong impressions were being created: "I very much fear that a mistake is being made in Greenwood in having too many dances," he fumed. When a Greenwood merchant opened his store on Sunday, Washington ruled that Tuskegee students should not patronize the store until the blue law was obeyed. In Washington's opinion, the entire village should reflect cleanliness, order, and good management, like the institute. Greenwood represented to him an example of black inculcation into the mainstream of American life. He wanted the stream of visitors to Greenwood to see a competent and successful life-style exhibited, conducted independently for and by blacks, with no evidence of the slipshod and reflecting pride in the Negro race.[77]

Other regional efforts extended Washington's mission of home- and landownership and improved housing for adults. In 1892, the Dizer Fund was established to help black farmers buy homes and farms at low interest rates. Silas C. Dizer of Boston granted $1,500, increased to $3,000 in 1895, to set up a revolving loan fund so that black farmers could buy the land and build model Christian homes as examples to surrounding shacks.[78] Other northern philanthropists, including such backers as Ellen Collins, a faithful financial and spiritual supporter, contributed to similar efforts by Washington. The Southern Improvement Company, originating at Hampton and extending to Tuskegee, also bought 4,000 acres near the institute and sold small plots—from forty to eighty acres with a house—to black farmers on extended credit. Backed by strong supporters like Robert C. Ogden and W. H. Baldwin, Jr., the Southern Improvement Company was generally successful during its operation.[79]

With the experience of the Southern Improvement Company's success and the financial support of Tuskegee trustees and friends, Washington established Baldwin Farms in 1914 as a memorial to his great personal friend and Tuskegee trustee, William H. Baldwin, Jr., who died in 1905. The plan for this farm was to allow Tuskegee graduates in agriculture to purchase forty-acre farms and build a $300 home which would allow for additional rooms for a growing family. The Tuskegee Farm and Improvement Company extended mortgage on the land at 6 percent and mortgaged crops and equipment at 8 percent. The idea was to promote independence, not charity, and Washington was enthusiastic about the project, stipulating five strict rules: all residents should pay as much as possible on their debts; rainy days should be used to fix up the interior of the house; soil should be carefully cultivated, using the agricultural principles taught at Tuskegee; home gardens should be maintained and foods preserved and canned; and, finally, all residents should raise pigs and chickens. On one occasion when a group of visiting summer-school teachers were being shown Baldwin Farms, Washington was embarrassed by the clear evidence of poor crops and a profusion of grass and weeds. "It seems to me," he wrote the farm superintendent, "that they are getting the spirit of looking for a hand-out from somebody rather than dig it out of the ground."[80] From his slave days, Washington had preached the value of a well-kept home; he would not tolerate the appearance of negligence. After all, he said, the most important result of a man's "struggles and sacrifice is a home and a farm paid for and clear of debt."[81]

An exciting project, at Hilton Head, South Carolina, began with the promise of independence but ended in failure. Washington and W. T. B. Williams of Hampton, with the assistance of Tuskegee graduates, tried to create an ideal settlement "as an illustration of what Tuskegee graduates can teach the people to accomplish," Washington said. William P. Clyde, a shipping magnate, owned 10,000 acres on this island, which he used as a hunting preserve. Too old to hunt, with great admiration for Washington, Clyde decided to finance a settlement if Tuskegee would undertake the project, and Washington and Williams worked out an acceptable plan.[82] Initially, 1,000 acres would be divided as an experiment into one-horse farms of about thirty acres each; each farm would have at least a two-room house with a shingled roof and an outhouse. If this first phase succeeded, more land would be divided into farms. Each farm would sell for $520, to be paid over a period from seven to ten years. Launched in 1906 under the supervision of Stephen T. Powell, a Tuskegee graduate with farm experience, the project was designed to be a model exhibition of housing, farming, and education. Powell was well advised by Joseph S. Shanklin, another Tuskegee graduate, who was principal of the Port Royal Agricultural School in Beaufort; by Williams, a Harvard graduate on the Hampton staff and a traveling agent of the General Education Board; and by Washington, from a distance.[83]

Two years into the experiment, Washington sent J. R. E. Lee from Tuskegee with some specific advice. "I am anxious that the industrial, moral and religious condition of the people be improved as fast as possible," he said. "I want them to begin the white-washing of their houses and fences, planting better crops and making better farms. They are a very primitive, backward people and cannot take ideas."[84] Lee returned and reported to Washington that Powell was setting a good example with his own farming, demonstrating the better use of the plow over the hoe. The school and all houses had been whitewashed. Lee recommended that more industrial training be added to the school, that another school be built, and that another Tuskegee graduate be added to the project, now staffed only by Powell and one Hampton graduate. There was a great need for demonstrations of the use and preparation of food and of home furnishing, Lee believed. "The people need to know how to live," he concluded.[85]

When Washington visited the project in 1908, he found good soil and possibilities, but the islanders were poorer and far more primitive than he had envisioned. Another two-room school was added, and a conference like Tuskegee's Negro Conference was implemented to demonstrate better ways of living and farming and to show the islanders that the purpose of the project was their education. In the following year, Washington made a concerted effort to infuse the island with new blood and to replace islanders in the housing project with Tuskegee graduates. Through the *Tuskegee Student,* he asked that more graduates put their training into practice at Hilton Head, buy or rent land there, and settle down to successful farming and teaching, demonstrating the Tuskegee principles at work in a first-rate colony. The ultimate economic goal at Hilton Head was to revive cotton production and operate a winter truck farm, thus providing the islanders with useful year-round work. With a secure economic base, good schools and increased literacy, better housing, and general improvement of living standards, Hilton Head could be a model of self-sufficiency; with success in the initial phase, the Clyde family would give more acreage and support to the succeeding stages.[86] Hilton Head had all the ingredients for a successful adult education program: a worthy mission; careful planning and good leadership; financial backing; community needs, which the program seriously tried to meet; stages of implementation; and serious evaluation. The program failed in spite of these ingredients, and the causes of its failure are both relevant and instructive to modern educators, demonstrating that success is never guaranteed.

The problems that ultimately doomed the Hilton Head project resulted largely from an age-old problem in adult education, resistance to change. Primitive and content in their ways, the native islanders often would not work to harvest the crops. Lying, stealing, and "traditional disorderliness" persisted, making the conscientious Powell wonder if it were worth the effort to keep trying to effect order and modernity out of the chaos. Other problems stemmed from the project's isolation, uncooperative weather, and dwindling funds. Clyde had invested in the initial project as an experiment; with so many obvious problems, the Clyde family felt disinclined to invest further. The project was closed in 1913, but its failure was never attributed to a lack of effort by Powell and his coworkers. Washington's evaluation was expressed in a letter to Clyde's son: "We have done the best we could under the circumstances I think." That Clyde agreed was evidenced by his continued connections with Washington and contributions to Tuskegee.[87]

Washington directed considerable attention, publicity, and assistance to other independent black enterprises, seeing in them a progressive step toward "moral, industrial, and political freedom."[88] In 1905 he visited and studied the black town of Boley, Oklahoma, and disseminated its story through his speeches and writing. In an article in *Outlook,* he praised the thirty-year progress of the northward and westward movement of blacks and noted that it had not been "a helpless and ignorant horde of black people" who had come to these new lands but rather "land-seekers and home-builders" prepared to expand the country. During the thirty years since the Kansas exodus, blacks from the South had learned how to establish schools, banks, and newspapers, Washington said. "They have recovered something of the knack for trade that their fore-parents in Africa were famous for." Through their churches and other groups, blacks had learned the "art of corporate and united action," which had enabled them to "set up and maintain in a raw Western community, numbering 2,500, an orderly and self-respecting government" like Boley.[89] Humorously, Washington also noted: "This was the town of Boley, where, it is said, no white man has ever let the sun go down upon him."[90] To the towns of Wilberforce, Ohio, and Allensworth, California, he gave similar attention, seeing in these all-black towns the dawning of race consciousness and cooperative independence. Such efforts, he said, "shall demonstrate the right of the Negro, not merely as an individual, but as a race, to have a worthy and permanent place in the civilization that the American people are creating."[91]

Mound Bayou, an all-black enterprise in Mississippi, initially provided the greatest promise of racial independence. Surrounded by white supremacy, which eventually helped to stifle the economic life of the struggling and isolated town, Mound Bayou was founded in 1887 by Isaiah Montgomery in partnership with a railroad company. Charles Banks, a black entrepreneur, moved his mercantile business to Mound Bayou in 1904, opened a local bank, and became a community leader in Washington's NNBL. Emmett Scott, Washington's secretary, invested in the bank and became one of its directors. Washington persuaded Andrew Carnegie to build a library in the town; he also arranged through the General Education Board for the town to have a farm demonstration agent and secured a demonstration Movable School wagon from Jesup for Mound Bayou. With the strong support of Tuskegee, Banks tried to broaden the economic base of the town by seeking funds from Washington's philanthropic connections to build a cottonseed oil mill in Mound Bayou.[92]

What started as a promising dream turned more into a nightmare, emerging as a failure in the harsh light of reality. Through a change in ownership of the original railroad partner, the failure to raise the necessary capital, and misdirection by Banks, the town's economic independence was not sustained. Robert E. Park summed up some of the difficulty in a letter to Emmett Scott: "Banks hasn't got a definite scheme to pursue to philanthropic people and he hasn't any one with sense enough and persistence enough to take it up and hammer it into the heads of the Northern people."[93] Having given a library which had no books, used only as the headquarters of the Masonic Beneficent Association, Andrew Carnegie would give no more. Washington and Scott searched for other assistance.

Julius Rosenwald, the Sears magnate and everlasting friend to black education and causes, built a Rosenwald school in Mound Bayou. He purchased some $25,000 worth of bonds to establish the oil mill.

Without Washington's knowledge, Banks sold out to B. B. Harvey, a white man from Memphis, and the oil mill went out of local hands. Harvey used the Rosenwald money for his own operation, and Rosenwald never received even the interest from his substantial investment. The mill went bankrupt in 1914.[94] If no more, the harsh economic lessons of Mound Bayou could serve as valuable experience, and, as Harlan concluded, the town did provide some refuge for many blacks from the prevalent practice of whitecapping, the deliberate obstruction of their opportunities by whites.[95]

📖 It was in the area of education, however, that Washington continued to make his greatest contribution in the South, across the nation, and around the world. At the root of most failures in economic ventures and the lack of progress in all areas, he contended, was privation in job training and education on all levels. If he leaned toward occupational readiness, it was not at the exclusion of higher education; he got tired, he sometimes said, of defending his philosophy and priorities in response to misinformation. When Thomas Fortune, a close friend and prominent black newspaperman, wrote Washington in 1903, asking him to come out with a clear-cut statement that he did not favor industrial education above higher education, Washington was exasperated. He had done this forcefully and plainly, he answered, in *The Future of the American Negro*, *Up from Slavery*, and the recent October issue of *Atlantic Monthly*. Yet "not one of the papers opposing me has dared to print a single line from the *Atlantic Monthly*" or from a Louisville speech on the subject. "They systematically avoid publishing anything that defines my position on all these vital questions."[96]

Washington's position was a simple one: Any education should contribute to the total improvement and welfare of the human race. Like Samuel Chapman Armstrong at Hampton, he believed that people should be judged on the good they did, not the economic class to which they belonged or the college from which they graduated. Of his white ghostwriter, Robert E. Park, Washington said: "I do not know whether Dr. Park is a graduate of any college or what college." The important thing was that Park was "a broad, sympathetic, strong, helpful man."[97] In this regard, he made his strongest statement in 1910: "This matter of defending and explaining these so-called higher institutions makes me tired. The sooner these institutions can learn that they are simply making a contribution to the general education of the people, the better it is going to be for all concerned."[98]

In spite of some suggestions to the contrary, Washington emerges through his papers as a strong supporter of institutions of higher learning. The first black man to receive an honorary master of arts degree from Harvard University in 1896, Washington was so honored for his "genius and a broad humanity which count for greatness in any man," and "for the value of whose services, alike to his race and country, only the future can estimate."[99] While assisting many black colleges, he made large and specific contributions to Howard and Fisk, serving as trustee and adviser for these two leading black universities.

Becoming a trustee of Howard in 1907, Washington helped the school get a Carnegie library and served as the school's liaison with the U.S. Congress and the General Education Board. Early in 1915, Washington helped to restore Howard's regularly approved federal appropriation, which a southern congressman had removed entirely from the appropriations bill.[100] According to Harlan, there is no evidence that Washington ever tried to change the nature of Howard University, but some tenets of his thinking cropped up in two incidents. When Wilbur P. Thirkield, the school's white president, gave his inaugural address, his remarks reflected some of Washington's philosophy: Although industrial education was not in itself sufficient for a completely rounded life of any people, Thirkield said, this body of "elect tenth" should never forget "that education involves obligation; that their election is not to privilege alone or to mere place and power above men, but rather to service and sacrifice for the downmost man."[101] The vocal infighting that had developed between William Trotter's radical group and Washington's followers erupted over the possibility of W. E. B. Du Bois's appointment to Howard's faculty. Washington and two other trustees had advised against appointing Du Bois because they believed that the argumentative Du Bois would hinder more than help the school and demand too large a salary. Washington, however, insisted to Thirkield that this was the kind of decision the president alone should make, and he would back the president's decision. "In the last analysis," Washington wrote, the president "bears the burden and should have the credit or censure for success or failure."[102] According to Emmett Scott, Thirkield should have the courage to decide the issue for himself and not "take refuge behind somebody else."[103]

Because Margaret was an 1889 graduate and Booker, Jr., a 1913 graduate from Fisk University, Washington had close personal links to the school. Serving as its trustee from 1909 until his death, he brought considerable expertise in administrative and fund-raising areas to help the struggling school. He visited and spoke at Fisk on many occasions and drew many of the Tuskegee teachers from its graduates. Through the influence of both Margaret and Washington, Andrew Carnegie was persuaded to give matching funds for a large library at Fisk.[104] Concerning this contribution, J. C. Napier, an influential black lawyer and banker from Nashville, wrote to Washington: "This one thing which you have done for Fisk University and the cause of higher education is more than *they* and their *kind* [the Du Bois faction] have done in all their lives."[105] Deploring the fact that so much philanthropic wealth was being poured into white schools, Washington worked to secure funding for Fisk and other black colleges. In the drive to raise $300,000 to stabilize the finances of Fisk, he used his influence with Julius Rosenwald, J. P. Morgan, Andrew Carnegie, and others to raise almost $200,000, with the General Education Board contributing $60,000 and Fisk alumni $45,000.[106]

It was for the education of the masses, however, that Washington reserved his larger energies. During the last five years of his life, he turned more and more from the idea of spreading Tuskegee clones across the country to the encouragement of public education. As an agent of the Southern Education Board, which sponsored his education train pilgrimages, Washington served in an advisory position, supporting the organization's expressed purpose of promoting public education across the South. In another irony of history, Washington was never invited to be a member of the board or even allowed to attend the meetings of the Southern Education Board, so closely were its white membership and promotion of white education guarded.

The general view of the Southern Education Board was expressed by one of its most democratic members, Charles D. McIver: "The less the Negro has to do with politics the more cheerfully will his white neighbors help him to work out his educational and industrial salvation."[107] According to Harlan, northern board members were often prevented from doing more for black education for fear that such efforts would jeopardize the board's position with southern white moderates. Although a few members would have welcomed Washington as a member of the board, he was never invited or allowed to report to them personally.[108] He stated his position often, becoming more specific in a letter to W. H. Baldwin, Jr., in 1903: "I have found it difficult to bring myself to the point where I could feel it proper to make a written report to a body which did not feel that it could afford to have me personally present at a meeting in order that I might make a report in the same way that the other officers made theirs."[109] In 1910 he wrote to Wallace Buttrick concerning the lack of black high schools. If the General Education Board continued to hire people to encourage white high schools while doing nothing for black high schools, it would be taken for granted by southern whites that Negroes were to have few if any high schools, Washington feared.[110]

Working from the sidelines and with some indirect influence through a few of its members, Washington continued to monitor and advise the Southern Education Board throughout its thirteen years of activities. Every effort had to be made, he wrote to Hampton's Hollis B. Frissell, "to watch carefully to see that nothing is done that would give the impression that Negro education is being shoved aside for white education."[111] As the separate and unequal policies of education worsened, Washington kept pressing the needs of rural education, charging that the board members were not putting "themselves on record in a straight and frank manner as much as they should," with the result that the movement "means almost nothing as far as Negro schools are concerned." In Alabama alone, he argued, the evidence pointed toward great reductions in black schools and pay for black teachers as more money was funneled to white education. One black teacher, for example, had a contract for a salary of only $1.60 per month.[112]

Primarily it was Washington who secured the important Jeanes Fund, money that helped to bridge the disparity for rural black education. Washington had known Anna T. Jeanes, a wealthy Quaker in Philadelphia, since the mid-1890s. In his correspondence with Hollis Frissell at Hampton, Washington frequently referred to Jeanes and the possibility of her assistance for black education.[113] Heir to a family fortune of more than five million dollars, Jeanes was in her eighties, living in the Friends Boarding Home in Germantown, Pennsylvania. (She would also leave $200,000 of her total estate to the home when she died in 1907.) Washington went to see Jeanes in 1905, appealing for $10,000 to build a new dining room at Tuskegee. Knowing exactly what she wanted to do with her money and still keen of mind, she warded off this and other suggestions for its use. "Is not aid for 'Rural Schools' more desirable and important than the Tuskegee dining room? That might benefit the few while the influence of Rural Schools might benefit the *many*," she told him.[114] Washington readily agreed that he could make excellent use of $10,000, especially in ways to stimulate self-help among rural blacks; he could, he assured her, find other funding for the dining room. Jeanes also frowned on Washington's idea of lending money to blacks for the purpose of building their own schoolhouses, using some of the interest to pay for them. After careful consideration, Jeanes enlarged the amount of her gift to rural black education to $200,000 and placed it under the General Education Board, with the stipulation that Washington and Frissell would administer the spending. Immediate matching grants were made for black schoolhouses near Tuskegee and Hampton.[115]

Wanting to free themselves from the General Education Board and its pro-white influences, Washington and Frissell carefully negotiated with Jeanes in secret, securing from her one million dollars for an independent fund, known as the Anna T. Jeanes Foundation. Her last wish was that her money should assist the southern country and rural schools and the large group of blacks for whom only the small community schools were available. The fund's main concern, she stipulated, should be industrial education, extension work, the improvement of rural education, and the elevation of black home conditions—all the chief concerns of Washington. James Hardy Dillard, a professor of classics and dean at Tulane University who was also active in the Carnegie Foundation for the Advancement of Teaching, reluctantly became the fund's executive officer. The board of trustees consisted of black members like Robert Moton of Hampton and whites like Andrew Carnegie, George Peabody, and William Howard Taft, all ardent advocates of the advancement of rural black education.[116]

Washington chaired the board of trustees and used his influence to spread the money to wider rural areas while securing the cooperation of country school boards for more funding. No private fund could last forever, and Washington wanted Jeanes teachers and workers to secure permission from county school officials and work in close cooperation with them, thus laying the groundwork for future public support of black education. Nothing should be done to lessen county and state responsibility in that direction. In 1908, Dillard started the innovative program of using supervising teachers, working in close conjunction with local school boards, throughout the rural districts of the South. With some help from the General Education Board, by 1915 the Jeanes Fund had placed black supervising teachers in 134 counties throughout the South; in many counties, additional funding was also secured from local school boards. Only a small counterweight to the great gap in black and white school funding, the Jeanes Fund did reach thousands of blacks in rural extension, while also laying the foundation for public responsibility toward black education.[117]

The Rosenwald school program was another extension of Washington's philosophy at work, inspired and directed by him. Julius Rosenwald, the Sears genius, had already given generously to almost every worthy self-help cause of black uplift, including the distribution of Sears clothes and products to institutions and the building of YMCAs in many cities through matching funds.[118] Rosenwald's first gift, in 1912, for his school program was $25,000 to be used for schools that perpetuated Tuskegee principles, and Washington got Rosenwald's permission to use some of this money to build six more model schools near the institute. Rosenwald wanted quality buildings erected at the lowest cost, with Sears products used only when they were cheaper than elsewhere. Communities were requested to match Rosenwald's gift in labor, materials, and money as much as they were able. Washington tried to implement Rosenwald's wishes to the letter, utilizing adult leadership in the joint effort of raising money, securing supplies, and providing skilled labor as community uplift projects.[119]

Rosenwald was so pleased with the successful first phase that he gave a second grant of $30,000. Applied first in Macon County, the Rosenwald school program was extended to five additional counties in Alabama by 1915. As with the Jeanes Fund monies, Washington had pursued his policy of involving adults in every community and cooperating with local school boards to insure their support; his double aim was to enhance public awareness and responsibility while minimizing old hostilities among whites toward black education and preventing the creation of new ones. In the spring of 1915, Washington told Rosenwald that a total of fifty new schoolhouses could be expected by October 1915.[120] This school project had started, in Washington's opinion, a revolution in public sentiment toward black education in the South. In his busy schedule during the last month of his life, Washington expressed his gratitude to Rosenwald, who continued the project after Washington's death. "I wish you could hear the expressions of approval that now come from white people—white people who a few years ago would not think of anything bearing upon Negro education. I wish you could hear the expressions of gratitude uttered over and over again by the most humble classes of colored people."[121]

In another leadership role, Washington suggested that a broad survey be made of some 600 southern black schools, using a special grant of about $10,000 from the Phelps-Stokes Foundation. He wanted the survey to amass comparative and comprehensive information concerning school locations, types, levels of education, and quality, to avoid duplication and misinformation. He suggested Robert E. Park, his press agent, for the job because Park could get information from all classes of people without offending them in the process. The foundation chose instead Thomas Jesse Jones to do the survey, and Washington worked with Jones, a former Hampton teacher, in the initial planning, even though Jones had not been his choice. Jones's survey report on black educational institutions was published in 1916 after Washington's death by the U.S. Bureau of Education. According to Harlan, this information was used by the sponsoring foundations to reorganize higher and secondary education according to their own and not the affected schools' standards—a result far removed from Washington's original purpose. Jones carried the Phelps-Stokes survey to Africa in the 1920s, concluding "that industrial education was the type best suited to the distinctive racial nature of black Africans." "This was a position Washington never endorsed," Harlan contended.[122] Washington had proved himself "a friend rather than an enemy" to higher education, never promoting industrial education as the panacea for his own or any race. In his multifaceted role of educational leadership, "Washington challenged the stereotype of mere accommodation and self-seeking," Harlan argued. In broad and skillful ways, he had secured money from philanthropists to meet the needs of "every level of black education," including a "great number and variety of black higher educational institutions," Harlan concluded.[123]

☞ Washington facilitated adult education in the world community, bringing pragmatic vision to international conflicts of the early 1900s that were harbingers of a new century. On foreign soil, his greatest impact was in the continent of Africa. Willie J. Ellison concluded that "Washington seems to have affected Africa in just as many ways as he affected America."[124] The problems that Africans faced at the turn of the century were much like those affecting American blacks, Washington believed. Although Washington never visited Africa, he sent Emmett Scott with a special delegation under the initial direction of President Theodore Roosevelt in 1908 to study the situation in Liberia and bring back recommendations.[125] Well informed about the economy, politics, and social conditions in Africa as a leader in the Congo Reform Association, Washington frequently advised presidents and State Department officials regarding African policies and served as interracial interpreter when African delegations came to America.[126] His recommendations for Africa always took the same pragmatic stance he followed for American blacks, however, stressing practical economics and education. He wrote to a Liberian editor: "Every time a Liberian eats a tin of canned goods imported from any other country, it means poverty for the Liberians; it means the Liberians are paying somebody else to manufacture the tin can, and paying the freight upon the cans, and all this of course means money taken out of Liberia."[127]

Washington and Tuskegee became actively involved in an African program of adult education in 1900. Three Tuskegee students and one faculty member started the Togo project in conjunction with the German government; five other Tuskegeans were later added. This mission sought to train native Africans in the interbreeding of local and imported cotton, with the objective of developing a commercially successful variety that would help the African economy and promote international trade.[128] After one year this group was able to grow, process, and ship to Germany some twenty-five bales of cotton. Although this shipment was perhaps insignificant, there had been no exportation of cotton before this one. By the end of a five-year period, the cotton export had increased to 950,000 pounds. The *Tuskegee Student* reported in 1906 that the cotton experiment had gained international recognition; English and French programs were adopting the principles, processes, and objectives of the Togo experiment.[129] A total of nine Tuskegeans participated in the African project from 1901 to 1909; unfortunately, four of the nine died in Togo. Promising self-help, economic improvement, and the extension of education, the African project demonstrated one road to economic independence, and Washington vigorously advised and supported it.

After the translation of *Up from Slavery* into Zulu, many Africans wrote and visited Washington for advice. Students from every part of Africa came to Tuskegee Institute, backed by whites, blacks, missionaries, and governments, to train and found similar schools in Africa. Among the African schools that were direct or indirect extensions of Tuskegee Institute and Washington's philosophy were two schools in the Cape of Good Hope, South African Native College at Fort Hare and Lovedale Industrial Institute. Other schools included the Zulu Christian Industrial School in Ohlange, Natal; the Pretoria Polytechnic Institute, Transvaal; the American Baptist Industrial Mission, South Rhodesia; the Church of Scotland Mission, Blantyne, Nyasaland; the Lumbwa Industrial Mission, Kenya; the Mittel and Gehelfen School of Kidugalo, German East Africa; the S. B. Thomas Agricultural Academy, Freetown, Sierra Leone; and the Booker T. Washington Industrial Institute of Liberia.[130]

The Reverend John Langalabalele Dube, who founded the Zulu Christian Industrial School, had studied at Oberlin College, becoming a Congregational minister in 1899 in New York. After studying the philosophy and purposes of Tuskegee Institute, he became an advocate of the Washington principle, "education for life." Dube later founded the Bantu Business League, based on Washington's NNBL. Although Dube became known as the Booker T. Washington of South Africa, the two men did not share a close relationship. Dube also founded a Zulu newspaper and helped to establish the African National Congress, which focused on black political activity in South Africa.[131]

Washington also significantly influenced other African intellectuals and helped to plan the Pan-African Conference, without actually attending its London meeting in 1900 or adopting its more militant stance. Such scholars as Mark C. Hayford and P. K. Isaka Seme visited Tuskegee, corresponded with Washington, and sought his advice, viewing Washington as a symbol of racial solidarity and self-help in theory and practice.[132] It was Velma Blackwell's impression that Africans viewed Washington and Du Bois with equal esteem, as evidenced by a plea for help from Harry Thuku, leader of the East African Association, in 1920; he wrote Tuskegee asking whether a "Booker T. Washington or a Du Bois [type] can be spared for founding a Tuskegee in the African world for the bold mission of uplifting and emancipating the hopeless, struggling 3,000,000 nude native souls from deep ignorance, abject poverty and grinding oppression of the white settlers of the colony of Kenya?" According to Blackwell, Thuku was not concerned with the rift that had developed in America between the Bookerites and the "Talented Tenth" faction; Thuku's main concern was for the African advancement that both had advocated—Washington through rural, self-help pragmatism, and Du Bois through his emerging importance as spokesman for higher education.[133]

Along with the steady stream of African students, Tuskegee also had many from the West Indies and Asia. After the Spanish-American War, students arrived from Cuba, Puerto Rico, Jamaica, Haiti, and English-speaking areas of the British West Indies. Many of these students carried the Washington philosophy back to their native regions, often founding schools modeled after Tuskegee and extending Tuskegee's programs beyond national boundaries. Requests for help came from other regions, exemplified by Joseph Sturge of Birmingham, England. With large holdings on the island of Montserrat in the British West Indies, Sturge himself, along with Francis J. Garrison, requested Washington's help in starting a Tuskegee-type school for the native population in Montserrat.[134] Wesley Warren Jefferson, who graduated from Tuskegee in 1899, was sent, with Washington's recommendation and instructions, and a Tuskegee clone school was started in Montserrat in the late summer of 1899. Jefferson's difficulties, repeating the problems of Togo and the Hilton Head experiment, illustrate the pioneering efforts, the raw courage, and personal sacrifices often involved in the extension of Tuskegee's adult education programs, especially in isolated, under-developed areas of the world.

On December 6, 1899, Jefferson wrote to Washington, depressed and homesick: "I know if you had only known where you were sending me, and under what disadvantages I would have to work you would not have sent me." Of the 9,000 Negro population, Jefferson lamented, some "8900 were in a condition of slavery." Starvation was rampant, fostering stealing and lying, and many of the natives had no clothes. Because of the monopoly of white men, who often would not hire the blacks, Montserrat natives were far worse off than American blacks, Jefferson wrote in July 1890. While strongly supporting Washington's philosophy, Jefferson feared that Tuskegee's programs would not prosper in

Montserrat. Montserrat was the "poorest place on earth," and, even though the people were willing to work, "there is nothing to do," Jefferson said. When Jefferson arrived on the island, there had been "no school building in which to teach nor house in which to live," but he opened his school on a former sugar plantation, implementing programs of agriculture, industrial training, academics, and family improvement.[135] Often discouraged and isolated in his efforts, Jefferson nevertheless persevered for two years until poor health and disappointment drove him home, leaving the seeds of his pioneer extension for others to nurture and harvest.[136]

Tuskegee influences also spread to Japan and China. "We have both Japanese and Chinese students," Washington wrote to the president of Fisk University in 1911, "and no adverse criticism has been made."[137] Iwana Kawahara of Tokyo graduated from Tuskegee in 1908; his sister and other Japanese students subsequently came. According to Harlan, the Japanese were greatly impressed with *Up from Slavery* in translation, seeing in the Tuskegee methods one way for the Japanese people to overcome their "technological lag behind the West" in the early 1900s.[138] Answering one of his frequent Japanese correspondents, Washington wrote in 1912 that the masses of his race had followed with great interest the fortunes of the Japanese people, more than any group living outside the United States. "The wonderful progress of the Japanese people and their sudden rise to the position of one of the great nations of the world has nowhere been studied with greater interest or enthusiasm than by the Negroes of America."[139]

When *Up from Slavery* was translated into Urdu by a Methodist teacher named Lilavati Singh, many prominent leaders in India took its message to heart. Christians, Sikhs, Buddhists, and Hindus alike often adopted the book as an official text on self-help and the dignity of labor. Indian visitors to Tuskegee studied its methods, hoping to adapt them across their country. One Sikh who had learned how to make pencils begged Washington for the chance to study at Tuskegee for four months and then get into an American pencil factory, wanting to establish a school in India like Tuskegee's: "I appreciate the system of education which simultaneously trains up head, heart, and hand. If there is any salvation for my nation I see it in such a course," he told Washington.[140]

In the spring of 1903, American newspaper reporters found an Indian man shivering on the streets of Chicago, dressed in ancient clothes. He was on his way to Tuskegee in Alabama, he told the reporters. "I am an admirer of your Booker Washington; I expect to visit his institution during my stay here, and if I am successful I will pattern the Indian institutions after his."[141] This man was Anagarika H. Dharmapala, a Singhalese patriot and Buddhist reformer who shared Washington's ideas on self-help and racial solidarity for his native Ceylon and India. Born in Colombo to a wealthy furniture manufacturer, Dharmapala had been educated in Catholic and Anglican schools. He had served earlier in civil service, ultimately finding his way to Buddhism as a counterforce to Western and missionary influences. He looked to Tuskegee for answers to the poverty of Ceylon and India, seeing in Washington a freedom from sectarian Christianity with the promise of material progress without serious challenge to India's caste system, Harlan observed. Dharmapala didn't think much of the Christian missionaries' "post mortem salvation," which gave little opportunity for "making man happy in this world where he is to live, at any rate expected to live at least for a generation."[142]

Dharmapala had already met Washington to California and was also familiar with Du Bois's *The Souls of Black Folk*. Noting that the two men took a somewhat different view of things, he concluded: "On the whole it is healthy that two parties are at work on two different lines; and there is no energy lost. The moral, political and industrial development are the three sides of a triangle."[143] When Dharmapala arrived at Tuskegee to study its methods, Washington was away from the school. The student later wrote to tell Washington that his visit had, nevertheless, been meaningful and memorable: "When I saw the Tuskegee Institute with its manifold branches under enlightened teachers I rejoiced that you have made all this glorious work a consummation within a generation; and I thought of the Viceroy in India who with the millions of children starving for education and bread that he should waste in sky rockets and tomfoolery and vain show to please a few loafing lords who came from England last January six million dollars in thirteen days! He is not worth to loose the latchet of your shoe."[144]

In spite of increasing world influence, Washington never traveled farther than Europe, however, and his three trips there were educational ones, used to support and extend his American work. Popular and influential in Europe, he spoke to large groups, met with national educators and leaders, and sometimes had occasion to meet writers like H. G. Wells, who came to America in 1906 to study the "colour question," anxious to meet "one or two representative educated men of colour." Although Wells basically disagreed with Washington's philosophy of patience, he viewed him more favorably than Du Bois, noting that Du Bois concealed his "passionate resentment all too thinly" and "battered himself into rhetoric." Meeting Washington in Boston, Wells studied his "rather Irish" face and listened to his "soft, low negro voice," observing also his great statecraft: "He looks before and after, and plans and keeps his counsel with the scope and range of a statesman. I use statesman in its highest sense; his is a mind that can grasp the situation and destinies of a people."[145]

Washington took a two-month tour of Europe in 1910 to study the conditions of the poor working classes. Traveling with Robert Park, Washington tried to avoid reporters, speeches, and regal visits until the end of the journey, intent on comparing the poverty of Europe with the conditions of blacks in America.[146] The journey took them through England, Scotland, Germany, Austria, Hungary, Italy, Sicily, Poland, and Denmark. Their findings were later transcribed from copious notes into a book, *The Man Farthest Down*, and various informative magazine articles. In the farmlands of Hungary, Washington was impressed with the technology of agriculture employed by large landowners; he was equally shocked by the sight of poor, barefoot Slavs who lived in mud houses being prodded to work by soldiers. He concluded that Hungary was improving the land, the trees, and the horses, but not "the man farthest down." The sulfur mines of Catania brought vivid memories of his own childhood work in the salt and coal mines of West Virginia, and Catania showed little improvement in the dehumanizing labor. Only 7 percent of the miners there voted, and robbers prayed to saints while entire families worked for seventeen cents a day. Poor farmers in villages of Austrian and Russian Poland were solemn, living in filth with dirt floors. Fifty beggars followed Park and Washington through the streets of Naples, a filthy city where a blacksmith shop existed in one bedroom of a house and a poultry yard in another. In Denmark, Washington found a kindred spirit; 12 percent of high school students were eighteen years or older, and the cottage schools were similar to Tuskegee, preparing students for useful occupations. Washington was also favorably impressed with the Jews of Europe, concluding that American blacks had much to learn from these people; they too had struggled against social ostracism, working their way up through education and economic progress. In London, Washington saw beneath the shining surface of the city the underlying problems of drinking. With women often doing the hardest labor, he concluded that the "man farthest down is women," not only in London but in other areas on his tour.[147]

Greatly lionized because of his international fame, Washington turned down "shoals of invitations to address meetings," according to newspaper reports, including an opportunity to address the House of Parliament in Vienna. He did speak in Prague, Vienna, and Liverpool to large audiences, and in London he addressed the National Liberal Club. In Denmark he was the dinner guest of the royal family, an event he later called the greatest surprise of his life except his honorary Harvard degree.[148] However, with his feet firmly back on American soil where his work and heart resided, he returned to the visions of poverty recorded in the notebooks. Washington's final conclusions, probably hypothesized before the European survey, reflected the main thrust of his philosophy and work. "He was an American and thought everything in America surpassed anything in Europe," Park later observed.[149] American blacks were not nearly as bad off as the down and out in Liverpool, the Italian miners, the Slavic peasants, or the East European Jews, Washington believed. Nor had the American Negro fallen backward: "If he is at the bottom of America, it is not because he has gone backward and sunk down, but because he has never risen," he wrote.[150] The man farthest down, in his ultimate judgment, was the man who made no effort to pull himself up from whatever the circumstances or place. In 1913, Washington was planning another trip to continue this survey, but the First World War and his own death preempted it. Writing to Park, who had finalized their notes for publication and to whom Washington had assigned the copyright of *The Man Farthest Down,* Washington spoke of the gathering war clouds in Europe. He suggested that their trip would have to be postponed until the majority of Europeans succeeded in killing themselves off, concluding that his own race would not act like the white people in Europe. "I do not know of a group of Negroes in this country or in any country who would have acted in the silly manner of these highly civilized, and cultured people."[151]

With his broadened world outlook and the extension of his philosophy and programs to many foreign countries, Washington hosted his first International Conference on the Negro in April 1912, at Tuskegee.

A 1906 article in the *Independent* had laid the groundwork for such a meeting, calling attention to the "permanent interests of the native peoples" of Africa. Washington here called for a permanent international society, composed of "scientists, explorers, missionaries, and all those engaged, directly or indirectly, in constructive work in Africa." While he did not specify just what work should be done, he did caution that efforts to help Africa should not be motivated by self-seeking, external force, or pious missionary zeal; the social, economic, and religious life of the people themselves should be the primary concern.[152] The seed of this idea continued to grow, taking firmer shape by 1911, when Washington wrote to Philander Chase Knox, U.S. Secretary of State, announcing the 1912 meeting, asking for help in publicizing it through the State Department, and stating his motivation. Many missionaries and officials of European governments had written him, he said, seeking information about methods used at Tuskegee. He was planning to provide an opportunity for representatives from Europe, Africa, and the West Indies to come to Tuskegee, see the methods of operation, and spend several days "in forming the plans for better work."[153]

Invitations for the international conference were sent to thousands of individual missionaries and societies, to the colonial powers of Africa and the West Indies through the State Department, and to leading black nationalists. Representatives from twenty-one countries and colonies came, mostly white and representing some thirty-six religious denominations. Because of the restrictive distance and cost, only one native African was present, Mark C. Hayford; others sent messages of agreement and encouragement, and the event was widely covered by the African and American press. The main theme of those who gathered was the need for the systematic development of constructive educational work in Africa and the West Indies. Although no definitive solutions were forthcoming, this international delegation discussed the problems of exploitation and inhumanity, with emphasis on methods of educational improvement. The general consensus was that Tuskegee was the most likely model for the preservation of racial pride and tradition, with its extensions of education, self-help, economic independence, and adult programs. Two other concerns expressed by the conference were fears that Africa would be completely Europeanized and that black nationalism would create greater upheaval, compounding internal problems.[154]

The conference was successful, and Washington wanted to extend its scope, drawing in other countries in the future and making Tuskegee a center for promoting international understanding, education, trade, and cooperation. Another meeting was planned for three years later; unfortunately, World War I and Washington's death intervened. By 1915, however, Washington's influence had virtually encompassed the globe, making Tuskegee Institute an international model in education.

Having reached the pinnacle of achievement and worldwide influence, Washington and Tuskegee had also become the focus of dissenting factions among blacks themselves. From 1895 to 1915, the churning racial discord would culminate in the organization now known as the National Association for the Advancement of Colored People. The most vocal of the dissenters against what they termed the "Tuskegee Machine" was W. E. B. Du Bois. His typical complaint was printed in the March 12, 1912, issue of the Indianapolis *Star*: "We can only come forward through the mind, not by digging or washing. There is no culture or uplift in washing clothes. The boys of brain are the wealth of a community." In response to such public assaults on Tuskegee programs, Washington replied in customary fashion, marked "Personal and Confidential" in his papers (vol. 11, p. 517). Du Bois was "puffed up with insane vanity and jealousy" that deprived him of common sense. "He knows perfectly well I am not seeking to confine the Negro race to industrial education nor make them hewers of wood and drawers of water." The battle lines were drawn. Washington had made his stand in the South, and his work would be evaluated from many perspectives.

"IN DIXIE LAND
I'LL TAKE MY STAND"

Private Politics, Public Perceptions,
and Pioneer Precedents

Let be be finale of seem.
The only emperor is the emperor of ice-cream.
Wallace Stevens, "The Emperor of Ice-Cream"

Progress, man's distinctive mark alone, not God's, and not the beasts':
God is, they are, man is and wholly hopes to be.
Robert Browning, "A Death in the Desert"

Burton Kreitlow identified the issue of social transformation as one of
the ten major controversies in adult education.[1] Gordon G. Darkenwald
and Sharan B. Merriam viewed the debate as two opposing extremes of
social intervention proposals in terms of degree and methods. While
Paulo Freire, Ivan Illich, or John Ohliger might advocate one extreme of
direct challenge and transformation of economic, political, and social
systems, the other extreme still advocates the protection of the status quo
and the preservation of inherited traditions. Between the two extremes,
the majority try to "maintain" and "reform."[2] Heightened by educational, social, and economic inequality—not far removed from Freire's
Third World conditions—the argument about social transformation was
a volatile one in the era of Booker T. Washington. In *Education for
Critical Consciousness* (1973), Paulo Freire refined his somewhat revolutionary stance defined in *Pedagogy of the Oppressed* (1970) as stages of
consciousness toward controlling forces.[3] Education, he observed in the
later book, helps to sponsor the highest level of critical consciousness,
characterized by a depth in interpreting problems, self-confidence in
discussions, responsibility, and dialogical discourse. Such critical con-

sciousness will not come, Freire argued, "as a natural by-product of even major economic changes, but must grow out of a critical educational effort based on favorable historical conditions."[4] As evidenced in the Washington papers, such critical consciousness characterized Washington's philosophy and work during the racially turbulent period of his leadership. Tuskegee Institute, whether secretly or openly, also fought for social transformation, making significant change in civil rights.

August Meier significantly noted that the centennial of Booker T. Washington's birth had slipped by without any national recognition in April 1956. Meier attributed this unfortunate blunder to Washington's perceived association with "a policy of compromise and conciliation toward the white South that is not in keeping with the trend of our times." Meier wrote to correct the record in 1957. He reported, "Yet Washington's own correspondence reveals such extensive efforts against segregation and disfranchisement that a re-evaluation of his philosophy and activities is in order."[5] When Washington's papers were made public, other observers like Louis R. Harlan also exposed "the secret life" of Booker T. Washington in revised historical perspective.[6] According to Meier, even southern whites had been beguiled by Washington's quiet, cooperative manner, mistaking his "short-range objectives for his long-range goals." People who knew him best had realized from the start, however, that "through tact and indirection he hoped to secure the good will of the white man and the eventual recognition of the constitutional rights of American Negroes."[7]

Addressing every aspect of adult social problems, Washington's protests bristle from the pages of his papers, marked by broad understanding, thoughtful responses, and overt or covert action. He protested against discrimination for coffee service denied in Selma, Alabama, the treatment of blacks in prison, separate and unequal education, discriminatory job and peonage practices, lynching, Jim Crow and conditions of railroad travel, voting restrictions, poor health and housing, and political inequities. His was a protest informed by facts, matched with action, and unmarred by heated radicalism that might spread discord with no significant results. Choosing his methods and priorities, Washington maintained the stability of his educational work through Tuskegee and the spirit of cooperation, while conducting secret maneuvers and court challenges to social injustice, often at great personal and financial risk to himself. Understanding the social structure of his environment, he countered with feasible, appropriate action; realizing the monopolizing power of the white press, he countered with a strong network of accessible black newspapers and publications for the purpose of informing, motivating, and acting.[8]

Through Washington's close ties to the Theodore Roosevelt and William H. Taft administrations, other governmental officials, and leading philanthropists, Washington lobbied for more black appointments and greater equality in laws, giving blacks for the first time an influential voice in high places.[9] Sought out by President Theodore Roosevelt for advice on black issues, Washington did not relish his role as black political arbiter; his limited role of suggesting people for positions and advising on policies became controversial among his own people. The record of his papers, however, indicates that he acted as a thoughtful statesman in such decisions, bringing to bear the best information he had available and the advice of trusted associates in making them. His role as black political arbiter often instigated public censure for circumstances over which he had no control. Although a trusted adviser, he could not dictate Roosevelt's decisions, for example. Often asked to read over the president's addresses and advise on policy and appointments, Washington did so in conjunction with other informed blacks. Polemics ensued, with Washington as target. When Roosevelt asked Washington to meet him at the White House for a conference in 1901, the resulting dinner, an innocent precedent, brought heated criticism from whites and blacks throughout the country. Militant blacks like William Trotter condemned Washington as a hypocrite.[10]

The Brownsville soldiers' dismissal involved Washington in a more serious controversy over which he had no control. Near midnight on August 13, 1906, in Brownsville, Texas, approximately twelve armed men charged down an alley and up main street in a ten-minute raid. They killed one white citizen, wounded two, and terrorized a section of the city. Suspicion immediately turned to a battalion of regular black soldiers who had recently arrived at nearby Fort Brown and caused white protest and racial unrest. In an atmosphere of predetermined guilt, the evidence introduced in the initial civilian and military investigations linked the black soldiers to this raid, but later investigations raised serious questions about the hastily collected evidence. A conspiracy of silence among the black soldiers also gave the appearance of shielding the possibly guilty ones. The military investigation concluded that the entire battalion of three black infantry companies should be discharged; their white officers were retained. President Theodore Roosevelt agreed with the military report and ordered the battalion discharged on November 5, 1906. The dismissal of the black soldiers created a loud protest across the country, and not without cause. Roosevelt had withheld his order for four days, possibly to insure black votes in congressional and state elections on November 9. The soldiers had been denied their rights of a trial by military court-martial, and innocent soldiers were punished with those presumed guilty. It was also decreed that none of the dismissed soldiers could ever enter the civil service, a ruling that Roosevelt later retracted. By November 26, all the black soldiers had been removed from military duty. Congressional wrangling continued over these men, with serious implications for Roosevelt, until August 13, 1910, when the case was closed. Fourteen of the dismissed soldiers were qualified for reenlistment, and eleven of them had reenlisted.

Newspaper headlines blazed with charges of political foul play, racial discrimination, and suppression of civil rights in the Brownsville incident. Roosevelt was severely castigated by many angry blacks and by some politically motivated whites. The question of the soldiers' guilt or innocence did not seem to concern the majority of blacks as much as the bungled handling of the case, inherently racial with subsequent inequities. It was to be expected, perhaps, that some blacks, feeling powerless, would turn to Washington, expecting him to change the president's decision, because they had an exaggerated view of Washington's political influence with Roosevelt. From the beginning, Washington stated emphatically that Roosevelt had blundered, especially in delaying his dismissal order until after the elections, and he staunchly maintained that position. It was not common sense, he believed, to turn completely against Roosevelt, however, for one bad decision. Roosevelt had done more for blacks than any other president, Washington said, and had favored blacks "in nine out of ten cases." Enmeshed in a catch-twenty-two situation, Washington correctly predicted in a letter of November 7, 1906, to his friend, Charles W. Anderson, "The enemy will, as usual, try to blame me for all of this."

Washington repeatedly asked Roosevelt to reconsider the case of the

Brownsville soldiers. Roosevelt refused to change his mind after dismissing the soldiers in question. By November 5, 1906, Roosevelt's decision was sealed in cement, as reflected in his letter to Washington: "I have your letter of the 2nd instant. I could not possibly refrain from acting as regards these colored soldiers. You can not have any information to give me privately to which I could pay heed, my dear Mr. Washington, because the information on which I act is that which came out in the investigation itself."[11] This hasty investigation had found the soldiers guilty. Washington continued to hammer the issue through his secretary, Emmett Scott, and friend, Charles W. Anderson, sending written pleas for the black soldiers; he told the president that "some wholly innocent men are being punished" and asked Roosevelt to modify his order.[12]

As late as November 5, 1908, Roosevelt wrote to Washington that "We may find it necessary to reopen the Brownsville business on account of the discovery of some, at least, of the men who were actively involved in the shooting."[13] On November 7, 1908, Roosevelt wrote to Charles Banks in Mound Bayou, Mississippi, that the Brownsville incident could come up again; he, therefore, wanted to "emphasize the other side of the question—the side typified by Mound Bayou, typified in another way by Tuskegee."[14] Although Washington tried to get President Taft, who succeeded Roosevelt, to modify the Brownsville decision, the incident was not then resolved, and Washington largely took the blame for failing to change the presidents' minds. Louis R. Harlan's judgmental conclusion is typical of revisionistic hindsight: "But Brownsville and the President's dismissal of the soldiers after a hasty and unfair investigation highlighted instead Washington's lack of one essential attribute for the leader of an oppressed minority—the capacity for righteous public anger against injustice."[15] One lone black man, however, hardly had the power to dictate presidential orders or to force their change, no matter his degree of influence or anger. Nor is such influence as yet in evidence as the twenty-first century approaches.

According to August Meier and the evidence in the Washington papers, Washington often gave the overt appearance of minimizing political and civil rights while fighting covertly against disfranchisement and other forms of discrimination. In 1899 he lobbied against the Harwick Bill of disfranchisement in Georgia. Seeking funds from philanthropists to fight the electoral provisions of the Louisiana constitution in 1900, Washington spent his personal funds in fighting the test case in Louisiana. In Alabama, he fought to prevent provisions discriminatory toward blacks in the state constitution in 1901, 1903, and 1904, spending at least $4,000 from his own pocket. So secret was this Alabama activity for fear of reprisal toward Tuskegee that Wilford Smith, his lawyer, Emmett Scott, and Washington developed pseudonyms and stated sums of money in code in their private correspondence.[16] Washington's letter to Walter L. Cohen in 1905 indicated his wide activism: "What I have attempted in Louisiana I have attempted to do in nearly every one of the Southern States, as you and others are in a position to know, and but for my action, as feeble as it was, the colored people would have been completely overthrown . . . in nearly every Southern State."[17]

In other secret work, Washington helped to eliminate black discrimination on jury panels, to provide protection for black tenants, and to stem the tide of lynchings. In the jury case, which involved Seth Carter of Texas and Dan Rogers of Alabama, Washington and Smith carried the case to its successful conclusion before the U.S. Supreme Court over several years, again with personal funding from Washington.[18] The Alonzo Bailey peonage case involved black violations of tenant contracts, often through ignorance or accident, with subsequent sentencing to chain gangs. The Supreme Court ultimately declared such peonage cases illegal, largely through Washington's efforts. "Some of us here have been working at this case for over two years," he confided to friends, using the free services of "some of the best lawyers in Montgomery" and other influential people in Alabama.[19] Neither ignorant of nor indifferent to acts of violence, Tuskegee kept close records on lynching, fighting and protesting its escalation.[20] Washington seldom missed a chance to inform the public in speeches, letters, and magazine articles.

Having national prominence, Washington himself was not greatly affected by discrimination in public transportation and hotel arrangements. He helped to lead the fight, however, against railroad segregation and the legislation that promoted it. With James C. Napier, a lawyer in Nashville, and W. E. B. Du Bois in Atlanta, Washington tried to gain access to Robert Todd Lincoln, the Great Emancipator's son and president of the Pullman Company, to register a complaint about the treatment of blacks by the railroad. When Lincoln refused to meet with them—in fact, refused to answer Washington's letters—Washington was anxious to file a suit, but others in the group failed to act.[21] Washington continued protesting through a steady stream of letters, keeping the horrible physical conditions of black compartments, incidents of raw discrimination, and unfair practices in plain view of railroad officials. When the Warner-Foraker amendment to the Hepburn Railroad Rate Bill came up in 1906, condoning railroad segregation across the country, Washington jumped into the fight to defeat it. Working through Professor Kelly Miller of Howard University and Archibald Grimké, a Boston lawyer, Washington also secretly paid former Senator Henry W. Blair of New Hampshire to lobby against the amendment. It was defeated.[22]

In the atmosphere of white supremacism and growing disfranchisement in the late 1800s and early 1900s, permeated with lynchings and whitecapping, the conclusion that C. Vann Woodward reached seems relevant: "It is indeed hard to see how [Washington] could have preached or his people practiced a radically different philosophy in his time and place."[23] If Martin Luther King, Jr., could be jailed and ultimately shot for his peaceful demonstrations for black equality as late as the 1960s, little imagination is required to understand the precarious difficulties of Booker T. Washington in the Black Belt during a far more racist period requiring secrecy in political agitation. Reviewing the covert actions and social intervention of Washington revealed in his papers, Meier concluded from such evidence: "It is clear, then, that in spite of his placatory tone and his outward emphasis upon economic development as the solution to the race problem, Washington was surreptitiously engaged in undermining the American race system by a direct attack upon disfranchisement and segregation; that in spite of his strictures against political activity, he was a powerful politician in his own right. The picture that emerges from Washington's own correspondence is distinctly at variance with the ingratiating mask he presented to the world."[24]

Social change is slow, hardly to be accomplished by one leader of the generation of slavery. Even with the work of the National Association for the Advancement of Colored People, coalitions, and massive civil rights activity in the mid-1900s, the Kerner Commission reported in 1968 that black unemployment was twice that of whites. Updating the Kerner report in March 1988, Fred Harris reported that "quiet riots" were ravaging American cities; less alarming and noticeable, these riots were "even more destructive of human life than the violent riots of 20 years ago." Dewayne Wickham, reviewing these facts, reported that unemployment of blacks was three times that of whites, that housing in America was still largely segregated, and that "most black children today attend schools that are overwhelmingly black, just as they did 20 years ago." With discriminatory employment practices and frequent jabs at "niggers," Wickham wondered "just how far we actually have come as a nation since 1968."[25] Washington was hopeful for his race, Charles W. Chesnutt observed, believing in "the ultimate triumph of the forces of progress, which in the end make for justice." But Washington was also the "prophet of the practical," Chesnutt said, believing that the black man's future "is that of to-morrow, as growing out of the conditions of yesterday and to-day." Chesnutt concluded that Washington believed in "getting the foundations of an argument, as well as of an education, properly laid," and he gave "the present a large part of his attention," knowing that each generation must build upon the socioeconomic conditions inherited from the past.[26] True progress for any race, however, required the philosophy "that there is as much dignity in tilling a field as in writing a poem," Washington said. "Nor should we permit our grievances to overshadow our opportunities."[27] Social change was inevitable, he affirmed: "One might as well try to stop the progress of a mighty railroad train by throwing his body across the track, as to try to stop the growth of the world in the direction of giving mankind more intelligence, more culture, more skill, more liberty, and in the direction of extending more sympathy and more brotherly kindness."[28]

☞ John Hope Franklin noted that the ascendancy of Booker T. Washington provided "the most dramatic and significant episodes in the history of American education and of race relations." So completely did he dominate the scene, Franklin argued, that he stamped his thirty years of leadership with his own name and personality, for better or worse, justifying the label "The Age of Booker T. Washington."[29] Horace Bond, in writing of the serious problems of evaluation in the "great man theory" of educational history, observed that two common errors affect the accuracy of such evaluations. First, there is a danger of "attributing momentous social and economic changes to the impress of a great personality whose life was contemporary with these changes," and, second, there is a common tendency to abrogate "the positive contribution of great personalities because we have no adequate statistical measure of their effect upon human history."[30] Evaluations of Washington's leadership in adult education are further complicated by the paucity of literature directed at his pioneer work in this field. With the exception of an introductory article by Leo McGee and a broad, loosely organized dissertation by Velma Blackwell, this writer has found no research or recognition of Washington's or any black leadership in the adult education movement, even though his contributions were highly significant to his age and relevant to the movement today.

According to Bond, who wrote his pioneer study of Alabama in 1939, Washington's statistically immeasurable influences lay in his immense influence on private philanthropy, which in turn affected public education for blacks; in the building of Tuskegee Institute and the wide influence its graduates had across the South and world; and in the profound effect the man himself exerted on public opinion, giving promise of increasing power through successive generations. Bond also noted other influences:

> The evidences of greatness are to be found, not in immediate institutional results, nor even in those claims upon which the personality itself rests its petition for present and future acknowledgment; but in the long-time contribution which that personality can make to the area of thought and feeling and opinion. It is so with Booker T. Washington. Another generation may evolve more delicate instruments for such appraisal; until that time, the historian of educational events may find in the builder of Tuskegee Institute perhaps the most illuminating point of departure from which to evaluate the times and the social and economic forces in which he was involved. In his own time Booker T. Washington was a vivid, towering personality; even in our time he has become a legend. And who shall deny the importance of legends, as social forces, in affecting the course of human history?[31]

These are intangibles, however, and Washington was a counter of dollars, programs, businesses, homes and acres owned, black school enrollment and teachers, lynchings, and other tangible, countable elements. Undoubtedly, the pragmatic Washington would want to be counted, too, in some accurate measurement of progress. Although Bond painted a gloomy picture of Alabama in the 1930s, his quoted figures reflected some measurable progress in Macon County during the Washington era. Without the benefit of the Washington papers or knowledge of Washington's secret work for social intervention, Bond neglected Washington's national and international influences, focusing primarily on Alabama's educational figures. In 1900, according to Bond, 69.1 percent of blacks in Alabama were reported illiterate, and by 1920, the figure was down to 31.3 percent, reflecting a drop of more than half in illiteracy in Alabama.[32] Actual enrollment in school increased from 44 to 62 percent from 1898 to 1929, and the rural school terms in length of days steadily increased, jumping from sixty-nine days in 1898 to 100 days in 1904. Unfortunately, however, expenditures for black teachers' salaries and appropriations for black schools were not substantially higher in the 1930s than they were in the early 1900s.[33]

Contributing to Bond's portrait of gloom was the Great Depression of 1929, which not only affected the poverty of Alabama but also devastated the rest of the South and the nation as well. Bond also put too much stock in a study done by Charles S. Johnson conducted in the throes of the depression in 1931 and reported in *Shadow of the Plantation* (1934), jumping to the harsh conclusion: "Making due allowance for exaggerations made by Washington and others in justifying the too-early success of their program, the results after fifty years are somewhat unsatisfactory."[34] As Mark Twain once observed, "Get the facts first and then you can distort them as much as you please." Andrew Lang also noted that statistics can be used as "a drunken man uses lampposts—for support rather than illumination." Some attention to the Johnson study, therefore, is in order for the purpose of illumination.

Without comparisons to rural Macon County before 1880, Johnson surveyed 612 rural families out of the black population, which was approximately 23,000 in 1910, before blacks' vast migration from Alabama beginning in 1916. Johnson failed to note that the majority of Tuskegee graduates also left the state to work in other areas across the nation or to seek industrial employment in areas like Birmingham. Trains packed with blacks were heading for railroad yards and rail work in the West in the fall of 1916, and authorities called upon Tuskegee to stop the outward flow of the black population.[35] From 1890 to 1930, the percentage of blacks living in Alabama cities increased from 10.3 to 28.4.[36] Based on his survey of rural families still living "in the shadow of the plantation," Johnson found that only a few people had returned to the outlying communities and were still working at their trades "with no great distinction." Washington was still remembered and liked by some of the older individuals, Johnson reported, and some of the cabins in the Sambo community that had been whitewashed twenty years earlier for a visit from Washington remained. The Baldwin land purchase project was no longer active, and the communities that Johnson studied reflected a Negro tenancy as "high as elsewhere in the Black Belt of Alabama, and the South," Johnson concluded in 1931. Of Washington, Johnson observed: "He came—a great man with a personality which took them in, which understood them, and which they could understand."[37]

Among the people surveyed, Johnson found only three people who had learned trades at Tuskegee, possibly because Tuskegee graduates sought employment where it was available. In educational assessments, Johnson reported that the successful heads of families were "those with an average education corresponding to the third grade in school." The surveyed families were literate enough "to take advantage of their surroundings," with no more schooling necessary "than is demanded by their dependent economic position," Johnson concluded.[38] To this regionally limited conclusion, based on limited statistical tools, Bond added a further note of gloom: Schooling had only served to equip citizens "with abilities and ambitions which they cannot satisfy in the 'shadow of the plantation'." The rural Negro school had conspired with other influences, therefore, "to hasten the movement from the rural South to the Northern cities," instead of the expected "settled class of Negro proprietors," especially after 1920.[39] Even the 1907 law that appropriated monies for building more schoolhouses in Macon County had backfired, Bond reported; Washington had supported the measure to help rural blacks, but it resulted in new buildings for whites from 1907 to 1909.[40] It was, as Bond was forced to admit, "fruitless to speculate regarding the degree to which Negroes might at any time have shared in the State Fund for schoolhouse construction had not philanthropy aided the race"—largely through Washington's influence, he might have added.[41] Limited by their geography, content, and methods and influenced by depression economy, the Bond and Johnson studies represent the largely ineffectual assessments of Washington's leadership in the 1930s. They lacked the careful and broad scrutiny that followed in the 1940s and 1970s with benefit of historical perspective and the publication of Washington's papers.

At the other end of the spectrum, Louis R. Harlan has emerged as the foremost Washington critic in the 1970s and 1980s, after his editorship of the thirteen volumes of *The Booker T. Washington Papers* from 1972 to 1984. Mining this rich vein, Harlan wrote a two-volume biography: *Booker T. Washington: The Making of a Black Leader, 1856–1901* (1972) and *Booker T. Washington: The Wizard of Tuskegee, 1901–1915* (1983), as well as numerous magazine articles. A professor of history, Harlan had done earlier work on racism and the separate but unequal public school campaign in the southern seaboard states. Gossipy and spirited, Harlan may also impress some as "anti" Washington, Tuskegee, and the South in quick, judgmental remarks that reveal his prejudices and uneven voice. While giving to Washington with one hand, he frequently takes away with the other, "damning with faint praise." With conflicting, stereotypical images fleeting across his pages, one is prone to ask, "Will the real Washington please stand up?" As early as the 1950s, Harlan observed that Tuskegee and Hampton had been led "up the blind alleys of manual skills," which were replaced by machines and mass production.[42] Harlan's view of the South was stated explicitly in 1983: The South, he said, "was a region not noted for thinking things through."[43] His general negativism toward the South is antithetical to the Washington philosophy and focus, and Harlan's greater empathy leans toward northern views in most cases.

Making enormous contributions to our understanding of Washington, the *BTW Papers* were generally well edited, providing a library of information in the main texts and extensive footnotes. There are errors, however, never corrected, in the early volumes; some papers were footnoted as having been destroyed by fire at Tuskegee when, in fact, they remain in the Tuskegee archives. The more dangerous and serious flaw of these volumes, however, lies in the judgmental introductions written by the editor and numerous co-editors. As if distrusting the reader's intelligence, introductions frequently spoon-feed the reader with liberal, revisionistic judgments and interpretations; the facts within the text itself often do not substantiate the editor's judgmental conclusions. Large and detailed, these volumes hardly invite the disinterested reader, and the danger that only introductions will be read without the subsequent serious reading of the text for clarification warrants some critical comment. One example of the slipshod occurs in the introduction to volume thirteen, in which wrong impressions are rendered concerning the circumstances of Washington's death; the actual facts within the text do not justify the introductory statement.

While extensive in selected details, Harlan's two-volume biography, based largely on the papers and funded by various grants, also demands some caution from the serious reader. Harlan seems to take more interest in the political maneuvers, infighting, and forays between the Bookerite vs. Du Bois/Trotter factions, with northern radical elements receiving more sympathetic treatment than the educational leadership at the center of Washington's life. In the introduction to the second volume, Harlan warns that readers should not expect a treatise on Washington's educational work. He justified this exclusion on the grounds that "this side of his life" had been detailed in Washington's papers, "and because I feel that he played an important but not remarkably innovative role in educational history." Harlan viewed the sources, nature, uses, and consequences of Washington's power as more important than educational work.[44]

Overall, Harlan's impressions of Washington may strike careful readers as tainted by revisionistic tendencies, personal bias, incongruities, and shifting perspectives, as evidenced by the following extract:

> There was also a more feral, more power-hungry Washington, inordinately involved in politics, and particularly the politics of patronage. Washington built the Tuskegee Machine by rewarding friends and punishing enemies, and political plums were his chief means for winning over individual members of the college-bred class, the Talented Tenth, his chief critics. A presidential appointment for a lawyer or a Republican party subsidy for a black editor were powerful solvents of opposition. Against the intransigent black critics of the Niagara Movement, headed by W. E. B. Du Bois, Washington was ready to employ secret methods of espionage, provocation, and sabotage that seem utterly at variance with the Sunday-school morality he publicly professed. Washington never tried to reconcile his secret machinations

with his public life, perhaps because, being secret, they did not pragmatically require justification.[45]

Onto the canvas of this unflattering portrait, equally inaccurate and unbalanced, Harlan splashes liberal streaks of hackneyed phrases and images: Samuel Chapman Armstrong is the "Great White Father"; Tuskegee is a "machine"; Washington is "Master of the Tuskegee Plantation," and, as such, is an absolute master, ruling his kingdom and "delegating none of his authority." A "benevolent despot," he left "his faculty and students little room for independence of action." While kowtowing as the "Great Accommodator," he controlled monies, newspapers, and politicians, bending all factions to his purposes. Unscrupulous, Washington spied on the Niagara Movement and the National Association for the Advancement of Colored People, sabotaging his enemies. Power-hungry, "his aim was not intellectual clarity, but power." A genius at the stratagem, "his mind was constantly devising new moves and countermoves." Searching for a suitable career, his "thirst for power and gift for manipulating others matured into a lasting pattern." Ever restless, like a runaway slave, he was "always running, only one step ahead of real or imagined pursuers." A "behavioral riddle," Washington ultimately landed on Harlan's couch for psycho-analysis:

> Perhaps psychoanalysis or role psychology would help us solve Booker
> T. Washington's behavioral riddle, if we could only put him on the
> couch. If we could remove those layers of secrecy as one peels an onion,
> perhaps at the center of Washington's being would be revealed a person
> with a single-minded concern with power, a minotaur, a lion, a fox, or
> Brer Rabbit, some frightened little man like the Wizard of Oz, or, as in
> the case of the onion, nothing—a personality that had vanished into the
> roles it played. Seeking to be all things to all men in a multifaceted
> society, Washington "jumped Jim Crow" with the skill of long practice,
> but he seemed to lose sight of the original purposes of his dance.[46]

Like the judgmental summaries in the introduction of the *BTW Papers*, this excoriating portrayal of Washington is not substantiated by the facts within his letters and papers. Washington was dominated by purpose, not power. That Tuskegee became an exemplary institution, singled out as a distinctive black college, was the result of careful management and hard work. Washington was tolerant, perhaps overly so, with such temperaments as George Washington Carver, wanting to utilize his great talent. If he fired or fussed there was justification. Depicted as the big house on the plantation, The Oaks, Washington's home, was no more than a comfortable, middle-class home befitting the leader of any institution who entertained visiting dignitaries. Having the role of political arbiter thrust upon him, Washington did not relish it, finding it more a curse than a blessing; nor did he make political suggestions for appointments or policies lightly. In consultation with other leaders, he tried to suggest the best people and policies for the entire race. It seems incongruous that a critic like Harlan, who so often denounced the power and racism of southern whites, would equally denounce the small influence, in comparison, that one black man was able to muster in politics and the press as a counterbalance to white supremacism. Hardly the behavioral riddle that Harlan wants to peel down like an onion, Washington's voice through letters, speeches, and other papers emerges as one sure of purpose and philosophy, unwavering throughout the course of his life, and motivated to the total uplift of his race. His secret and overt actions were unified toward one purpose, the educational, economic, social, and political enfranchisement of blacks in the American mainstream.

Harlan's suggestions that Washington was the sinner and the Du Bois/Trotter faction was the saint and that Washington tried to sabotage the National Association for the Advancement of Colored People require more accuracy and balance. Washington never opposed true civil rights champions, but he did oppose radical methods. William M. Trotter, a radical newspaperman from Boston and leader of the Niagara Movement that ultimately merged with the NAACP, took it upon himself to mount an obsessive attack upon Washington. "Week after week in his editorials Trotter mounted an extended attack on the person, prestige, and racial policies of Booker T. Washington," Trotter's biographer, Stephen Fox, observed.[47] The Niagara Movement was also "a radical document, even without any direct reference to Washington as it set down the program for a radical organization," Fox reported.[48] Trotter's great campaign against Tuskegee's leadership was the main cause for which Trotter had started his newspaper, the *Guardian*, and plunged into racial work, Fox noted.[49] After the Trotter faction violently broke up a Washington meeting in Boston and led other similar disruptions, harmful press attacks, and secret meetings, the Bookerites mounted some counteroffensives to determine where the next strike from the enemy would fall. Making no contribution to his race in the role of hate monger, Trotter grew steadily more radical. Falling off a roof, he may have committed suicide in 1934. Harlan did not complete the radical puzzle of the Trotter portrait.[50] As he explained in a letter to Oswald Garrison Villard in 1910, Washington had neither the time nor the inclination for such infighting. So much remained to do, he said, in punishing those guilty of lynching and peonage and in securing school funds and the right to vote that it was difficult to understand "how people can throw away their time and strength in stirring up strife within the race instead of devoting themselves to bringing about justice to the race as a whole."[51]

Influenced by the radical tactics used by Trotter and subsequent incidents such as the distribution of a paper in Europe that was highly critical and embarrassing to Washington, many black leaders were leery of the fledgling movement that evolved into the NAACP in 1912. There was some concern that the organization was too much influenced by its white northern leadership like Villard.[52] Mary Terrell, wife of Judge Robert H. Terrell, worked inside the embryonic movement and began to have some doubts. Ray Stannard Baker, author of *Following the Color Line,* had difficulty deciding between Washington and Du Bois as well as some doubts about the NAACP; he recorded his qualms in a notebook after attending an NAACP meeting in New York in 1915 and spending an evening with Washington:

[Washington] is one of the comparatively few men I have met who always impresses me as being great—somehow possessing qualities beyond & above the ordinary (February 13, 1915).

[The NAACP] emphasize rights, not duties & just as Washington attacks them in an indirect way, so they attack Washington. I find myself with them, too, though there are some aspects of their work I do not approve. Agitation for rights is necessary as well as emphasis upon duties. Probably Dr. Washington is attacking the problem from the South in the wisest way; & probably these people are doing the most useful thing here in the North. But always I find myself instinctively leaning toward those who teach duty and service. It is so easy to clamor for rights & so hard to earn or deserve rights (February 15, 1915).[53]

Robert Moton, of Hampton and soon to succeed Washington, was also questioning the leadership and the methods of the new movement in April 1914. Seeing the possibilities of the organization for national unity, he nevertheless expressed reservations: "I don't think we can accomplish anything for them or with them" as the group was then constituted, he wrote.[54] In a letter to Villard, Moton criticized the personal attacks on Washington and the organization's methods: "I am in no sense lacking in appreciation of what you are doing for the Negro and the Nation," he wrote, but "I do question seriously, sometimes, the methods of the National Association. There is no doubt that there is plenty to do and the Association has a splendid opportunity."[55]

As the central target of initial radical tactics and leaders, Washington understandably did not rush to embrace the NAACP, feeling that "Nothing that has real sense in it would be received by any degree of enthusiasm" and "What they want is nonsense." Like offering candy to a sick child when castor oil was needed, Washington was afraid that white influences in the organization were persuading blacks to fight for their rights "by merely making demands, passing resolutions and cursing somebody."[56] When an open letter signed by Du Bois and other members attacking Washington and his policies was circulated in England on the national organization's stationery, in 1910, Washington was deeply embarrassed, growing more skeptical of the organization's purpose. Other prominent blacks were equally alienated by the incident, seeing no positive purpose in airing racial division worldwide. Du Bois had stated in the open letter that Washington's optimism was leading him astray, causing a failure of leadership and turning both white and black intellectuals to his opponents.[57] Washington continued to view Du Bois's work as divisive and his own efforts as constructive.[58] The rift never healed, but Washington had softened his views of the NAACP near the end of his life, as the organization became better focused and less radical.

Du Bois was founding editor of the NAACP's *Crisis* magazine; for several years, he contributed his efforts to the organization and produced several published works. Often disgruntled, however, he once described his difficult personality: "I do not doubt in the least but that my temperament is a difficult one to endure."[59] In the ironic postscript to the Du Bois–Washington role in the NAACP—one that Harlan certainly makes no effort to elucidate—Du Bois himself left the NAACP fifteen years later in a controversy over its ideological compromise on segregation. "To have started out in this organization with a slogan 'no segregation,' would have been impossible. What we did say was no increase in segregation; but even that stand we were unable to maintain."[60] Disgruntled with American politics, Du Bois turned to communism in 1961. Disgruntled with America in general, Du Bois denounced it too, becoming a citizen of Ghana in 1963.[61]

The sum of Harlan's scholarship on Washington, however, spanning over four decades, has contributed to a revival of interest and to a multi-dimensional view of the man and his era. Although revisionistic, often judgmental, and sometimes uneven in focus and tone, Harlan has nevertheless dared to plow new ground in the secret, political fields of Washington's life, leaving an impressive canon for future scholars.[62] There are special moments, too, when Harlan captures Washington with significant insight, especially in details about Washington's role in helping institutions of higher learning, his family relationships, and his distinctly southern attributes. Although Washington "knew the harsh injustices of southern society," he was fond of the physical environment there, Harlan recorded. "Southernness came naturally to Washington, for he was born in the South, chose to remain there, achieved the zenith of his fame there . . . and, when his time came, he chose to die there."[63] Whatever else Washington may have been, "he was always indelibly a southerner," blending "into his time and place like an old tree in a woodland landscape." Washington dressed and looked like a prosperous peasant, and his speech reflected the rural South, "never salty but always earthy and direct." According to Harlan, Washington "abhorred abstractions as he lived among people to whom mathematics was a foreign language and polysyllables a Yankee invention." His southern inclinations were also reflected in his closeness to nature, love for the outdoors, and pleasure in working with animals. Washington seemed to have a fear and distrust of cities and city dwellers, "whether white or black," Harlan surmised.[64] Washington's "great and almost unique gift as a black political leader," Harlan concluded, was that "he could immediately and intuitively, without formal questioning, see through the masks and intellectual superstructure of those he met to the main-springs of their behavior."[65]

Falling between Harlan and the depression studies, Gunnar Myrdal's study of racial problems in America provided the best placement of Washington in historical perspective. Myrdal's work was begun in 1938, assisted by Richard Sterner and Arnold Rose and funded by the Carnegie Corporation. Interrupted by World War II, the two-volume *An American Dilemma: The Negro Problem and Modern Democracy* was not published until 1944. Carnegie President Frederick P. Keppel had originally directed that the study "be undertaken in a wholly objective and dispassionate way as a social phenomenon." Keppel looked for a social scientist "from a foreign non-imperialistic country, and with no background of domination of one race over another, who could approach this task with a fresh mind, uninfluenced by traditional attitudes or by earlier conclusions." Myrdal and Sterner, both from Sweden, had at their disposal the experience of many experts and scholars, a top staff of six members, thirty-one independent workers outside the staff, thirty-six assistants and outside members, and a corps of secretaries and typists. The first phase of the study consisted of forty-four monographs on the full range of subjects related to Negro problems in America.[66]

When the Germans invaded Denmark and Norway in April 1940, Myrdal returned to Sweden, and Samuel A. Stouffer of the University of Chicago, with the help of Arnold Rose, completed the forty-four monographs (over 15,000 typewritten pages) by the September 1940 deadline. According to Myrdal, this first phase had "embraced in friendship and concerted effort, white and Negro men and women of different specialties, ages, and previous accomplishments" and laid the groundwork for the second phase, picked up by Myrdal when he returned to America in 1941. The study continued as a major collaboration of digging "into primary sources in many fields of social science" and broad fieldwork. Myrdal later reported that the study's structure of hypothesis, data, and conclusions made no effort to "solve" the Negro problem, just as it is not solved in American society. Looking over the manuscript, however, Myrdal came to one explicit conclusion: "Not since Reconstruction has there been more reason to anticipate fundamental changes in American race relations, changes which will involve a development toward the American ideals."[67]

With more than forty evaluations of Washington's work, viewed in relationship with the broad spectrum of the study, Myrdal also concluded that Washington had made significant contributions to every aspect of black life in America. Calling Washington "the supreme diplomat of the Negro people through a generation filled with severe trials," Myrdal reported that "there is no reason to think that Washington did not firmly believe in the fundamental equality of inherent capacities."[68] With the initial publication of Washington's papers more than two decades later, the editor of *Intellectual Digest* echoed Myrdal's conclusion: Washington had begun his life as a "nonperson," and "the magnitude of his achievement has to be measured against the obscurity and anonymity out of which Booker T. Washington emerged." From the *Digest* overview, even Washington's controversial Atlanta address in 1895 had been "the charter for racial peace, not an acceptance of second-class status."[69]

The findings of *An American Dilemma* substantially support the guiding hypothesis and final conclusion of this writer's research: Booker T. Washington effected significant change in every area of adult life and provided pioneer leadership in the adult education movement from 1856 to 1915. General consensus, therefore, with Myrdal's earlier postulates will serve as a parallel summation to this study of Washington as a social change agent through adult education.[70]

Education. Concerned for all education, whether public or private, industrial or higher, Washington effected considerable change in education at all levels for the black population. Educated himself through the early medium of night school, Washington helped to lead the movement at Hampton and Tuskegee toward providing night school for working adults. Washington extended from Tuskegee local, regional, national, and international programs of adult education in the areas of literacy, agriculture, occupational training, business, health, family uplift, moral improvement, and interracial cooperation. According to Myrdal (vol. 2, p. 889), Washington salvaged "Negro education from the great danger of being entirely destroyed." Washington's extremely timely message helped "to reconcile Southern white men to the idea of Negro education" in the "actual power situation of the Restoration." Even the great dispute that erupted between the Du Bois faction of the "Talented Tenth" and the Bookerites served as an important development of Negro ideologies, raising the demand for teachers with broader educational background (pp. 889–90). Washington was also responsible for the large flow of philanthropic money to southern education, expanding rural schools and assisting black colleges.

Land- and Homeownership and Tenant Relationships. Myrdal minced no words about how crucial landownership had been to the black race's independence. He often reiterated the Washington theme: Their future "in agriculture would have been a rather different one if the Negro farmer had had greater opportunity to establish himself as an independent owner," firmly attached to the soil. Myrdal's figures also demonstrated Washington's influence, illustrating peak landownership by black farmers between 1910 and 1915, with a maximum of approximately 220,000 farms owned. After 1920, the figures declined, dropping to a low of 174,000 in 1940 (vol. 1, pp. 237–38). Contrary to Charles Johnson's suggestions of lingering "plantation shadows," Myrdal found that the majority of tenants in 1910 were on small holdings rather than plantations, receiving too little attention, with the exception of leadership like Tuskegee's. The rising number of white tenants increased the problems of black rural farmers, bringing about greater peonage problems. Attached to the soil to a larger degree—another Washington conclusion—blacks were more likely to remain in the same place longer, and with rising white competition and peonage trouble, the plight of black tenant farmers was crucial, Myrdal concluded. These farmers had "most of the disadvantages of being an independent entrepreneur without having hardly any of the rights that ordinarily go with the position," Myrdal argued (vol. 1, pp. 237–48). The great emphasis that Washington placed on the problems of rural farmers through the Tuskegee annual Negro Conference and the Movable School, as well as court action to eliminate unfair peonage, was, therefore, highly significant in Myrdal's long view of rural farm problems. Closely connected to farmers' problems were matters of improving the soil and methods of agriculture, family housing and health, and general family uplift through the education of women, all largely taught through extension and demonstration from Tuskegee. These innovative and relevant regional programs of rural education and demonstration laid the groundwork for county extension work and spread to national importance.

Industry and Business. "What Booker T. Washington saw," Myrdal said, "when he started out with his endeavor to give Negroes vocational training in crafts and trade" was bias and inequities. Fewer and fewer blacks could "keep up skills when they were not allowed to compete under the better working conditions and the improved techniques, and when they had difficulty in getting training" (vol. 1, p. 284). The general attitude of white southern employers was that "the Negro is not so satisfactory as formerly. The old-time Negro, trained in slavery to work, has about passed away and his successor is far less efficient and faithful to duty." Too many blacks had left the farms, seeking work on railroads, in sawmills, and in cities; large numbers had migrated to cities of the North. "They like to work in crowds . . . making more work for the police" (vol. 1, p. 284). Others argued that blacks had regressed as workers, and their ability to compete in areas where once they had no competition was diminishing. Therefore, "as has been shown a generation ago all the mechanical work of the South was in the hand of the Negroes, only a small proportion of it is done by them to-day" (vol. 1, p. 283).

Contributing to bias and inequities, fierce competition from poor whites for industrial jobs was another problem Washington encountered. As reported earlier from Bond's study of Alabama, southern white employers made similar complaints as they hired poor whites and barred blacks from the textile industry, an important job market in the South, largely on the false pretext that blacks could not read instructions or operate complicated machinery. According to Myrdal (vol. 1, p. 286), blacks had also been pushed out of the tobacco and building industries in the late 1800s, maintaining only some representation in the trowel trades of bricklaying and masonry. By 1930, white workers were in the majority in many of the jobs traditionally held by blacks. Although the Great Depression hit the industrial South less severely than the North, blacks were greatly affected during this period (vol. 1, p. 289). In the face of growing industrialization, increased white competition, and negative attitudes about the abilities of black workers, Myrdal suggests that any training that would give black workers some edge in the job market could hardly have been a false direction.

Myrdal also strongly supported Washington's drive to create more black business enterprises. "Business will stimulate the Negro's initiative, give him valuable training and experience, increase his self-confidence, increase his wealth, create a relatively secure middle and upper class, give employment to Negroes in the lower classes, and provide a reservoir of resources" necessary to compete with whites (vol. 2, p.

801). Robert Moton had pursued similar lines, believing that blacks would get "more honest consideration and a fairer deal [in business] than in any other of his contacts with the same white men, not even excepting religion." Money, after all, could solve most of the problems of blacks, according to Sir Harry Johnston's review of black problems at the beginning of the twentieth century; money could help the black vote, found and shape black educational institutions, establish newspapers, and fight diseases, alcoholism, and oppression while giving people good homes with some of the amenities of life. "The one undoubted solution of the Negro's difficulties throughout the world," Johnston concluded, "is for him to turn his strong arms and strong legs, his fine sight, subtle hearing, deft fingers, and rapidly-developed brain to making of Money" (Myrdal, vol. 2, p. 801).

Sometimes criticized for preaching materialistic progress, Washington did believe that black influence would come in economic progress, balanced, however, by moral and educational strength. The preamble to the constitution of Washington's NNBL had stated its purpose: "The promotion of commercial achievement" to help the black race achieve economic independence and a "position of influence in American life." Myrdal concluded that the NNBL's greatest contribution was in shaping the psychology and thinking of blacks; it had not contributed significantly to the economic change of many communities in various parts of America which he observed (vol. 2, p. 815). Washington was hardly the sole preacher of economic progress, however. Myrdal reported that practically all black businessmen and professionals met in the course of his study advocated economic growth. It was "preached in church and taught in school" (vol. 2, p. 801). The movement begun by Washington in the NNBL for unified efforts in business had contributed to organization for concerted action, orderly cooperation, and experience in planning and working together (p. 817).

Religious Life. Although Washington had preached an educational and economic gospel, he had also preached a moral one. He was appalled at the frequent evidence of illiteracy and what he regarded as low moral standards in rural ministers of Alabama in his early days at Tuskegee, as well as their emotional influence on blacks and failure to lift up the general standards of the community; Washington instituted the Bible School at Tuskegee, included ministers in the annual Negro Conference, and held night school and special training seminars in the summer for their instruction. In view of Abraham H. Maslow's hierarchy of needs, people with little food, poor housing, poor health, and no income could hardly concentrate on aesthetics of the soul; from improved life standards would flow the self-actualization of the spirit. Quoting Washington's summation of religious problems, Myrdal concluded that these conditions had sprung from "ignorance, poverty, cultural isolation, and the tradition of dependence" that also held the black population down in other areas of life (vol. 2, p. 874). In religious teaching all through slavery, the future world had been emphasized, rather than life in this world, Washington said. "The Negro was prevented from discussing many points of practical religion which related to this world," and white ministers had found it more convenient to talk to slaves about heaven. As a result, religious meetings among blacks even after emancipation followed the same pattern: "It is the Negro's feelings which are worked upon mostly, and it is description of the glories of heaven" rather than practical attention to problems that fills the minister's sermon (BTW, *Future of the American Negro*, p. 170). Myrdal found that various schisms worked to break down the institutional strength of black churches that had once provided the greatest "outlet for Negro ambition." Poverty and the poor economic base of a region also contributed to the weakened church. Like Washington, Myrdal criticized the emotionalism that was too frequently played on, low educational training for ministers, and the failure of black ministers to lead in larger community needs, such as education, housing, health, agriculture, and industry (vol. 2, pp. 874–76).

Self-Image, Racial Pride, and Leadership. Myrdal concluded that Washington exemplified the successful black man with national and international prestige, in the tradition of Frederick Douglass; other successful black leaders like W. E. B. Du Bois and James Weldon Johnson were, in Myrdal's opinion, of equal stature but "virtually ignored by whites" (vol. 2, p. 987). On a level just below these men were leaders like Charles S. Johnson and Mary McLeod Bethune. Myrdal also found blacks with great political wisdom across America in many organizations and in all governmental levels. The one factor that Myrdal seemed to view as significant in determining leadership levels was the "defeatism" that stemmed from historic circumstances, sensitivity, and frequent poverty. Feeling overwhelmed by the continuous struggle to overcome deprivations and humiliations, even the upper classes were often victims of defeatist philosophy, reacting angrily to personal incidents of discrimination and insensitivity (vol. 2, pp. 758–59). A positive image of self, race, and country, with the absence of defeatism, was an integral part of the philosophy on which Washington bet his life; instructive to all leadership, positive attitudes contributed to that extra height of his leadership, as contrasted with Du Bois, for example. Although providing some leadership to intellectual blacks through protest, Du Bois left a dubious legacy to the solution of fundamental, grass-roots problems. Blessed with freedom, broad education, and brilliance, Du Bois lacked a philosophy to bet his life on, often succumbing to defeatism. Protesting industrial education, he later wavered from that position. Leading the NAACP, he left that organization in protest after fifteen years (Myrdal, vol. 2, p. 797). Fighting racial segregation, Du Bois also became pessimistic "about erasing the color bar in a reasonable future" in his old age, according to Myrdal, urging the building up of a "cooperative black economy for defense and mutual aid" (vol. 2, pp. 797–98). Myrdal argued that the "determination to hold to the American Creed" was the one consistent scheme that directed blacks toward positive goals (vol. 2, pp. 808–9). Whereas Washington placed great priority on black inculcation into the American mainstream, discouraging any consideration of black colonization outside the United States, Du Bois's ultimate protest resulted in his giving up on the American creed altogether.

Interracial Interpretation and Cooperation. Robert E. Park once observed that racial prejudice in the southern psyche was basically "the resistance of the social order to change." The North was also susceptible to such resistance. "The white North definitely became more prejudiced when hundreds of thousands of crude Southern Negroes moved in," Myrdal reported (vol. 2, p. 662). Understanding the geographic and historic roots of prejudice and the slow process of change, Washington brought patience and a futuristic vision to his interracial interpretation and leadership, helping to link southern and northern resources with black-white cooperation. Myrdal concurred with Washington's bedrock principle that what affected one race also affected the other; whites could not hold blacks in the gutter without falling in themselves. Myrdal said that throughout his studies he had been forced to "notice the low economic, political, legal, and moral standards of Southern whites—

kept low because of discrimination against Negroes and because of obsession with the Negro problem," and these things were "true of the North as well . . . with other minority groups and Negroes" (vol. 1, p. 644).

As interracial interpreter, Washington served his race well as political advisor to presidents and government officials (vol. 1, p. 504) and in bringing blacks and whites together for cooperative change as illustrated by the Atlanta riot of 1906 (vol. 2, pp. 843–44). Washington "boarded the first train for the city," Myrdal said, crediting him with what Ray Stannard Baker called "the first important occasion in the South upon which an attempt was made to get the two races together for any serious consideration of their differences." As reported earlier in this study, it was also Washington's interracial effectiveness that had secured the Jeanes Fund, the Rosenwald schools, the Carnegie libraries, and various other philanthropic funds that helped in bridging educational inequities and other social and economic injustices.

The Southern Perspective. Both Washington and Myrdal identified slavery's moral, economic, and social dilemma as a national one, defying the American creed. Washington frequently argued that blacks were as well off in the South as they were in the North, well suited to agriculture and with other economic opportunities available to them: "Whatever other sins the South may be called upon to bear, when it comes to business, pure and simple, it is in the South that the Negro is given a man's chance in the commercial world," Washington said. Henry W. Grady had expressed the idea that blacks "had ten avenues of employment" in the South to one in the North, and Edgar G. Murphy made a similar observation in the early 1900s: "The race prejudice is . . . as intense at the North as it is anywhere in the world." Only in some places in the North could Negroes be waiters in hotels or restaurants, butlers or footmen in clubs or households or haircutters or bootblacks in barber shops. Murphy emphasized "in some" because even the more menial offices of industry were denied. As early as 1853, the influential black leader Frederick Douglass had lamented dwindling black opportunities in the North. "Every hour sees the black man elbowed out of employment by some newly arrived immigrant whose hunger and whose color are thought to give him a better title to the place." Douglass believed this trend would continue "until the last prop is leveled beneath us." White men took away jobs as house servants, cooks, stewards, porters, and barbers from blacks. "A few years ago, a white barber would have been a curiosity," he said.

Quoted in Myrdal (vol. 1, pp. 291–92), the suppositions above could hardly be supported without statistical measurement, but they were common knowledge. The greater industrialization of the North generally worked to the advantage of blacks. The few advantages that did occur in the North from the Civil War until 1940 resulted from a "series of unique happenings" that included the scarcity of labor after the First World War and the decline of immigration, Myrdal said. Even then, blacks were "completely, or almost completely, kept out of many manufacturing lines in the North" (vol. 1, p. 293). Race prejudice was in little evidence during this period among native white workers, but "later many of them developed a deep race prejudice," Myrdal noted. Even the unique happenings that had afforded some black gains were a "combination that could not last." Wanting to keep a heterogeneous labor force, many northern employers used blacks to prevent unionization and to serve as strikebreakers, especially before World War I, and dismissed the blacks when the conflict was over. Myrdal also concluded the following:

This should be emphasized: *large employment gains for Negroes in the North—except for the present war boom—occurred only during the short period from the First World War until the end of the "twenties."* During the "thirties," the upward trend in number of Negro workers was broken even more definitely than was the case of the urban South—and this in spite of the fact that the Negro population in the large Northern centers of Negro concentration increased by as much as 23 per cent between 1930 and 1940. The white population of the urban North, on the other hand, was almost stationary, as was the white labor force. Thus, while the proportion of Negroes in the total population continued to increase, there was scarcely any change at all in the relative number of Negro male workers. Further, . . . the unemployment among these Negro workers was much greater in the North than in the South (vol. 1, p. 295).

The black population continued to outgrow employment opportunities in the North, largely because the North treated blacks better in "other respects," but the record of the North was not a good one. "Many labor unions discriminated against the Negro worker. So did many employers, especially when it came to skilled work," Myrdal reported (vol. 1, p. 296). As he had agreed with Washington's agricultural emphasis, Myrdal also supported his view of work opportunities in the South. Often criticized as narrow and geographically limiting, Washington's southern perspective, according to the Myrdal findings, was as clearly in focus as other aspects of his leadership.

Politics and Compromise. Myrdal worked without the benefit of the published Washington papers, but he thoroughly addressed Washington's role in fighting segregation and the frequent charge that he was a "compromiser," a subservient extender of southern white supremacism. In this respect, Myrdal had some emphatic observations, possibly his strongest in the study:

It is a political axiom that Negroes can never, in any period, hope to attain more *in the short-term power bargain* than the more benevolent white groups are prepared to give them. This much Washington attained. With shrewd insight, Washington took exactly as much off the Negro protest— and it had to be a big reduction—as was needed in order to get the maximum cooperation from the only two white groups in America who in this era of ideological reaction cared anything at all about the Negroes: the Northern humanitarians and philanthropists and the Southern upper class of "parallel civilizations." Both of these liberal groups demanded appeasement above all. And so *the Southern conservatives were actually allowed to set the conditions upon which Washington and the Southern and Northern liberals could come to terms.*

But this was hardly Washington's fault. It is not proven that he could have pressed the bargain he made for the Negro more in their favor. Remembering the grim reaction of the period, it is difficult to study his various moves without increasingly feeling that he was truly a great politician, probably the greatest one the Negro people ever had. For his time, and for the region where he worked and where then nine-tenths of all Negroes lived, his policy of abstaining from talk of rights and of "casting down your buckets where you are" was entirely realistic. Even today it is still—in local affairs where the short-range view must dominate—the only workable Negro policy in the South. . . . Practically all Southern Negroes have actually to accept much more, including disfranchisement and gross arbitrariness and laxity in justice (vol. 2, pp. 740–41).

Myrdal also noted that Washington's long-range perspective came under serious attack from leaders of the Niagara junto, Monroe Trotter, Du Bois, and George W. Forbes, co-editor with Trotter of the Boston *Guardian*, who once told a public meeting that the black race would benefit if Tuskegee Institute burned down. They railed at Washington's "gradualist and conciliatory policy," but Myrdal wisely suggested that these northern intellectuals had produced themselves little progress in the social and political ills of their race after Washington's death. The same discussions were still going on in the 1940s among black leaders "in much the same terms as at the beginning of the century," and the racial climate was little improved (vol. 2, pp. 742–43). Nobody had accomplished the miracle which many had expected from Booker T. Washington.

Nor has that miracle yet transpired. In a special ABC report in August 1989, "Blacks in White America," black reporters concluded that racism in America is a fact of life, that blacks are still segregated and disadvantaged, and that racial genocide is possible as a result of rampant drugs, crime, unemployment, poverty, illiteracy, disintegrating families, teenage pregnancy, and AIDS. Carole Simpson, a successful journalist with the network, concurred with others that the race had not come very far as a people: "When you're black in white America, the top has a ceiling and the bottom has no floor." Still hampered by what Myrdal called the main stumbling block to great leadership—defeatism—many capable black leaders are restrained by real fears of bodily harm, social isolation, and racial insults which render them incapable of assuming full responsibility for the race's destiny. After two decades of unparalleled economic and educational opportunities, it is perhaps ironic that not only blacks but countless other minorities and disadvantaged people still view the American dream as an impossible one in a restrictive and racist society.

Reviewed in conjunction with current attitudes and problems, Washington's leadership takes on new distinction and relevance for the social, economic, and educational dilemma that confronts all adults in the next century. Hardly one to minimize the scope of the problems, Washington was, however, a master at maximizing the meager opportunities for freedmen struggling for survival after the Civil War. He would be the first to say that the black race's progress has been significant; he had walked that long road with his people from slavery to world leadership, knocking down barriers of social, educational, economic, and political inequities. A prophet of possibilities, he laid claim to minuscule means, bringing to his desert a wellspring of resolution and vision; there was no room in his mind-set for defeatism, even when facing seemingly insurmountable obstacles. The sureness of his purpose, the soundness of his programs, and the thorough, patient groundwork he laid for future generations still provide guidance, understanding, and hope for the path that stretches precariously before us. "I have learned that success is to be measured," he wrote in *Up from Slavery*, "not so much by the position that one has reached in life as by the obstacles which he has overcome while trying to succeed."

⚲ Bill Allain, a Jackson lawyer and the recent governor of Mississippi, selected Booker T. Washington as one of seven important people of the world whom he'd most like to meet (Jackson *Clarion-Ledger*, Sept. 17, 1989). Allain explained that Washington's contributions to the field of education at a difficult period in history had been impressive. "I think he could offer good insight and maybe help us bridge the educational problems facing all of us." The examination of Washington's life and work certainly has important implications for the field of adult education—to its continuing professionalization and its mission of social change in a complex, racially mixed society. An integral part of adult education history, Washington embodied the head-hand-heart philosophy from which innovative programs for adult freedmen emanated, thus changing the course of their lives and history. As adults approach the new problems of the twenty-first century, what might we learn from his "good insight," his pragmatic vision, that will help us "bridge the educational problems" which confound and overwhelm our society?

Washington speaks first to our racial divisiveness and the lingering shadows of white supremacist attitudes. As early as 1896 he sounded his note of warning: "I beg of you to remember that wherever our life touches yours we help or hinder . . . wherever your life touches ours, you make us stronger or weaker. . . . There is no escape—man drags man down, or man lifts man up" *(The American Standard)*. Inexplicably, Washington in particular, blacks in general, and other minorities have been virtually ignored in the frequently used histories of adult education. This is a significant oversight, creating unbalanced perspectives, encouraging the attitude of white supremacy, and eliminating one of the most interesting and relevant chapters in adult education relating to freedmen's education and Washington's contributions to the field. Continued research into the area of black contributions to the adult education movement will enhance the field, broaden its perspective, and give greater historical balance toward encompassing all people under the American creed.

The education of Native Americans has been equally ignored in adult education history. Explored in conjunction with Samuel Chapman Armstrong's and Washington's pioneer work at Hampton in this study, Indian education also contributed an important chapter that enriches American adult education history. Innovative and progressive, Hampton Institute became a laboratory for the study of interracial exchange, enhancing Washington's skills as interracial interpreter. Expanded focus on Indians and other minorities will greatly facilitate our progress in international understanding and world peace as we move into the next century.

The subject of mentoring influences has been explored rather extensively in professional circles. In connection with the area of interracial mentoring, however, there has been relatively little research; further research into interracial influences will prove instructive and beneficial to adult education leadership. Some attention was initiated in this study with regard to Armstrong and Washington that might inspire continued investigation into interracial relationships and the subject of mentoring. With his uncanny ability to size up people by character, not color, Washington set an early example of interracial exchange, launched by the white Armstrong who had influenced his philosophy and work; the chain continued as many influential whites were equally influenced by the strength and wisdom of Booker T. Washington, including writers, industrialists, philosophers, politicians, and educators. There is much we can all learn from each other once the barrier of color has been eliminated.[71]

As Allain has suggested, the insight that Washington applied to the social, economic, and educational problems of his era is still relevant, serving as an aid in solving the present onslaught of upheavals in the family, work place, school, and society at large. A headline in a local paper recalled for this writer the situation of unskilled workers and unemployment that Washington confronted when he first went to Alabama to open Tuskegee Institute: " 'Smart' Worker Supply Drying Up in U.S." (Hattiesburg *American*, May 30, 1989). According to John Omicinsky of the Gannett News Service, American business has a deepening shortage of skilled, productive workers, and panic is setting in. Qualified workers are disappearing, and zealous, highly trained overseas competition is rushing in to fill the gap. "The level of basic education, the level of the American worker's training, is the most serious problem we face in the country," Suzanne Berger of the Massachusetts Institute of Technology asserted. The Institute for the Study of Adult Illiteracy at Pennsylvania State University has warned that the United States may be producing "a permanent underclass of unskilled workers," and the workforce decline will grow steadily worse through the turn of the century.

Despite enormous expenditures on public education, illiteracy still gnaws, like silent termites, and weakens our national fiber. Omicinsky reported that the "much-ballyhooed" national crusade shows no evidence of cutting into the U.S. population of 23 million functional illiterates. The National Assessment of Educational Progress found that one in four 1989 graduates could not read well enough to handle simple tasks after twelve years in school. Three out of five twenty-year-olds could not add up a lunch bill, and seven of ten high schoolers could not write an effective job inquiry. Approximately 82 percent of all colleges have to offer remedial courses. One employment recruiter observed, "We get high school grads who can't spell the name of the street they live on." And Jonathan Kozol, author of *Illiterate America*, has reported 750,000 dropouts yearly and yet another 750,000 who finish school as functional illiterates, with an additional 500,000 immigrants. The problem of illiteracy weakens our place in the international market while strengthening the upsurge of unemployment, drug abuse, crime, homelessness, disintegrating families, and chronic despair in America among increasing numbers of ghettos. It is a scenario not far removed from the Washington era, with less than 5 percent of the freedmen literate and the majority lacking job skills, homes, and opportunity after their emancipation.

What did Washington do, and what does he still have to say about societal problems facing the twenty-first century that in many ways parallel those of four million freedmen more than 100 years ago in spite of more schools, more opportunities, more freedom, and more abundance? In the severe trials of his own age, Washington found courage and solutions to lead his generation out of the morass of illiteracy, homelessness, poverty, joblessness, disfranchisement, and despair, largely through his philosophy of educating the hands, the head, and the heart. Imperative to freedmen, training for logical minds, skilled hands, and strong moral fiber still provides a workable course of action. A teacher skilled in the art of remedial work with adults and familiar with education history told this writer recently: "We should have listened to Booker T." Her litany of reasons was instructive to all adult educators. "He wanted us to stabilize the family, rooting out the homelessness and drifting—and now the plague of drugs, of teenage pregnancy, of crowding up in city ghettos," she said. "Think smart, train smart, and work smart, he taught us; make yourself a credit to the work place, the community, and the country. He took hold, using his past. Time was a train to Booker T. He got on in the present, rode on to the future, never a victim," she concluded.

And, finally, the study of great leaders and the forces that molded their philosophies has relevance to adult education and other disciplines. In the last decade, there has been a general complaint that history texts focus on trivia, not substance. In the ABC report "Blacks in White America," one of the black journalists observed that too many blacks have lost their connection with the past and its heroes, and that criticism perhaps sums up our main failure in the study of history, according to most critics. In 1979, teams of Russian and American scholars and educators began a study of history and geography textbooks in the two countries, concluding their work in June 1989 (The U.S./USSR Textbook Study Project). The general conclusions of this project are instructive for the writing of adult-education histories and for methods of teaching: Too little attention has been paid to significant historical events and people, and this limited attention has been, at best, superficial and diluted, omitting the analysis of people and events in depth. The role of people has too often been replaced by countless facts and figures, "isms" and graphs, and the narrative fabric that enlightens the why of things has been drowned in a sea of cold facts. The project participants also noted that Russian history texts are more likely to be built around a narrative fabric, explaining in depth the how and why of events, with bold interpretations. The analysis and interpretation of vital personal forces that shaped the philosophies of people like Washington and Armstrong, beliefs that each man embraced whole-heartedly, help us understand and measure the qualities of leadership, give substance and stimulation to otherwise dogmatic, ritualistic, and uninspiring perusals of educational history and philosophy, and refocus content and methods. Again, Washington's words have proved to be prophetic: "Instead of studying books so constantly, how I wish that our schools and colleges might learn to study men and things!"[72]

Behind the dusty volumes of history was Washington the man, merely human like us, who nevertheless emerged with an entire era attributed to him.[73] It is his humanness we search for, walking again over the path he walked from a slave cabin in Virginia to the salt mines of Malden, West Virginia, moving on to Hampton and Tuskegee, and watching the metamorphosis of an illiterate slave into an acclaimed world leader. It is his humanness that inspires, proving that ordinary people and journeys may somehow be transformed into majesty and honor. His triumph helps to waken the slumbering possibilities in the ordinariness of individual days and journeys. From the dark soil of Alabama to the shores of Africa, human problems not unlike our own claimed his attention and leadership. Over the dangerous waters of prejudice and disfranchisement, Washington built a bridge to interracial understanding, and where no roads existed, he opened new paths in education, employment, housing, and economic independence. In the turmoil of his age, he made bricks without straw, building toward a nebulous future and embracing in totality the American ideal—a thing for him of biblical faith, "the substance of things hoped for, the evidence of things not seen." Washington challenged and mastered the great American crucible that sometimes scorched and seared his own soul, leading the first generations of freedmen into the American mainstream—that crowded highway still inspired by the dream and encumbered by realities.

At Tuskegee in the Deep South, Washington took his stand, fighting for and building racial equality throughout the world. Washington's city on a hill, Tuskegee Institute, continues to be what Thomas Fortune called "a lighthouse of knowledge in the Black Belt, . . . blinding the eyes of ignorance and prejudice" through successive generations, a distinctive university carved from its distinctive mission of adult education.[74] The pragmatic voice of his age, Washington still speaks to the purposes of adult education and the unifying but unfulfilled creed of human justice. Contrary to stereotypical images of the man, which dart like missiles fired from two opposing camps to collide in space, Washington's voice rises from the words of his own pages, vibrant above the tenuous images and the passage of time itself. With a vision defined, it is a voice of purpose, not power. However distant, the voice is distinct, couched in plain language and liberated from despair and defeat. As modern educators must confront the universal crucible that continues into the twenty-first century, Washington's voice remains relevant to our social problems and their possible solutions.

BOOKER T. WASHINGTON
AND ADULT EDUCATION
Crucible, Creed, and Crossroads

In the economy of God there is but one standard by which an individual can succeed—there is but one for a race. *This country demands that every race shall measure itself by the American standard.* By it a race must rise or fall, succeed or fail, and in the last analysis mere sentiment counts for little. *During the next half century and more, my race must continue passing through the severe American crucible.* We are to be tested in our patience, our forbearance, our perseverance, our power to endure wrong, to withstand temptations, to economize, to acquire and use skill; in our ability to compete, to succeed in commerce, to disregard the superficial for the real, the appearance for the substance, to be great and yet small, learned and yet simple, high and yet the servant of all. This, this is the passport to all that is best in the life of our republic, and the Negro must possess it, or be debarred.
BTW, Alumni Address, Harvard University, June 1896 (emphasis added)

While Washington cannot, in learning and philosophy, be ranked with Herbart, Pestalozzi, Froebel, . . . he may be truly classed among those who have wrought grandest results on mind and character.
J. L. M. Curry, November 1889, introduction to BTW,
The Story of My Life and Work, *p. 7*

When Washington referred to the American crucible, which he frequently did, he had in mind the testing that occurs in the process of acculturation. In his view, the assimilation of former slaves into the American mainstream after the Civil War ended the "peculiar institution" of slavery involved the "great questions of the Anglo-Saxon race," with attendant responsibilities and opportunities. For the flood of immigrants flocking to America during his era of leadership, the crucible of Americanization was no less real, however different in origins and nature. For these two crossroads in American history, adult education has been actively involved in the process of assimilation, unified to a large degree by the American creed, which buttressed our governmental principles. Horace M. Kallen has argued persuasively that the American dream and idea have unified the diversity of adult education philosophies directing this process of assimilation in our melting-pot society. Using the American creed as a unifying theme, Gunnar Myrdal also spoke of the many crossroads of history that have propelled American blacks "a permanent step forward." He argued that "history is not the result of a predetermined Fate" and that "nothing is irredeemable until it is past." According to Myrdal, the outcome of history is determined by actions of people, and the reconstruction of society is a never-ending and supreme task, demanding practical solutions in the face of world catastrophe.[1]

With tenets of the Declaration of Independence, the "American Creed" was stated explicitly by William Tyler Page in 1917 and accepted by the House of Representatives on behalf of the American people on April 3, 1918. Often viewed as an abstract and grandiose phrase, it was, nevertheless, a concrete document that stipulated that America was a "government of the people, by the people, for the people"—a democracy "established upon those principles of freedom, equality, justice and humanity for which American patriots sacrificed their lives and fortunes."[2] In the context of adult education, Kallen argued that the American idea, based on this creed, has been a "directive" to adult education in private lives, the nation's history at home, and our democratic cooperation with foreign countries, giving substance to the teaching and the behavior of adults.[3]

According to Kallen, adult education has moved, willy nilly, toward Henry Adams's concept of education as depicted in his autobiography and expressed by Robert Peers: "to help men and women to work out for themselves an effective attitude to life based on wider knowledge, to find their place in the universe, and to discover a philosophy which will enable them to face up to life's problems individually and collectively."[4] As an authentic, unifying directive in the American epic, "Is not 'the American Dream' a sufficient motivation for adult education?" Kallen asks.[5] Theodore Parker, a minister of religion, introduced the concept of the American idea in Boston on May 29, 1850. Repulsed by slavery and committed to the issue of equality for all human beings, Parker argued that the American ideal was antithetical to the premise that one man "has a right to hold another in thralldom." Not peculiarly American, slavery was, furthermore, "irreconcilably hostile to the American Ideal." Parker defined the American idea as a democracy, a government of, by, and for the people "after the principles of eternal justice, the unchanging law of God"—the idea of freedom. The idea provided the basis, Parker believed, for all our original and distinctive American institutions. Complex in itself, it was further divided into three subordinate ideas: "that all men have unalienable rights; that all men are created equal; and that government is to be established and sustained" to guarantee these inalienable rights for everyone to enjoy and develop.[6]

Such an idea, Kallen argues, depends on choices, "on the philosophy of existence and value, which the chooser and all who share his philosophy, bet their lives on." Inherent in both the American idea and the Universal Declaration of Human Rights, according to Kallen, is the notion that the "American Idea can guide, and shape man's struggle to go on struggling without the American Dream." The dreamer, however, is "doomed to a deadly awakening without the American Idea." The dream without the idea is suicidal, but the idea without the dream "is still the upkeep of life so long as life is."[7] In the diversity of America's melting pot, with the ultimate aim of liberation in all aspects of adult life, philosophic ideas can be "neither nostrums nor cure-alls," however. From the time of Socrates and Aristophanes, philosophies have been, at best, mere "articulations of beliefs, of aspirations, and of experiment." Kallen further argued that "one man's solution has turned out consistently to be another man's problem." Philosophies of education, first and last, can only express a faith on which the "believer is ready to bet, if not his own future, other peoples' futures," Kallen concluded.[8]

Guided by diversity of ideology, the history of adult education reflects a slow but steady movement toward the American idea in the United States and universal justice and liberation. Adult education has shifted with the maturation of the country toward democratic ideals and common people. During the colonial period from 1600 until the American Revolution, educational thought in America was still linked to European aristocracy, limiting education to the elite. Private schools and societies marked the beginning of education for the few, with little enlightenment for the masses. The growth of the nation from 1780 to the Civil War reflected also the growth of democracy and the quest for diffusion in education. Democratization began to uproot aristocratic and elitist notions of educational thought as opportunities for working people proliferated in agricultural education, evening schools, the Lyceum movement, and practical higher education. Only after the Civil War, which threatened to dissolve the Union, did the country mature from 1866 to 1920. Within that period, workers' education would find acceptance, and industrial education was popularized. Chautauqua, the Freedmen's Bureau, and organizations like the American Missionary Association made immense contributions to educational opportunities for the masses. Public education, however separate and unequal, made its uneven journey into the American mainstream.[9] In this exciting period of American maturation and democratization, Booker T. Washington appeared on the scene, helping to build, according to Emmett J. Scott and Lyman B. Stowe, an entire civilization from the first generations of freedmen.[10] Pioneering adult education programs, Washington was well centered in the adult education movement—its history, philosophy, aims, and theories—in the United States and the rest of the world.

Although adult education did not take the shape of a unified movement with national organizations in the United States until the modern period between 1924 and 1961, Malcolm Knowles wrote in a 1964 article that adult education has deep historical roots. Noting that the movement might be the educational frontier of the twentieth century, Knowles traced the beginnings of adult education to Confucius, Isaiah, Socrates, Plato, Aristotle, and Jesus Christ—all teachers of mature adults rather than children. As an organized movement, adult education began to evolve in the nineteenth century, taking different shapes in various countries. For Denmark, it was evidenced in the folk movement, institutionalized in the folk high schools that helped to refashion the national culture. The working class spearheaded the adult education movement in Sweden, and it was centralized in labor unions, temperance societies, cooperative associations, and the Social Democratic party. Adult education in Great Britain was rooted in labor unions, workers' education, voluntary organizations, local education authorities, and universities. Totalitarian countries have characteristically used adult education as an instrument of government to propagate political philosophy, Knowles reported.[11]

In the United States, "adult education might be said to have begun when the early settlers learned from the Indians how to grow corn, conquer the elements, and survive in the inhospitable New World," Knowles concluded. As early as the colonial period, adult education was evidenced in town meetings and colonial legislatures, teaching the tools of liberty and self-government.[12] In the national movement toward common people and away from aristocracy, adult education has followed history, accelerating the processes of maturation and democratization through four centuries. If the Americanization movement was a crossroads in the early 1900s, certainly the same must be said for the education of more than four million slaves set free at the end of the Civil War and, for that matter, the efforts to educate all blacks prior to that war as substantiated by such noted historians as Carter G. Woodson and Bell Irvin Wiley.

Washington's work in many respects reflected and benefited from the national tenor and focus on practical aspects during his era of leadership in adult education. The Morrill Land Grant Act of 1862 turned attention to the pragmatic college through agriculture and mechanical arts, breaking away from classical traditions. Passed when the southern states were out of the Union, this act awarded federal land grants of some 30,000 acres each toward the establishment of land grant colleges. It would naturally have been opposed by the southern states, which resisted any violation of states' rights. The subsequent Morrill Act of 1890 resulted in some seventy black colleges with its stipulation that if southern states would not admit blacks into existing land-grant colleges, new ones would be established. The Hatch Act of 1887 (strengthened by the Purnell Act of 1925) supplemented the 1862 act, providing for the diffusion of practical information on subjects connected with agriculture as well as scientific investigation of and experimentation with the principles and application of agricultural science. A sum of $15,000 yearly was provided initially for each state to establish and maintain agricultural experiment stations. The Smith-Lever Agricultural Extension Act of 1914 provided extramural instruction and continued diffusion of information to American farmers, greatly benefiting rural areas like the Black Belt in Alabama. Coming shortly after Washington's death, the Smith-Hughes Act of 1917 helped to fund vocational education through public education, bringing wider acceptance to occupational training.

Two important private funds prior to the Jeanes Fund also reflected the national trend toward the practical, helping Washington and other educational work in the South. In 1867, George Peabody established the Peabody Education Fund with an initial gift of one million dollars; ultimately his gift amounted to nearly four million dollars for educational work in the South. Born poor himself, Peabody had clerked in his uncle's grocery store before going into business; through sheer industriousness, he amassed a large fortune in the banking and mercantile business in America and England. In London, he built model tenement houses for the poor, and his total gift to philanthropy was nearly nine million dollars. His southern fund in America was administered until 1881 by Dr. Barnas Sears, president of Brown University; the fund was later headed by J. L. M. Curry and provided an example for the Slater Fund.[13]

Established in March 1882, the John F. Slater Fund was "for the lately emancipated population of the Southern states, and their posterity, by conferring on them the blessings of Christian education." Slater was a wealthy industrialist, and his son John built upon his father's work, amassing a large fortune in the textile industry. The Slater Fund had income from one million dollars initially and was gradually increased during the next decade; in 1890–91 alone, nearly $50,000 was used to help black education in the South. Former President Rutherford B. Hayes was president of the Slater Fund.[14] Atticus Green Haygood, a Methodist minister and president of Emory College in Georgia, was chosen as its first agent, largely as a result of his influential book, *Our Brother in Black*. Bold for his time and place of work, Haygood had asserted in his work that blacks were in the South to stay and that the South was the best place for them. Slavery could never be undone, he argued, and black citizens should be educated and prepared for civic responsibilities; blacks should be trained in available occupations, encouraged to buy land, and taught how to farm wisely in preparation for their responsible place in society, including the right to vote.[15]

In choosing between strong arguments on both sides for practical versus classical education, the Slater Fund's board was influenced to a great extent by what Samuel Chapman Armstrong had accomplished at Hampton Institute.[16] In Haygood's first report of 1883, he praised the work of Armstrong, convinced that Hampton provided the best model for freedmen's education. In 1884, Haygood declared that the fund would support those schools "best prepared to teach well and those that made 'industrial training' a part of their educational system." By 1889, Haygood informed the Slater trustees that industrial training was a vital part of every school aided by the Slater Fund and that "there is a growing sentiment that industrial training, in some degree, at least should be in every school, the small as well as the great."[17] J. L. M. Curry replaced Haygood in 1891 as agent for the Slater Fund, ultimately administering both the Peabody and Slater funds in the South. As indicated in Horace Bond's study of Alabama, Curry had enormous influence on educational philosophy and policy throughout the South in the late 1800s.[18]

Born in Georgia in 1825 and later graduated from Harvard Law School, Curry became a great admirer of Washington; both had witnessed firsthand the special problems of the South, understanding its racial tensions, educational needs, and possible areas for change. A noted Baptist minister and educator, Curry had also served as a congressman from Alabama before the Civil War; during the war he served in the Confederate Congress and Army. From 1866 to 1868, he was president of Howard College in Alabama, and he subsequently became professor of English philosophy and constitutional/international law at the University of Richmond. Influenced by Horace Mann, Curry believed in universal education and worked to improve education in the South, especially for blacks.

When Curry took over the Slater Fund in 1891, his general aims were to clean up the slipshod management of his predecessor, Haygood, to eliminate student grants-in-aid, and to give careful scrutiny to programs of industrial education. With limited funds, he believed that greater concentration on a few salient points was essential, that "diffusion is weakness." He correctly suspected that "many [industrial] programs were primarily window-dressing instituted by schools in order to obtain money from the Slater Fund, and that mere manual training without instructions in the principles of mechanics was of little help in training teachers." Within two years he had reduced the number of schools receiving Slater funding from thirty-six to fifteen. According to Louis D. Rubin, Curry's admiration for Washington was such that "during the years ahead Washington's influence undoubtedly loomed large in the program that Curry set forth for the Slater Fund." Curry's aims and those of the Slater trustees "were completely in accordance with those that Washington advocated, and the Slater Fund came to stand for industrial education above all."[19] The Slater and Peabody funds, with the later Anna T. Jeanes Foundation and the Virginia Randolph Fund, gradually merged into the Southern Education Foundation of Atlanta. Representing national trends in the late 1800s and strongly influenced by Washington's philosophy of the practical, these funds helped to advance the cause of black education in the South, supplementing the separate and unequal public funding for black schools.

While Washington did not rank with a philosopher like Johann Heinrich Pestalozzi, according to Curry, he was nevertheless in the mainstream of adult education philosophy. According to John L. Elias and Sharan B. Merriam, six ideologies have provided the philosophical foundations for adult education: liberalism, progressivism, behaviorism, humanism, radicalism, and analytical philosophy. The debate about classical versus practical education that erupted between the Bookerites and the Talented Tenth faction was as old as the Greek civilization of Socrates, Plato, and Aristotle; it remains a lively debate among practitioners of adult education, with strong roots in realism and idealism. While Sophists had argued for utilitarian training for statesmen and politicians, Socrates and Plato distrusted the idea of democracy, advancing classical intellectual inquiry and elitism. In Rome, Cicero and Quintilian continued the Sophist tradition, holding to the storing of facts and utilitarian training, and the debate has continued through the centuries, becoming no less viable today.

Anchored by the polarized opposites of Platonic idealism and Aristotelian realism, philosophical thought in adult education is more often blurred with mixed tenets than it is clear-cut. While Eduard Lindeman leaned to Plato's philosophic idealism and believed that education should revolve around nonvocational ideas, he nevertheless placed high value on experience. "Education is life," he said, and it should treat situations, not subjects. Nor did he rule out radicalism, allowing for the possibility of revolution when faith in intelligence breaks down. The progressivism of John Dewey, connecting education with life and rooted in realism, is also evident in the Lindeman philosophy, as well as in that of other adult educators like Malcolm Knowles, Carl Rogers, Ralph Tyler, and Cyril Houle. Radicalism, or social reconstruction, carries Dewey's pragmatism one step further, recommending not only connection with life but also the transformation of the social order. Adult education radicals like Ivan Illich, John Ohliger, and Paulo Freire follow the realism polarization to its extreme limits, urging drastic social reconstruction. Behaviorists like Tyler and Houle also have strong roots in realism, recommending measurable tasks and programs harking back to John Watson, B. F. Skinner, and E. L. Thorndike. Certainly, such analytical philosophers as R. W. K. Paterson and K. H. Lawson are clearly classical in tradition, recommending the intellectualism of Socratic inquiry, but they represent a minority elitism in adult education. The majority of adult educators represent the democratic, humanistic philosophy derived from liberalistic tendencies going back to China, Greece, and Rome. Dwelling on freedom and design for the individual and the whole man, humanism moves from the past to the present. Carl Rogers expresses the modern extension of humanism through existentialism, and Abraham H. Maslow's self-actualized individual represents the fully functioning person, the desired objective in humanistic programs of adult education. Expressive of the full gamut of society, the variety of adult education philosophies have covered like an umbrella the many crucibles of change in historical perspective.[20]

If sometimes muddled and frequently overlapping, the conglomerate ideology affecting the wide range of programs—from individual self-help learning to military training, from the analytical writing of Stephen Brookfield to the machine shop of vocational education—reflects the democratization of the movement itself. Maintaining ideological links with the past, adult education lives in the present, reaching out to the future beyond national borders. From such ideology has sprung also a diversity of aims, as defined by Gordon G. Darkenwald and Sharan B. Merriam. Eager to embrace a melting-pot society, adult education has perhaps aimed with its broad philosophical base to be all things to all people. There is room in the movement for intellectual development and the analytical philosophy of a Lawson or Paterson; there is also room for the social transformation of an Illich, a Freire, or Ohliger. Adult education abundantly provides for personal and social improvement, espoused by such practitioners as Lindeman and Paul Bergevin. Individual self-actualization, preached by Maslow and practiced by Knowles and Leon McKenzie, provides another option. For organization effectiveness, promoted by Leonard Nadler, a broad space has been reserved, providing for job training or human-resource development, as Nadler views it, in the private or public market place.[21]

From its philosophical orientations and resultant aims, adult education has also developed a conceptual framework of theories as broad based as its philosophical foundations. Patricia Cross has identified the four trends in the theoretical approach to adult education as andragogy, humanism, developmentalism, and behaviorism. With its roots in the

1800s, the word andragogy has been defined by Malcolm Knowles to mean the art of teaching adults—as opposed to children—how to learn. Central to the andragogical theory is the assumption that adults are different, requiring a different learning environment from the pedagogical approach used with children. Viewed in this light, adults are self-directed, having a reservoir of life experiences to bring to the learning environment. They want their learning experiences to complement their social roles as farmers, mothers, factory workers, or business executives. In their busy social roles, adults may be persuaded to take a night class, a weekend seminar, or a summer course, assuming that the learning objective is one with immediate application—a job promotion, certification, better parenting skills, literacy, or education for personal enjoyment.[22]

The humanist theory makes the assumption that people have a natural inclination toward learning and that such learning will flourish in atmospheres in which it is encouraged and in which options are available. That adults do and will learn without a structured setting has been demonstrated by Allen Tough; they learn in the workplace, in the community, in the home, and in their hobbies, as individuals or groups, in structured or unstructured settings. Humanism allows for the broad spectrum of planned and unplanned learning, directed toward the total development of an individual and Maslow's hierarchy of human needs, culminating in self-actualization.[23]

Developmentalists like Robert Havighurst hold to stair-step stages of learning theory—what one learns as an adult is just another step on the ladder of development. Each step is part of an integrated whole from childhood to old age. One stage, successfully completed, leads to the next, each replaced by the new stage. Every individual passes through all stages, always building toward the next, and this succession of stages is considered universal and constant. All people differ, however, having their own frameworks of learning; individuals experience their own stages, which may be disconnected to family and society. Just as individuals pass through stages of development, so do societies, cultures, and countries, according to the development theory.[24]

Behaviorism is a more exacting theory, requiring specific and measurable terms, tasks, and content. There will be small steps to master and immediate feedback. Learning will be sequential, capable of mastery, providing its own reward, and it will depend on materials, not teachers. A "correct response" may be sufficient reward, assuring learning and desired behavior. However cold and "conditioned" behaviorism may appear, it still provides one of the largest segments of adult education, according to Patricia Cross. Job and skills training, programmed instruction, computer-assisted learning, and personalized systems of instruction are examples of behavioristic systems that provide convenience for off-campus instruction, motivation for self-directed adults, improvement of job skills in the marketplace, and the connection of adult education to modern technology. Although behaviorism is useful in its application to practical skills, humanism is directed toward self-understanding, and developmentalism is relevant in teaching ego, intellectual, and moral development, Cross concluded. Each theory has an important place in the broad spectrum of adult education learning.[25]

In broad and general review, the history, philosophy, aims, and theories of the adult education movement provide some perspective of Booker T. Washington in its mainstream. Historically, Washington's era of leadership occurred from 1866 to 1920, the greatest period of democratization and maturation of the United States and of the country's adult education movement. As the nation's attention turned more to common people and practical education in agriculture, workers' education, and industrial education, schools, colleges, libraries, and museums also proliferated. Washington's quest for the acculturation of former slaves through education reflected the national tenor evidenced in other significant crossroads of history, such as the Americanization of immigrants at the turn of the century. The assimilation of Afro-Americans from centuries of slavery into the mainstream of the American creed certainly was a gargantuan crossroads, testing the fiber of the American idea and dream. It was the initial testing of a nation, precariously reunited through the conflict of civil war and unprepared for its own crucible of assimilating the people it had fought to free. Hesitant and uncertain, the federal government essayed to correct its lack of foresight, giving its best effort through its military leaders and the Freedmen's Bureau—if far too late, of short duration, and never sufficient to address the centuries of oppression in education, social justice, and human dignity. Offering some relief in its schools, hospitals, and work arrangements, the bureau also represented a nation's failure to provide the freedmen with land, a missed opportunity that might have changed the course of their journey to freedom. It was also a time of testing for grand ideas and noble aspirations expressed through philanthropy and organizations like the American Missionary Association. If sometimes paternalistic and doctrinal, philanthropists, religious organizations, and relief societies from the North aimed to and often succeeded in picking up the pieces of failed state and federal policies—or the lack of them. In providing physical relief, schools, colleges, and libraries, such efforts helped to bridge the great gap in public moneys and relieve human suffering, leaving a lasting legacy of black colleges. Tasting the first fruits of freedom, former slaves would be tested, seeking a promised land in education. It was also a time of testing for leadership and the strength of philosophies, exemplified by men like Samuel Chapman Armstrong and Booker T. Washington, both imbued with the reality of the present and a vision for the future.

Washington was not an intellectual philosopher, but there was at the center of his work much of the ideology that still directs adult education programs. Molded in slavery and the harsh realism of his youth, Washington was, above all else, a pragmatic realist; he cared for the past only as it illuminated the present and directed the future. Utilitarianistic, Washington abhorred the idea of a freedman studying Latin and Greek when he had no house, no job, and no solid occupational skill. Washington believed in priorities: First get the training, the job, and the house, and then study Latin and Greek for self-actualization—a Maslow principle, after all. Carrying pragmatism to the extreme of radicalism, however, was also abhorrent to his style and philosophy; he could never embrace the radical actions of the Trotter faction or the early clamoring demands of the fledgling NAACP. At the same time, Washington was fighting both covertly and overtly for social transformation through peaceful negotiation, education, the dissemination of information, and court battles. Washington certainly had strong behaviorist tenets of thinking. He wanted measurable progress in job skills, homes owned, acres purchased, black businesses, black schools and teachers, and dollars to black education. Robert E. Park, Washington's coworker and cowriter who perhaps knew Washington better than any white man, later observed that Washington was not an intellectual, but "he seemed to me to be doing something real." He was a man "engaged in a fundamental task who has a sense of reality . . . who knows what should be done, and how to do it."[26]

Not inclined toward the philosophical, analytical ramblings of

R. W. K. Paterson, Washington did have some of the critical reflectivity of Stephen Brookfield, however. Skilled in the analysis of problems, needs, and people, he was equally able at debate, effective writing, and dynamic public speaking. The Great Communicator, Washington reflected in his spoken and written words his pragmatic concern for problems and people. He could communicate his simple but eloquent message to diverse audiences; homilies were accompanied by cushions of optimism and hope. There was—there had to be—a large streak of idealism in the man who could make bricks from naught, keep faith in the American creed, and maintain a vision of progress in the political climate of his era. If the foundation of his house rested on realism, then surely the spires of his temple were built of idealism, reaching toward an unseen future. Eschewing fiction, Washington accepted as faith the great idea of inalienable rights, the equality of men, and a government of, by, and for all the people.

If the aims of adult education have been the cultivation of the intellect, individual self-actualization, personal and social improvement, social transformation, and organizational effectiveness, what were the aims of Booker T. Washington 100 years ago? Washington and Armstrong stated their aims far more simply as improvement of head, hand, and heart, a unified triumvirate. Both men put the development of the mind first, although they often have been labeled as hand educators only. For their time and place, they were hardly advocating the scholarship of Lawson, Paterson, or Brookfield; nor were they discrediting such intellectualism when the freedmen were ready. Washington and Armstrong aimed for clear heads and clear thinking that could bring intelligence to bear on the practical affairs of life; such clear-headedness would bring both personal and social improvement. They wanted trained and skilled hands, capable of operating successfully in a machine shop, on a productive farm, in a business operation, in a hospital, or in the classroom—in other words, the organizational effectiveness proposed by Leonard Nadler. Their heart objective was for moral and spiritual development that unified people and their work, whatever the task, toward self-actualization and personal and social improvement. Both men aimed and directed considerable efforts toward social transformation in their era; theirs was a peaceful revolution for social change through education for the democratization and assimilation of freedmen into the mainstream of American life—a radical revolution of sorts at a significant crossroads in history.

With our conglomerate, melting-pot society, there is no general consensus of opinion as to the priority of aims. We do not, for instance, believe that organizational effectiveness should take priority over the cultivation of the mind, or vice versa. And how can there be personal and social improvement without some elements of all our aims? We don't want a mindless, unintelligent workforce any more than we want a breaking down of effective systems by the forces of radicalism. In the tradition of humanism, our main objective is fully functioning individuals, capable of taking their responsible place in a democratic society, capable of bringing intelligence to bear on the everyday tasks at hand— whether in the machine shop, the medical operating room, or the highest levels of government, business, and education. We want personal improvement and self-actualization that can translate into social improvement and positive change toward the equality of all people. In retrospect, such humanistic aims were at the center of Washington's objectives as he pioneered adult education programs 100 years ago, urging the development of head, hand, and heart for a fully functioning individual.

A practitioner first and last, Washington did not hold to intellectual theorizing. Viewed from the perspective of adult education theories, however, Washington's philosophy and work reflect interesting and instructive elements of andragogy, humanism, developmentalism, and behaviorism. Washington did not know Malcolm Knowles, of course, but his early view of adults clearly meshed with Knowles's assumptions about adult learners. In his night classwork with adults at Malden, Hampton, and Tuskegee, in his association with older students at Hampton, and in his assessment of rural black farmers before starting the annual Negro Conference at Tuskegee, Washington spoke of their basic common sense stemming from a variety of practical experiences, their high motivation or self-directedness, their need to learn practical things to match social roles, and their desire to find relevant solutions to practical problems. With his pragmatic approach to adult programs, Washington assumed the principles of andragogy without the use or knowledge of the popular term in adult education today. In the tradition of humanism, he certainly believed that adults have a natural inclination to learn, that they learn in structured and unstructured environments as proposed by Allen Tough, and that learning moves individuals through levels of self-knowledge and responsibility toward self-actualization in the Maslow hierarchy.

In many respects, Washington also exemplified the theories of developmentalism and behaviorism. For individuals and cultures, he believed there were stages of development; neither could enter on the eighth floor. Basic stages of development had to occur in some sequential order. White civilization had taken centuries for the development of its culture, and basic development was essential for freedmen and their civilization, which had been suppressed in slavery for centuries. In the Washington lexicon, it was simply a matter of keeping things in proper order. In tracing Washington's origins and the development of his ideology through earlier chapters of this study, it has been noted that his learning followed rather closely the developmental stages, proposed by Havighurst, from early childhood through maturity. There was much of the developmental theory in his proposals for his race as well, based on stair-step progression from the infancy of freedom through total assimilation into the mainstream of American culture.

With occupational readiness and measurable progress central to Washington's work, he showed strong tenets of the behavioristic theory, of course. He wanted specific and duplicatable instruction, processes that could be perpetuated through extension. He had, however, a strong moral emphasis too—abstractions that cannot be measured—that paralleled the measurable tasks, mixing again humanistic and behavioristic tendencies. Looking for labels then, we search for neat little slots into which adult educators can fit: For instance, we want to say that Lindeman or Washington was this or that in philosophical leaning, theory, and practice—to sum it all up neatly with one broad label—but it is not possible. From the historical perspective of guiding philosophies, aims, and theories, the practice of adult education has reflected a mixture of ideologies and objectives, broad based and generally overlapping, influenced by our past and present crossroads with an eye toward the future. Like Lindeman, Washington was a pragmatic realist, connecting all education to life. Influenced by the democratic idea, both were also idealists, placing faith in intelligence for the survival of the creed of justice and democracy. Even the more radical Freire embraced the faith of idealism, that "authentic union of action and reflection" made possible by a "critical educational effort," or that level of critical consciousness exemplified by discussion, responsibility, and intelligent dialogue.

In the flux of our crossroads, in the diversity of ideologies, aims, and theories that intermingle and confound us, we naturally search for a point of unity, a common ground of purpose and practice. One adult education philosopher, Horace M. Kallen, has provided the only clear map this writer has found to guide us through the muddled jungle of ideology toward the clearing, a point of unification for all purposes and practices of adult education. Kallen initially called it the American idea, that notion that all men are created equal and that all governments should be of the people, by the people, and for the people. Although this creed of justice was an American creation, it was universal in its application, as Kallen extended its meaning to the liberation of all adults in the diverse cultures of the world. The way of adult education, he concluded, was the opening of the doors of freedom, the task of achieving perspectives:

> Would it be altogether a trope to say that the education of the adult is also a task of achieving perspectives? Whatever the level, whatever the area, the task is to take anything or everything in the personal experience—day life and night life together—that seems inwardly low and mean and dirty, and to set it in the transforming perspectives of the historical and biographical sequences of the arts and sciences. A person seeing whatever it be that he is or has, at the time he is or has it, spanned by these perspectives, experiences them as passages into growing freedom. They serve him as vehicles he can propel himself with, out of the isolations of habit and the segregations of prejudice, into felt fellowship with all persons of all times and places. By means of such perspectives, his learning can follow from, instead of merely following after, whatever he is or has at hand, here and now.[27]

After tracing the influence of educational philosophy and purpose through 2,000 years of history, Robert Ulich posed the central question: "Where do we stand?" In many respects, Ulich argued, the thinking of our present age is not far removed from the educational thought at the end of the Roman Empire. With all the blessings of democracy, modern culture, science, and self-determination, the philosophic purposes of education have been unable to prevent the consequences of global war, the menace to the social order, inhumanities on every continent, and the curse of unemployment spawned, in part, by modern technology. In the atmosphere of such cultural failures, however, rational frameworks of ideology are all the more necessary for the survival of civilization itself, Ulich further argued. On philosophic concepts and purposes falls the greater responsibility: to transmit the wisdom of governing principles from one generation to the next, helping people find their place in "the great workshop of history." A free and wise society must expect the educator "to point courageously at the faults from which it suffers, and to seek remedies for them."[28] Ulich saw the future of philosophic purposes as relevant in the important areas of international education, the constructive use of human talents, the connecting of man with the cultural values of humanity, and the linkage of education with real life in vocations. Education has not only the task of liberating people "from," but it must also liberate people "toward" critical convictions and purposeful actions throughout the world, Ulich contended. Unfortunately, educators, governments, and social planners have been incapable of viewing the complete wholeness of humans and "the totality of the conditions" under which they can fully develop. People are not just the *homo economicus* concerned with mere material needs; nor are they the *homo politicus*, who depends on the external organization of society. Neither are they *homo sapiens* following the voice of reason, nor the *homo contemplativus* reflecting on spiritual matters. They are also not the *homo practicus*, who finds pleasure only in business and adventure. People are all of these things combined, Ulich reminds us:

> Man wishes to have his bread and some security; he wishes to be
> a decent citizen in a decent state; he wishes to think and argue;
> he needs faith in a deeper meaning of his life; he needs time for
> withdrawal from the hustle and bustle lest he lose the inner peace and
> strength which come from perspective; yet he wishes also to breathe from
> time to time the exciting air of action. . . . Each of us tends toward one
> way more than toward another and organizes his life and values
> accordingly. Yet some desire for totality lives in every sound person, and
> a wholesome civilization must give sufficient scope to all the different
> talents and aspirations of its members.[29]

If Kallen provides some unity in themes of adult education, the equality of people, Ulich offers some unifying perspective in the multiplicity of objectives as well. In our diversity, adult education has tried to view the wholeness of people in the totality of their conditions, trying to liberate them from the "isolations of habit and the segregations of prejudice" toward their individual totality, whatever their specific temperaments may be. Pestalozzi once observed that people are the same, whether a king on a throne or a peasant in a hut, but what are their innermost natures? "Why do not the wise tell us?" he asks. "Does your wisdom help you to understand your race and is your goodness the goodness of enlightened guardians of the people?" In his answer, Ulich suggests that educators must have a comprehensive knowledge of the fundamental conditions of people and their civilization. Only then can we "distinguish means and ends (achieving perspectives, Kallen called it) and dare be revolutionary with respect to the instruments of society, without being destructive of the permanent interests of man."[30]

In our continued quest for the comprehensive understanding of people's innermost natures and the conditions of people and their civilization, trying to achieve perspective upon their deeper and permanent interests, adult education has followed the flux of history. At significant crossroads, the movement has adjusted to the crucible of assimilation, unified to some degree on the principle of universal justice for everyone, that American idea or creed. The era of Booker T. Washington from 1856 through 1915 was an important chapter within that movement, using the instruments of society for the education and assimilation of freedmen. Washington's pioneer leadership in adult education accelerated that assimilation, assuring its survival. In his acceptance of the American creed and its total implications for human justice, Washington assumed the universality of its justice for his turbulent present and for the future of the human race. In an address before the Alabama State Teachers' Association in June 1892, Washington posed the questions: "What are the ends in view for which we are laboring, what are the results for which we are toiling, what is the type of humanity which education seeks, and what is the goal towards which all in common are struggling?"

> In this utilitarian age when hands and minds are so largely occupied with things material—with that which seeks for shelter, food and clothing we are tempted as educators to forget the end and mistake the means for the end to be attained. Some of us seek to make a skilled hand, to give practical knowledge of agriculture, to give a technical and scientific knowledge that will enable one to help supply the immediate wants of the body—that will not only enable one to make himself independent by supplying himself with this world's good, but will put him in a position to

administer to the material necessities of his fellows. All this is well and most praiseworthy, but this is not the end of education—to provide the stomach, to fill the pocket, to shelter the body. . . . Let it ever be borne in mind that these are but *means* not *ends*—that these studies are but instruments to lead up, up into that higher atmosphere of truth, virtue, love and unselfishness and higher still till [people] learn to lose themselves in service for others and it can be said of them as of the great Teacher: "They went about doing good." This, fellow teachers, I consider the true end of all education.[31]

Expressing a similar idea, James Truslow Adams wrote in his preface to *The Epic of America* (1931) that the American dream has been the force that has most deeply moved its people and shaped its successes. It is not a dream, however, of bigger and better materialism. It is that dream of "a better, richer, and happier life for all our citizens of every rank which is the greatest contribution we have as yet made to the thought and welfare of the world."[32] Such a dream shaped the work of Booker T. Washington. It remains the dream that shapes and influences the adult education movement throughout the world. While orthodox education may be a preparation for life, "adult education is an agitating instrumentality for *changing life*," Eduard Lindeman maintained. Using the instrumentality of adult education, Washington was an agent of change in his own turbulent era. Reviewing his commitment to social progress, educators facing the approaching century with its inherent problems are reminded again of the purpose of adult education, as stated by Lindeman and practiced by Washington: "Adult education will become an agency of progress if its short-time goal of self-improvement can be made compatible with a long-time, experimental but resolute policy of changing the social order. Changing individuals in continuous adjustment to changing social functions—this is the bilateral though unified purpose of adult learning."[33]

I Have a Dream
A New Heaven and a New Earth

AFTERWORD

Booker T. Washington, a little-known black school principal, gave his Atlanta Exposition Speech in 1895. Who will commemorate, in 1995, its historic centennial? Like Martin Luther King, Jr.'s message in "I Have a Dream," the words of Washington were also forged from dark southern soil and years of subjugation. Washington also voiced the eternal hope that has propelled mankind toward positive change through the ages: the dream of a new heaven and earth. Only thirty years removed from bondage, Washington was the first black man to share the stage with former slaveholders and speak to an audience including southerners, northerners, and former slaves. It was a momentous crossroads in history that linked Washington's dream with ours. It also lifted an obscure but eloquent black educator from Tuskegee to subsequent preeminence around the world.

Surveying thirty years of progress for his race, Washington reminded his audience of a shared heritage, a commonality of purpose, and an inescapable destiny that could not avoid the laws of man or God. As his words spiraled through the hot Georgia hall in 1895, they reiterated the dream that still inspires our most noble achievements, regardless of color, creed, or circumstance: With material benefits, "that higher good, let us pray God, will come, in a blotting out of sectional differences and racial animosities and suspicion, in a determination to administer absolute justice, in a willing obedience among all classes to the mandates of law. This, then, coupled with our material prosperity, will bring into our beloved South a new heaven and a new earth."

NOTES

CHAPTER 1

A special note: The Booker T. Washington papers, edited by Louis R. Harlan with Raymond Smock and various assistant editors, were published by the University of Illinois Press (Urbana) as follows: vol. 1 (autobiographical writings), 1972; vol. 2 (1860–89), 1972; vol. 3 (1889–95), 1974; vol. 4 (1895–98), 1975; vol. 5 (1899–1900), 1976; vol. 6 (1901–2), 1977; vol. 7 (1903–4), 1977; vol. 8 (1904–6), 1979; vol. 9 (1906–8), 1980; vol. 10 (1909–11), 1981; vol. 11 (1911–12), 1981; vol. 12 (1912–14), 1982; and vol. 13 (1914–15), 1984. An invaluable reservoir of material, the Library of Congress collection of Washington's papers contains a large assortment of speeches, correspondence, and other documents. Citations from these volumes are noted as *BTW Papers*, with volume and page numbers. Sizable collections of Washington's papers are also held by the archives of Tuskegee University in Alabama and by Hampton University in Virginia.

1. Booker T. Washington, *BTW Papers*, 9:145.

2. Multiple sources shed light on Lincoln's evolution of thought concerning the Negro question: Harry S. Blackiston, "Lincoln's Emancipation Plan"; Charles H. Wesley, "Lincoln's Plan for Colonizing the Emancipated Negro"; and Richard N. Current, "The Friend of Freedom." See also Richard N. Current, *The Lincoln Nobody Knows*.

3. Gunnar Myrdal, *An American Dilemma: The Negro Problem and Modern Democracy*, 1:xliii.

4. Ibid., 1:xli.

5. Ibid., 1:220. See also Stanley M. Elkins, *Slavery: A Problem in American Institutional and Intellectual Life* (1959; reprint, New York: Grosset and Dunlap, 1963).

6. Myrdal, *American Dilemma*, 1:xlix.

7. Population Census of 1860, Franklin County, Va., Reel 1346, Free Schedule, and Reel 1390, Slave Schedule (National Archives); estate inventory of James Burroughs, November 23, 1861, Will Book 12, Franklin County, Va., Courthouse, Rocky Mount, pp. 148–51. *BTW Papers*, 2:5–11.

8. John Hope Franklin, *From Slavery to Freedom*, p. 133.

9. I. A. Newby, *The South: A History*, pp. 50–51.

10. Lillian Smith, *Killers of the Dream*, pp. 168–71.

11. J. R. V. Daniel, *A Hornbook of Virginia History* (Richmond: Virginia Department of Conservation and Development, 1949), p. 14. See also Marshall Wingfield, *Franklin County, Virginia: A History*.

12. Booker T. Washington, *Up from Slavery*, p. 28.

13. Harold W. Ramsey, *Franklin County Public Schools: A Century of Progress*.

14. Charles H. Ambler, *Sectionalism in Virginia from 1776 to 1861*, pp. 198–200, 330. See also John S. Wise, *The End of an Era*, pp. 219, 227.

15. Arnold Gesell and Frances L. Ilg, *The Child from Five to Ten*, p. 423.

16. Ibid., pp. 423–24.

17. Robert J. Havighurst, *Developmental Tasks and Education*, pp. 6–28.

18. Ibid., p. 27.

19. Ibid., pp. 27–28.

20. Ibid., p. 3.

21. Ibid., p. 5.

22. See, for example, Washington's article in *World's Work*, 27 (Nov. 1913), pp. 101–7, or *BTW Papers*, 12:351–62.

23. *BTW Papers*, 9:350.

24. Ibid., 4:366–77.

25. Ibid., 5:376, 13:463–64.

26. Ibid., 13:22, 144. See also Howard N. Rabinowitz, *Race Relations in the Urban South 1865–1890* (1978; reprint, Chicago: University of Illinois Press, 1980).

27. *BTW Papers*, 11:56, 216.

28. Ibid., 3:282–84; 5:530; 6:408.

29. "The Negro in Business," *BTW Papers*, 6:76–83; "Negro Self Help," *BTW Papers*, 8:445–48; "A Town Owned by Negroes: Mound Bayou, Miss., An Example of Thrift and Self-Government," *BTW Papers*, 9:307–20; 11:581.

30. *BTW Papers*, 7:470. See also Melville J. Herskovits, *The Myth of the Negro Past* (1941; reprint, Boston: Beacon Press, 1969), pp. 292–99.

31. Hartford, Conn., speech on Jan. 28, 1914, *BTW Papers*, 12:421. See also "Looking at the Bright Side of Life," *BTW Papers*, 9:183–87; and Rabinowitz, *Race Relations*, pp. 259–81.

CHAPTER 2

1. Washington, *Up from Slavery*, p. 83.
2. Joel Williamson, "The Meaning of Freedom," p. 193.
3. Joel Williamson, *After Slavery: The Negro in South Carolina.*
4. Willie Lee Rose, "Old Allegiance," chap. 8 in *Reconstruction*, ed. Stampp and Litwack, from Willie Lee Rose, *Rehearsal for Reconstruction: The Port Royal Experiment.* See also Williamson, "The Meaning of Freedom," pp. 213–17.
5. Quoted in Williamson, "The Meaning of Freedom," p. 201.
6. Ibid., p. 202.
7. Ibid., pp. 203–4.
8. Ibid., p. 204.
9. Ibid., p. 206.
10. Ibid., p. 207.
11. Ibid., p. 218.
12. Joe M. Richardson, *Christian Reconstruction: The American Missionary Association and Southern Blacks, 1861–1890*, p. 238.
13. Ibid., p. 239.
14. Ibid., pp. 239–40.
15. Paul Skeels Peirce, *The Freedmen's Bureau: A Chapter in the History of Reconstruction*, p. 129.
16. Ibid., pp. 9–10.
17. Ibid., p. 131.
18. Claude F. Oubre, *Forty Acres and a Mule: The Freedmen's Bureau and Black Ownership*, p. xv.
19. Ibid., p. 196. See Sherman's plan in James M. McPherson, *The Negro's Civil War* (New York: Ballantine, 1991), pp. 303–4.
20. Myrdal, *An American Dilemma*, 1:237.
21. Ibid., p. 225.
22. Oubre, *Forty Acres and a Mule*, p. 196.
23. Ibid., p. 196; Myrdal, *American Dilemma*, p. 237.
24. *BTW Papers*, 13:24.
25. Peirce, *Freedmen's Bureau*, p. 32.
26. Richardson, *Christian Reconstruction*, p. vii.
27. Ibid., p. 6; Edward Pierce, "The Contrabands at Fortress Monroe," pp. 624–40. See also Richard S. West, *Lincoln's Scapegoat General: A Life of Benjamin F. Butler, 1818–1893.*
28. Richardson, *Christian Reconstruction*, p. 37; Jacqueline Jones, *Soldiers of Light and Love: Northern Teachers and Georgia Blacks, 1865–1873.* See also Ronald E. Butchart, *Northern Schools, Southern Blacks, and Reconstruction.* Butchart argued that the association's main objective was social control in a

sectarian society fashioned in the organization's image and that the Freedmen's Bureau was a failure.

29. Henry Allen Bullock, *A History of Education in the South From 1619 to the Present*, p. 30. See also *History of the American Missionary Association with Facts and Anecdotes Illustrating Its Work in the South;* Augustus Field Beard, *A Crusade of Brotherhood: A History of the American Missionary Association;* Frederick L. Brownlee, *American Missionary Association, 1935, Annual Report: A Review of the American Missionary's Eighty-Ninth Year*, pp. 25–38; and Frederick L. Brownlee, *A New Day Ascending*. Brownlee was the association's executive secretary in 1935; the Reverend A. F. Beard was a corresponding secretary for the association in the late 1800s.

30. Peirce, *Freedmen's Bureau*, p. 87.

31. Ibid., p. 88.

32. Ibid., pp. 89–90.

33. Ibid., p. 93.

34. Ibid., pp. 94–99.

35. Ibid., pp. 99–104. See also Rabinowitz, *Race Relations*.

36. Peirce, *Freedmen's Bureau*, pp. 129–60.

37. Ibid., pp. 161–71.

38. Washington, *Up from Slavery*, pp. 21–22.

39. See possible route to Malden, W. Va., in *BTW Papers*, 2:13. Washington gave his memories of this journey in *Up from Slavery*, pp. 24–25. Louis R. Harlan, *Booker T. Washington: The Making of a Black Leader, 1856–1901*, pp. 29–30.

40. Washington, *Up from Slavery*, p. 22. See also Otis K. Rice, *The Allegheny Frontier: West Virginia Beginnings, 1730–1830*, pp. 167–70, 304, 306.

41. Rice, *Allegheny Frontier*, pp. 309–13. See also George W. Atkinson, *History of Kanawha County, from Its Organization in 1789 until the Present Time*, pp. 223–50.

42. Washington, *Up from Slavery*, pp. 25–26, 30–32, 38; Harlan, *Booker T. Washington: Making of a Black Leader*, p. 32. See also Basil Mathews, *Booker T. Washington: Educator and Interracial Interpreter*, pp. 32–44.

43. Washington, *Up from Slavery*, pp. 26–27.

44. Harlan, *Booker T. Washington: Making of a Black Leader*, p. 43; Washington, *Up from Slavery*, pp. 43–45; and Washington, "My Life Work at Tuskegee, Alabama." In this article, Washington attributed his learning to read at the age of twelve to Viola Ruffner, who was "kind enough to teach me" (p. 37).

45. Washington, *Up from Slavery*, pp. 43–44.

46. Ibid., pp. 6–7.

CHAPTER 3

1. BTW, 1914, *BTW Papers*, 13:60.

2. Myrdal, *American Dilemma*, 2:887. The Census of 1870 reported that 18.6

percent of all Negroes ten years old and above were literate (U.S. Bureau of the Census, *Negroes in the United States: 1920–1931*, p. 231). This figure probably included many blacks who could only write their names and free antebellum Negroes, some with access to northern schools.

3. Carter G. Woodson, *The Education of the Negro prior to 1861*, p. 228.

4. Ibid., p. 3.

5. Herbert Aptheker, "The Quaker and Negro Slavery," p. 355. See also Thomas E. Drake, *Quakers and Slavery in America;* Joanne Grant, ed., *Black Protest: History, Documents, and Analyses, 1619 to the Present*, pp. 26–28.

6. George K. Hesslink, *Black Neighbors: Negroes in a Northern Rural Community*, p. 33. Hesslink noted that his reference to Myrdal's famous title was particularly relevant to the Quakers; they had solved their dilemma, and the country had not.

7. Booker T. Washington, "Two Generations under Freedom," p. 293.

8. Booker T. Washington, *The Story of the Negro: The Rise of the Race from Slavery*, 1:245.

9. Woodson, *Education of the Negro*, p. 51.

10. Franklin, *From Slavery to Freedom*, p. 83.

11. Ibid., p. 104.

12. H. A. Washington, *The Writings of Thomas Jefferson* (Washington, D.C., 1853–54) 6:455–58, 8:380–82. See also Matthew T. Melton, *Early American Views on Negro Slavery* (1934; reprint, New York: New American Library, 1969), pp. 5–28, 85–123.

13. Newby, *The South*, pp. 45–46.

14. Joshua Coffin, *Slave Insurrections* (New York, 1860), quoted in Woodson, *Education of the Negro*, pp. 170–71.

15. Herbert Aptheker, *Nat Turner's Slave Rebellion*, pp. 48–50.

16. Ibid., p. 109.

17. Stephen B. Oates, *The Fires of Jubilee: Nat Turner's Fierce Rebellion*, p. 161.

18. Ibid., p. 164.

19. Ibid., pp. 152–53.

20. Woodson, *Education of the Negro*, pp. 172–75.

21. Ibid., p. 175.

22. Ibid., 175–78.

23. Bell Irvin Wiley, *Southern Negroes, 1861–1865*, pp. 260–61; Henry Lee Swint, *The Northern Teacher in the South, 1862–1870*, chap. 1.

24. *History of the American Missionary Association*, pp. 2–15; Pierce, "The Contrabands at Fortress Monroe," pp. 626–40.

25. Rev. Horace James, *The Annual Report of the Superintendent of Negro Affairs in North Carolina for 1864* (Boston, 1865), pp. 10–42.

26. Peirce, *Freedmen's Bureau*, pp. 5–6, 8, 12, 16, 25–26; Wiley, *Southern Negroes*, p. 263. See also Richard S. West, *Lincoln's Scapegoat General: A Life of Benjamin F. Butler, 1818–1893*, and J. Parton, *General Butler in New Orleans*.

27. Wiley, *Southern Negroes*, p. 263; Mrs. A. M. French, *Slavery in South Carolina and the Ex-Slaves or the Port Royal Mission.*

28. Edward L. Pierce, "The Freedmen at Port Royal," pp. 291–315; Wiley, *Southern Negroes*, pp. 263–64; Peirce, *Freedmen's Bureau*, pp. 5, 8–9, 13–14, 20–22. See also John R. Rachal, "Gideonites and Freedmen: Adult Literacy Education at Port Royal, 1862–1865," 453–69. According to Rachal, black literacy was "perceptibly advanced" by the Port Royal experiment through day and night classes. Fueled by the Gideonites' humanitarian and evangelical impulses toward freedmen education, Port Royal was one of many seeds that germinated into the Freedmen's Bureau.

29. Peirce, *Freedmen's Bureau*, pp. 16–17.

30. Richardson, *Christian Reconstruction*, pp. 31–32; Robert R. Macdonald, et al., eds., *Louisiana's Black Heritage* (New Orleans, 1979), pp. 145–50; Peirce, *Freedmen's Bureau*, pp. 18–20.

31. Wiley, *Southern Negroes*, pp. 265–67; Peirce, *The Freedmen's Bureau*, p. 20; A. D. Mayo, *Southern Women in the Recent Educational Movement in the South*, p. 80.

32. Peirce, *Freedmen's Bureau*, p. 9. General Grant instructed Eaton to employ the freedmen to cut wood for the government and do agricultural work, with food, medicine, and some returns from crops as compensation. Grant in his *Memoirs* (New York, 1886), 1:424–26, credited this labor as the origin of the Freedmen's Bureau, thus discrediting some of the efforts of Butler, Sherman, Banks, and others.

33. John Eaton, Jr., *Report of General Superintendent of Freedmen, Tennessee and Arkansas, 1864* (Memphis, 1864), pp. 30–60, 80–87. Wiley, *Southern Negroes*, p. 268; and John Eaton, Jr., *Colored Schools in Mississippi, Arkansas, and Tennessee, April, 1865* (Memphis, 1865).

34. Swint, *The Northern Teacher in the South*, chap. 5, especially pp. 106–7, deals with the reaction of southerners; Richardson, *Christian Reconstruction*, chap. 12, pp. 213–33.

35. Richardson, *Christian Reconstruction*, p. 216.

36. Ibid., p. 218.

37. Wiley, *Southern Negroes*, p. 275.

38. Pierce, "The Freedmen at Port Royal," pp. 304–6; Wiley, *Southern Negroes*, pp. 278–79.

39. Wiley, *Southern Negroes*, pp. 276–77.

40. Ibid., pp. 279–82.

41. Ibid., pp. 288–92.

42. Richardson, *Christian Reconstruction*, pp. 42–46.

43. Ibid., p. 43.

44. Ibid., pp. 46–49; Wiley, *Southern Negroes*, pp. 282–84.

45. Wiley, *Southern Negroes*, pp. 287–88.

46. Pierce, "The Freedmen at Port Royal," pp. 302–5. See also Elizabeth Hyde Botume, *First Days Amongst the Contrabands*, pp. 40–130.

47. Pierce, "The Freedmen at Port Royal," p. 307.

48. Quoted in Wiley, *Southern Negroes*, p. 293.

49. Ibid.

50. Washington, *Up from Slavery*, p. 62; Jacqueline Jones, *Soldiers of Light and Love*. Although focusing on northern teachers in Georgia, Jones also depicts the motives, hardships, and work of the majority of such teachers. Jones follows the American Missionary Association's theme: "The war with bullet and bayonet is over at the South; the invasion of light and love is not." See also Beard, *A Crusade for Brotherhood*.

51. Richardson, *Christian Reconstruction*, p. 37. See Beard to Washington, August 28, 1898, Tuskegee Archives, box 1.

52. Richardson, *Christian Reconstruction*, pp. 37–38.

53. Ibid., pp. 38–39.

54. Ibid., p. 39.

55. Ibid., p. 53.

56. Peirce, *Freedmen's Bureau*, pp. 78–79, 86; Richardson, *Christian Reconstruction*, pp. 123–24.

57. Richardson, *Christian Reconstruction*, chap. 8, pp. 123–40. See also Horace M. Bond, *The Education of the Negro in the American Social Order*.

58. Elisabeth S. Peck, *Berea's First Century, 1855–1955* (Lexington: U. of Kentucky Press, 1955); Brownlee, *A New Day Ascending*, pp. 181–85.

59. Joe M. Richardson, *A History of Fisk University, 1865–1946* (University: U. of Alabama Press, 1980).

60. Clarence A. Bacote, *The Story of Atlanta University*.

61. Richardson, *Christian Reconstruction*, pp. 128–31; Addie L. J. Butler, *The Distinctive Black College: Talladega, Tuskegee, and Morehouse*.

62. Richardson, *Christian Reconstruction*, pp. 131–33; John W. Blassingame, *Black New Orleans: 1860–1880*, pp. 125–30.

63. Vernon L. Wharton, *The Negro in Mississippi, 1865–1890* (Chapel Hill: U. of North Carolina Press, 1947), pp. 254–56; Clarice T. Campbell, "History of Tougaloo College" (Ph.D. diss., University of Mississippi, 1970); Beard, *Crusade for Brotherhood*, p. 187.

64. Louis D. Rubin, Jr., ed., *Teach the Freeman: The Correspondence of Rutherford B. Hayes and the Slater Fund for Negro Education, 1881–1887*, vols. 1 and 2. This correspondence indicates that schools gave more emphasis to industrial education to secure needed money from the Slater and other funds. See also August Meier, *Negro Thought in America, 1880–1915: Racial Ideologies in the Age of Booker T. Washington*, chap. 6, pp. 85–99; Richard B. Drake, "The American Missionary Association and the Southern Negro, 1861–1888" (Ph.D. diss., Emory University, 1957), pp. 205–10. As Meier reaffirms, the idea of

industrial and agricultural education had its roots long before 1890, when Washington "simply brought it to a climax" (*Negro Thought*, p. 85).

65. Richardson, *Christian Reconstruction*, pp. 136–37.

66. Ibid., pp. 135–37.

67. Ibid., p. 137.

68. Ibid., pp. 139–40; Brownlee, *New Day Ascending*, pp. 180–84. See also Frederick L. Brownlee, *American Missionary Association, 1935 Annual Report*, pp. 25–38. Brownlee, executive secretary of the AMA in 1935, contended that the organization had helped change the "over 80 percent" illiteracy rate of the liberated slaves in 1865 to "fewer than 20 percent" illiteracy in 1935.

69. *BTW Papers*, 13:410.

70. *BTW Papers*, 13:411. See also Louis R. Harlan, *Booker T. Washington: The Wizard of Tuskegee, 1901–1915*, p. 448; E. Davidson Washington, ed., *Selected Speeches of Booker T. Washington*, pp. 277–83.

71. Peirce, *Freedmen's Bureau*, pp. 75–76.

72. Ibid., pp. 76–78.

73. Bullock, *History of Negro Education*, pp. 33–34; E. Franklin Frazier, *The Negro in the United States*, pp. 475–77; Rayford W. Logan, *Howard University, 1867–1967* (New York: New York U. Press, 1969); Dwight O. W. Holmes, "Fifty Years of Howard University," *Journal of Negro History* 3 (October 1918): pp. 368–74.

74. Peirce, *Freedmen's Bureau*, p. 79.

75. Ibid., pp. 82–83.

76. Ibid., pp. 84–85. For more background on Curry's role, work, and attitudes, see also Rubin, *Teach the Freeman*, vols. 1 and 2; J. L. M. Curry, *The Negro since 1860*.

77. Washington, *The Future of the American Negro*, p. 25.

78. Washington, *Up from Slavery*, pp. 29–30.

79. Ibid., 28–30.

80. Harlan, *Booker T. Washington: The Making of a Black Leader*, pp. 34–35.

81. Carter G. Woodson, *Early Negro Education in West Virginia*, pp. 26–32; Thomas E. Posey, *The Negro Citizen of West Virginia*, pp. 90–95; Washington, *Up from Slavery*, p. 31; Rice, *Allegheny Frontier*, pp. 215–20; and Charles H. Ambler, *A History of Education in West Virginia from Early Colonial Times to 1949*.

82. Harlan, *Booker T. Washington: The Making of a Black Leader*, pp. 36–37.

83. Ibid., p. 37.

84. Ibid., p. 38.

85. See for example, William Davis to John Kimball, Nov. 20, 1868, in BTW *Papers*, 2:17.

86. Harlan, *Booker T. Washington: The Making of a Black Leader*, p. 39.

87. Washington, *Up from Slavery*, p. 37.

88. Ibid., p. 31.

89. Ibid., pp. 42–43.

90. Ibid., pp. 57–58.

91. Ibid., p. 46.

CHAPTER 4

1. Horace M. Kallen, *Philosophical Issues in Adult Education*, pp. 9, 19, 54.

2. Ibid., p. 24.

3. Quoted in Edith Armstrong Talbot, *Samuel Chapman Armstrong: A Biographical Study* (New York: Doubleday, Page and Co., 1904), p. 210.

4. Ibid., p. 155. Emphasis added.

5. Samuel Chapman Armstrong, *Twenty-Two Years' Work at Hampton Normal and Agricultural Institute*, pp. 2–3.

6. *Annual Report* of 1876, quoted in Luther P. Jackson, "The Origin of Hampton Institute," p. 148.

7. *BTW Papers*, 2:36, 41. See chap. 3, "Great White Father," in Harlan, *Booker T. Washington: The Making of a Black Leader*, pp. 52–77. Meier expressed a similar view in *Negro Thought in America*, pp. 88–89. Meier saw a "conservative racial bias" in Armstrong's work. Also Donald Spivey, *Schooling for the New Slavery;* W. E. B. Du Bois, *The Education of Black People: Ten Critiques, 1906–1960*. Born free in the North, Du Bois was the leading proponent of the "Talented Tenth" intellectualism and was in frequent conflict with the Hampton and Tuskegee philosophy. The first speech in this series, delivered at Hampton in 1906, was openly hostile to the Hampton idea; Du Bois's speech at Fisk in 1908 helped to destroy the plans for agricultural and industrial courses, creating financial hardship for Fisk from 1908 to 1925. By 1930 (pp. 68–69), Du Bois acknowledged some value in industrial education. In 1933, Du Bois believed that the black college should train "for life and making a living." The last two speeches in this series reflect Du Bois's communist sympathies. A graduate of Fisk and Harvard, Du Bois also studied in Berlin, Germany. Ironically, Du Bois's studies abroad were financed by the Slater Fund, which strongly advocated industrial education. See also *The Autobiography of W. E. B. Du Bois;* Rubin, *Teach the Freeman*, vols. 1 and 2 for Slater policies, and vol. 2 for Du Bois's letters regarding Slater scholarship and loan.

8. M. F. Armstrong and Helen W. Ludlow, *Hampton and Its Students*, pp. 122–23.

9. Ibid., pp. 124–25.

10. Washington, *Up from Slavery*, pp. 61–62.

11. Keith L. Schall, ed., *Stoney the Road: Chapters in the History of Hampton Institute*, p. 181.

12. Armstrong and Ludlow, *Hampton and Its Students*, p. 161.

13. Ibid., pp. 121–22.

14. Harlan, *Booker T. Washington: The Making of a Black Leader*, pp. 80–85.

15. Washington, *Up from Slavery*, p. 75.

16. *BTW Papers*, 2: 68, 76.

17. W. T. McKinney to BTW, September 11, 1911, *BTW Papers*, 11:308. This letter (pp. 304–8) gives vivid details of Washington's teaching methods, debating, church activities, and impact on his students.

18. Reported of Washington's speech at the Greenbrier County Courthouse in the Lewisburg *Greenbrier Independent*, July 21, 1877, quoted in Harlan, *Booker T. Washington: The Making of a Black Leader*, p. 95. Important state officials also took note of Washington's successes. More than twenty years later, in the spring of 1899, the citizens of West Virginia honored him at the Opera House in Charleston.

19. Washington, *Up from Slavery*, pp. 87–88.

20. Ibid., pp. 88–91.

21. Constance M. Green, *The Secret City: A History of Race Relations in the Nation's Capital* (Princeton: Princeton University Press, 1967), pp. 119–54; quoted in Harlan, *Booker T. Washington: The Making of a Black Leader*, p. 99. Harlan called Booker's year at Wayland "the most obscure year of his life" because the school's records were destroyed by fire and Washington did not talk much about it (p. 96).

22. *BTW Papers*, 2:75.

23. *The Congregationalist* 31 (May 28, 1879), p. 169; *BTW Papers*, 2:76.

24. Armstrong to Washington, *BTW Papers*, 2:76.

25. Washington, *Up from Slavery*, pp. 97–99. Washington indicates on p. 97 that Armstrong brought him to Hampton initially to be "house father" to the Indian men. Washington's articles in *Southern Workman* indicate that the night school was begun this first year also.

26. Ibid., pp. 102–3.

27. Quoted in William H. Robinson, "Indian Education at Hampton Institute," p. 1.

28. *Annual Report of the Principal*, 1878, Hampton Archives, p. 12.

29. "An Indian Raid on Hampton Institute," *Southern Workman* 7 (1878), p. 36.

30. *Annual Report of the Principal*, 1879, p. 11.

31. "An Indian Raid on Hampton Institute," p. 36.

32. Ibid.

33. Robinson, "Indian Education," p. 8.

34. Ibid., pp. 8, 31.

35. *Annual Report of the Principal*, 1878, p. 12.

36. *Annual Report of the Principal*, 1882, pp. 2–6.

37. Robinson, "Indian Education," pp. 14–16.

38. Estelle Reel, "Industrial Training for Indian Children," *Southern Workman* 29 (1900), p. 201.

39. Samuel Chapman Armstrong, *Annual Report to the Commissioner of*

Indian Affairs (Washington, D.C.: Government Printing Office, 1882), p. 3.

40. *Annual Report of the Principal*, 1881, p. 13.

41. Ibid., 1886, p. 12.

42. Ibid., 1879, p. 16.

43. Robinson, "Indian Education," p. 17.

44. Washington, *Up from Slavery*, pp. 98–99.

45. Robinson, "Indian Education," p. 21.

46. Helen W. Ludlow, ed. *Ten Years Work for the Indians*, pp. 10–15.

47. Robinson, "Indian Education," pp. 23–24. Robinson also reported that an Indian basketball team played an all-white local team and that all Indians were allowed to worship in local churches; both activities were denied to the black students. Some discrimination existed "within the school itself and in the community," he concluded.

48. Washington, *Up from Slavery*, pp. 97–98.

49. Hollis B. Frissell, "Annual Report," *Southern Workman* 32 (1903), pp. 243–44.

50. Robinson, "Indian Education," pp. 18, 21, 27, 30–31. Robinson stated that the "race problem" persisted to the end of the Indian experiment and "was directly responsible for the withdrawal of federal support" in 1912 (p. 18). Although Frissell tried to give public assurance that no intermarriages had occurred, Robinson indicated there were reports to the contrary (p. 21).

51. Cora M. Folsom's untitled and unpaginated 1928 study is kept in the Hampton Archives. A dedicated teacher at Hampton, she worked extensively with Indian students and did an impressive follow-up study of 460 Indians in their native situations after the Hampton experience. See also Armstrong, *Twenty-Two Years' Work*, pp. 315–46.

52. Samuel Chapman Armstrong, "Concerning Indian Education," *Southern Workman* 13 (1884), p. 44.

53. Walton C. John, *Hampton Normal and Agricultural Institute: Its Evolution and Contribution to Education as a Land Grant College*, Bureau of Education, U.S. Department of Interior, Bulletin No. 27 (Washington, D.C.: Government Printing Office, 1923), p. 89.

54. *Annual Report of the Principal*, 1879, p. 16.

55. Samuel Chapman Armstrong, *Annual Report to the Commissioner of Indian Affairs*, 1883, p. 9.

56. Robinson, "Indian Education," p. 27. Armstrong considered the training of teachers of greatest importance, Robinson stated. It could not be overemphasized "because some of the tribes would soon be thrown on their own resources, having to provide for their own education."

57. Washington, *Up from Slavery*, p. 103. Washington states here that the night school work came after his Indian work, but records at Hampton indicate the reverse order. He may have performed both activities simultaneously.

58. Washington, *Up from Slavery*, pp. 104–5.

59. *BTW Papers*, 2:92–94; Washington, *Up from Slavery*, p. 105; Harlan, *Booker T. Washington: The Making of a Black Leader*, pp. 102–3. A letter in *Southern Workman* 11 (1882), p. 42, indicated that General Marshall, not Washington, originated the name "Plucky Class."

60. Booker T. Washington, "Seven Months Well Spent, More about the 'Plucky Class'," *Southern Workman* 10 (1881), p. 57.

61. Booker T. Washington, "The Plucky Class," *Southern Workman* 9 (1880), p. 112; Booker T. Washington, *The Story of My Life and Work*, pp. 70–72.

62. From September 1880 through May 1881 a series of articles appeared in *Southern Workman*, all titled "Incidents of Indian Life at Hampton" by Booker T. Washington. They are rich in details, both humorous and serious, concerning the Indians' daily life, education, and customs. See *BTW Papers*, 2:78–126, 128–31.

63. *BTW Papers*, 2:127.

64. Washington wrote extensively of Tuskegee's struggles in *The Story of My Life and Work* and *Up from Slavery*, often repeating the story in numerous articles and speeches. See also Max Bennett Thrasher, *Tuskegee: Its Story and Its Work*, and Emmett J. Scott and Lyman B. Stowe, *Booker T. Washington: Builder of a Civilization*, for important primary sources. Thrasher, a newspaper reporter, traveled with Washington and observed the inner workings of the school until his early death in 1903 from peritonitis. Scott, a brilliant newspaper editor from Houston, Texas, was Washington's private secretary from 1897 until Washington's death in 1915. Loyal, devoted, and efficient, Scott was so submerged in his "wizard" Washington that he could write letters, speeches, and articles under the other man's name that accurately expressed Washington's thoughts. Scott contributed unselfishly to Washington's power and influence. Warren Logan, treasurer of Tuskegee for forty-two years, and John H. Washington, Booker's older half brother and jack-of-all-trades at Tuskegee, helped to manage the school during Washington's frequent absences to raise money. Like Scott, both men devoted their lives to the success of Tuskegee and Booker T. Washington, faithful and loyal through years of grinding, unheralded, day-to-day operations of the school.

65. Armstrong had a stroke in 1886, with subsequent poor health and paralysis in November 1891. See Washington, *Up from Slavery*, pp. 293–95. Six months before Armstrong's death, one of his last requests was to visit Tuskegee. Practically helpless, he was a guest in Booker's home, The Oaks, for about two months, dying at Hampton a few weeks later. The Tuskegee Railroad ran a special train to bring Armstrong from Chehaw to Tuskegee; on campus, the students and staff gave him a "pine-knot torchlight reception." During this visit, he spoke to students in a fervent but weak voice and was transported by students eager to push his wheelchair. Of the last conversations with his great mentor,

Washington recorded: "Almost wholly without the use of voice or limb, [Armstrong] spent nearly every hour in devising ways and means to help the South. Time and time again he said to me, during this visit, that it was not only the duty of the country to assist in elevating the Negro of the South, but the poor white man as well. At the end of his visit I resolved anew to devote myself more earnestly than ever to the cause which was so near his heart" (p. 294).

66. Washington, *Up from Slavery*, p. 146.

67. Ibid., pp. 178–80.

CHAPTER 5

1. Addie Louise Joyner Butler, *The Distinctive Black College*, chap. 4, pp. 55–79.

2. Ibid., chap. 5, pp. 80–99.

3. Velma L. Blackwell, "A Black Institution Pioneering Adult Education, Past and Present (1881–1973)," p. 8.

4. Ibid., p. 16.

5. Leo McGee, "Booker T. Washington and George Washington Carver: A Tandem of Adult Educators at Tuskegee," p. 16.

6. Quoted in Thrasher, *Tuskegee*, pp. 162–63.

7. Horace Mann Bond, *Negro Education in Alabama: A Study in Cotton and Steel*, p. 125.

8. Ibid., pp. 125–26.

9. Ibid., p. 124.

10. Ibid., p. 121.

11. Ibid., pp. 12–13, 36–37.

12. Washington, *The Story of My Life and Work*, pp. 194, 200. See also Washington, *Up from Slavery*, p. 294.

13. Bond, *Negro Education*, pp. 126–27.

14. Quoted in Washington, *The Story of My Life and Work*, pp. 138–39.

15. Bond, *Negro Education*, p. 144.

16. *Montgomery Advertiser*, August 1, 1900, quoted in Bond, *Negro Education*, p. 146.

17. Bond, *Negro Education*, p. 146.

18. Ibid., pp. 144–45.

19. *Montgomery Advertiser*, Feb. 2, 1885, quoted in Bond, *Negro Education*, p. 143.

20. Bond, *Negro Education*, p. 119.

21. Washington, *Up from Slavery*, pp. 111–15.

22. Bond, *Negro Education*, p. 121.

23. Washington, *Up from Slavery*, pp. 115–16.

24. Ibid., p. 116.

25. Clifton Johnson, "Tuskegee: A Typical Alabama Town."

26. Thrasher, *Tuskegee*, pp. 37–38.

27. Washington, *The Story of My Life and Work*, pp. 75–77. Washington quoted Screws's report verbatim from the *Montgomery Advertiser* for Tuskegee's early history.

28. Washington, *Up from Slavery*, p. 107.

29. Ibid., pp. 120–21; Washington, *The Story of My Life and Work*, p. 87. See also Harlan, *Booker T. Washington: The Making of a Black Leader*, p. 113.

30. Washington, *Up from Slavery*, p. 119.

31. Harlan, *Booker T. Washington: The Making of a Black Leader*, pp. 115–16; *Tuskegee News*, August 5, 1880.

32. Act No. 292, *Acts of the General Assembly, Session of 1880–1881*, Montgomery, Alabama, pp. 395–96. This act awarded Tuskegee $2,000 annually. Lewis Adams was one of the three Tuskegee residents who served as commissioners of the Institute.

33. *Tuskegee News*, February 12, 1880, and May 20, 1880, quoted also in Harlan, *Booker T. Washington: The Making of a Black Leader*, p. 112.

34. Washington, *Up from Slavery*, p. 118.

35. Washington, *The Story of My Life and Work*, pp. 400–401.

36. Washington, *Up from Slavery*, pp. 204–6.

37. See August Meier, "Booker T. Washington and the Negro Press." Washington had an "orbit" of black press influences, many of them far more radical in expression than his public image. His papers seem to suggest—as does Meier—that Washington could utilize newspapers for more militant stances than he could publicly take in politics and civil rights. Although he had influence, he hardly controlled the black press, which was led by independent thinkers like T. Thomas Fortune of the *Age*, W. Calvin Chase of the *Bee*, and Fred R. Moore of the *Colored American Magazine* and the *Age* (after Fortune gave it up).

38. Wendell to Washington, April 12, 1901, *BTW Papers*, 6:87.

39. *Atlantic Monthly* 87 (June 1901), p. 882.

40. *North American Review* 173 (Aug. 1901), pp. 280–88; *BTW Papers*, 6:191–200.

41. Harris to *Washington*, Jan. 8, 1901, quoted in *BTW Papers*, 1:xxix. Volume 1 of the *Papers* contains excerpts from Washington's primary autobiographical works.

42. Horace J. Smith to Washington, June 16, 1901, quoted in *BTW Papers*, 1:xxxiv.

43. Laijiro Yamamasu to Washington, March 1, 1915, quoted in *BTW Papers*, 1:xxxiv.

44. Robert E. Park, Washington's press secretary and ghostwriter, to Washington, March 19, 1910, quoted in *BTW Papers*, 1:xxxviii.

45. Washington, *Up from Slavery*, p. 214.

46. Ibid., p. 213. See also pp. 208–37, which detail the circumstances, preparation, and importance of the Atlanta address.

47. See text of speech in Washington, *Up from Slavery*, pp. 218–55. Original is in the Tuskegee archives.

48. See Hugh Hawkins, ed., *Booker T. Washington and His Critics: The Problem of Negro Leadership*, especially Rayford W. Logan's "The Atlanta Compromise," pp. 21–27, and C. Vann Woodward's "The Atlanta Compromise," pp. 98–105. See also Harlan, *Booker T. Washington: The Wizard of Tuskegee*, pp. 33, 129, 205, 250, 265; W. E. B. Du Bois, *The Souls of Black Folk*, especially his essay "Of Booker T. Washington and Others"; Harlan, *Booker T. Washington: The Making of a Black Leader*, pp. 207–28.

49. There were, however, some charges of discrimination in the displays themselves. Some blacks objected to the "separate" black building, preferring that black exhibitions be distributed throughout appropriate departments. See August Meier and Elliott M. Rudwick, "Come to the Fair?"

50. Harlan, *Booker T. Washington: The Wizard of Tuskegee*, p. 263.

51. *BTW Papers*, 8:440–42, "An Account by Emmett Jay Scott of a Speech in Little Rock," Nov. 15, 1905.

52. Ibid., 10:60–68, "A Cheerful Journey Through Mississippi," February 1909.

53. See *BTW Papers*, 9:652–58, for more details on the lynchings that occurred in Lula, Mississippi, in October 1908. The Eupora, Miss., *Warden*, Nov. 5, 1908, referred to the circumstances of Washington's birth as quoted in Harlan, *Booker T. Washington: The Wizard of Tuskegee*, p. 264.

54. *BTW Papers*, 10:64–65.

55. Ibid., 10:67–68.

56. Ibid., 10:67.

57. Ibid., 10:200–236.

58. See Washington's tribute to Rogers in the *New York Evening Post*, May 29, 1909, in *BTW Papers*, 10:122–26.

59. Quoted in Harlan, *Booker T. Washington: The Wizard of Tuskegee*, p. 264.

60. *BTW Papers*, 10:201.

61. Ibid., 10:203.

62. Ibid., 10:230.

63. Ibid., 10:230.

64. Ibid., 10:235.

65. William Henry Lewis recorded details of the North Carolina trip for the Boston *Transcript*, Nov. 12, 1910, in *BTW Papers*, 10:455–68. Washington pleaded for tolerance from both sides in Greensboro (p. 459), and in Washington, N.C., argued strongly against lynchings (p. 466).

66. *BTW Papers*, 11:322–30, 331–43, Texas tour of Oct. 1911.

67. The Louisiana tour occurred in April 1915, about seven months before

Washington's death on Nov. 15, 1915; *BTW Papers*, 13:266–68. See also Charles Vincent, "Booker T. Washington's Tour of Louisiana."

68. Washington, *Up from Slavery*, p. 199.

CHAPTER 6

1. Edgar J. Boone, R. J. Dolan, and Ron Shearon, "Programming in the Cooperative Extension Service, A Conceptual Schema," Extension Publication 72, North Carolina Extension Service, 1971; Ralph Tyler, *Basic Principles of Curriculum and Instruction* (Chicago: U. of Chicago Press, 1949). See also Malcolm Knowles, *The Modern Practice of Adult Education*, pp. 120–25, and Ronald Lippitt et al., *The Dynamics of Planned Change* (New York: Harcourt, Brace, and World, 1958).

2. Washington in "Aims of Tuskegee Institute" speech printed in *Southern Letter* 28 (Dec. 1912), Tuskegee Archives.

3. Blackwell, "A Black Institution Pioneering Adult Education," p. 20. Blackwell noted that "adult education did not herald a revolution but it was an evolution from the very inception. . . spanning the years of 1881" until the present. Beginning as an adult education movement to train teachers, farmers, preachers, and artisans, Tuskegee carried education to "rural, isolated, by-passed people, not only in Alabama, or the Southeast, but throughout the world" (p. 206).

4. Ibid., p. 21.

5. Thrasher, *Tuskegee*, pp. 53–54. *Southern Letter* 29 (Oct. 1913) cited 1,618 students from thirty-three states and eighteen foreign countries.

6. Thrasher, *Tuskegee*, pp. 93–103.

7. Ibid., pp. 52–64, 68–74, 75–92.

8. Ibid., p. 59.

9. Washington, *The Story of My Life and Work*, p. 122. In *Up from Slavery*, pp. 196–97, Washington gave the year of 1884 as the start of night school. See also Thrasher, *Tuskegee*, pp. 66–67.

10. Washington, *The Story of My Life and Work*, pp. 408–9; Thrasher, *Tuskegee*, pp. 112–13.

11. Thrasher, *Tuskegee*, p. 79; *Southern Letter*, July 1907; undated manuscript (box 119, ca. 1909, Tuskegee). Cooking classes were conducted on Tuesday and Friday afternoons and attended by heads of families and women who cooked for local white families (Blackwell, "A Black Institution Pioneering Adult Education," p. 68). In Washington's manuscript of an address to the Tuskegee trustees (ca. 1909), he mentioned these classes, stressing other extension work: a night school for county ministers, the monthly farmers' institute, and yearly short courses for farmers. According to this report, Tuskegee had offered some 250 extension lectures during the year on various phases of

education. In addition to regular students, Washington estimated that 100,000 people had been reached that year through extension work.

12. Washington, *The Story of My Life and Work*, p. 303.

13. Ibid., p. 304.

14. Ibid., pp. 305–6.

15. Thrasher, *Tuskegee*, pp. 164–65.

16. Ibid., pp. 172–73.

17. Thomas Monroe Campbell, *The Movable School Goes to the Negro Farmer*, pp. 83–86.

18. Ibid., pp. 87–88.

19. Ibid., p. 90.

20. Thrasher, *Tuskegee*, p. 182.

21. Campbell, *Movable School*, pp. 90–91.

22. George Washington Carver (1864–1943) played a significant role at Tuskegee Institute. As temperamental as he was brilliant, however, Carver was at odds with Washington most of the time, according to the *BTW Papers*, which contain frequent letters between the two. Linda O. McMurry's biography, *George Washington Carver: Scientist and Symbol*, shatters the myth of Carver, who lived, according to McMurry, in Washington's shadow for twenty years. Whiny and demanding, Carver threatened to resign with regular frequency. He was also "almost completely inept at administrative duties, a disastrous shortcoming in Washington's mind" (p. 53). McMurry concluded that "Carver was a dreamer and idealist" and that Washington was preeminently a "realist and pragmatist," thus ensuring a stormy relationship. Recognizing his brilliance, Washington tried to keep Carver placated while insisting on some conformity to the general standards required of all staff members. *BTW Papers*, 10:486–87, 592–96; 12:93–94. See also George Washington Carver, "Twelve Ways to Meet the New Economic Conditions in the South." Carver's papers are in the Tuskegee Archives.

23. Campbell, *Movable School*, pp. 92–93.

24. Ibid., p. 94.

25. Ibid., pp. 95–100.

26. Ibid., pp. 106, 111–16.

27. Ibid., p. 119.

28. Ibid., p. 120.

29. Ibid., pp. 120–22.

30. Ibid., pp. 133–36.

31. Ibid., p. 135.

32. Thrasher, *Tuskegee*, p. 174.

33. Ibid., pp. 175–78.

34. Ibid., pp. 179–81.

35. Ibid., pp. 123–24.

36. Ibid., pp. 123–24.

37. Ibid., p. 127.

38. *BTW Papers*, 3:257–58, Washington to Bedford, Aug. 18, 1892.

39. Washington, *The Story of My Life and Work*, p. 420.

40. *BTW Papers*, 5:572–73. Washington to Scott (from Boston), July 8, 1900.

41. Ibid., 5:594–95. Interview of Aug. 11, 1990.

42. Ibid., 5:573.

43. Quoted in Harlan, *Booker T. Washington: The Wizard of Tuskegee*, p. 268.

44. Speech of Aug. 23, 1900, Boston in *BTW Papers*, 5:600–603. Washington also gave a brief closing address on Aug. 24, 1900, *BTW Papers*, 5:603–5.

45. Blackwell, "A Black Institution Pioneering Adult Education," p. 59.

46. Nov. 20, 1915, *BTW Papers*, 13:463–64.

47. *BTW Papers*, 7:10. By 1960, local affiliates of the Urban League operated in sixty-three cities of thirty states and the District of Columbia, supported by private and group philanthropy.

48. Ibid., 13:94–95.

49. Ibid., 13:171.

50. Washington to Moton, Nov. 4, 5, 1915, quoted in Harlan, *Booker T. Washington: The Wizard of Tuskegee*, p. 449.

51. Washington, *The Story of My Life and Work*, pp. 412–13.

52. *Tuskegee News*, December 3, 1908; Harlan, *Booker T. Washington: The Wizard of Tuskegee*, p. 233.

53. *Montgomery Advertiser*, January 23, 1914; Harlan, *Booker T. Washington: The Wizard of Tuskegee*, pp. 233–35.

54. Washington to Anson Stokes, Oct. 26, 1914, and quoted in Harlan, *Booker T. Washington: The Wizard of Tuskegee*, p. 235.

55. Richard W. Thompson, March 29, 1915, and quoted in Harlan, *Booker T. Washington: The Wizard of Tuskegee*, p. 235.

56. Wilma King Hunter, "Three Women at Tuskegee," pp. 76–78, 81.

57. *Montgomery Advertiser*, May 23, 1884; Harlan, *Booker T. Washington: The Making of a Black Leader*, pp. 146–47.

58. Helen Ludlow, quoted in Armstrong, *Twenty-Two Years' Work*, p. 177.

59. Hunter, "Three Women at Tuskegee," pp. 73–80; Jessie P. Guzman, "Olivia A. Davidson: Educator and Co-Founder of Tuskegee Institute," pp. 1–9; Carolyn A. Dorsey, "Olivia Davidson Washington's Story," p. 71; Harlan, *Booker T. Washington: The Making of a Black Leader*, pp. 126–33, 147–53.

60. Harlan, *Booker T. Washington: The Making of a Black Leader*, pp. 149–54.

61. Ibid., p. 155.

62. Hunter, "Three Women at Tuskegee," p. 83.

63. Washington, *The Story of My Life and Work*, pp. 131–32.

64. Hunter, "Three Women at Tuskegee," pp. 84–85; Emmett J. Scott, "Mrs. Booker T. Washington's Part in Her Husband's Work," p. 42.

65. Margaret to Booker T. Washington, July 17, 1892, *BTW Papers*, 3:248. See also letter of July 10, pp. 243–46; letter of July 15, pp. 246–48; and of July, pp. 254–55. Earlier letters in the same volume reflect Margaret's honesty in confronting her love for Washington while worrying about taking on his children. See also Harlan, *Booker T. Washington: The Making of a Black Leader*, pp. 176–90. Portia, the musician who studied in Europe, ended in dire straits, as depicted in Ruth Ann Stewart's biography, *Portia: The Life of Portia Washington Pittman*. Stewart suggests that Portia had been spoiled and never got out of her famous father's shadow. She died in 1978. Margaret related more easily to "Baker" and "Dave." Davidson later edited a volume of his father's speeches, published in 1932. He died in 1938. Baker died in 1945 in California, where he worked as a successful real estate broker. If not distinctive, the lives of Washington's children were generally productive.

66. Scott, "Mrs. Booker T. Washington's Part," p. 42.

67. Ibid.; Thrasher, *Tuskegee*, pp. 183–85.

68. Scott, "Mrs. Booker T. Washington's Part," p. 42.

69. Thrasher, *Tuskegee*, pp. 152–59; Scott, "Mrs. Booker T. Washington's Part," p. 42. This was generally called the Russell Plantation Project; the extended project on the ten acres was called the Rising Star Model School.

70. Thrasher, *Tuskegee*, pp. 160–61.

71. Hunter, "Three Women at Tuskegee," pp. 86–87.

72. Ibid., pp. 87–88; Scott, "Mrs. Booker T. Washington's Part," p. 42.

73. Hunter, "Three Women at Tuskegee," pp. 88–89. Douglass's home did not become a national shrine until February 1972.

74. Quoted in *Tuskegee Alumni Bulletin*, August 1925. See also the *Tuskegee Messenger* 1 (June 27, 1925), pp. 1–6, and (August 1, 1925), pp. 3–4.

75. Washington, *Up from Slavery*, pp. 267–68.

76. See "A Model Negro Village" pamphlet and "An Education Center for Colored People," undated in Tuskegee Archive files.

77. Harlan, *Booker T. Washington: The Wizard of Tuskegee*, p. 170.

78. Boston *Evening Transcript*, Dec. 22, 1894, p. 16; Washington to Warren Logan (from Boston), July 5, 1895, *BTW Papers*, 3:563–64.

79. Harlan, *Booker T. Washington: The Wizard of Tuskegee*, p. 213.

80. Ibid., pp. 213–14.

81. *Montgomery Journal*, Jan. 7, 1915.

82. Washington to R. C. Bedford, March 21, 1905, *BTW Papers*, 8:221, and "Proposed Scheme for Hilton Head Settlement," undated typescript.

83. Harlan, *Booker T. Washington: The Wizard of Tuskegee*, p. 215.

84. Ibid.

85. Ibid., p. 216.

86. Washington in *Tuskegee Student* 22 (May 14, 1910); Harlan, *Booker T. Washington: The Wizard of Tuskegee*, p. 216.

87. Harlan, *Booker T. Washington: The Wizard of Tuskegee*, pp. 216–17. That modern developers are now displacing native residents in Hilton Head illustrates Washington's vision and the lingering effects of failed economic opportunities.

88. *BTW Papers*, 9:435.

89. Ibid., 9:430–31, from Jan. 4, 1908, article, "Boley, a Negro Town in the West."

90. Ibid., 9:433.

91. Ibid., 9:435.

92. References to Mound Bayou are summarized from two larger discussions: August Meier, "Booker T. Washington and the Town of Mound Bayou," and Harlan, *Booker T. Washington: The Wizard of Tuskegee*, pp. 218–26.

93. Park to Scott, quoted in Harlan, *Booker T. Washington: The Wizard of Tuskegee*, pp. 220–21.

94. Ibid., p. 223.

95. Ibid., pp. 225–26.

96. Washington to Fortune, Nov. 3, 1903, *BTW Papers*, 7:333. T. Thomas Fortune was editor of the *Globe*, the *Freeman*, and the *Age*, the last of which came into the Washington orbit. Emma Lou Thornbrough's biography, *T. Thomas Fortune: Militant Journalist*, provides insight into Fortune's influence in the black press and friendship with Washington. The letters between Fortune and Washington in the *BTW Papers* provide further clarification relating to black thinking of the period. Unfortunately, Fortune's continued bouts with drinking and other problems became a source of embarrassment to Washington, clouding their friendship in later years.

97. Washington to Leslie P. Hill, March 29, 1906, *BTW Papers*, 8:557–58.

98. Washington to Robert R. Moton, March 24, 1910, *BTW Papers*, 10:283.

99. Washington, *Up from Slavery*, pp. 295–302.

100. Harlan, *Booker T. Washington: The Wizard of Tuskegee*, pp. 177–78. Washington interceded with Woodrow Wilson, members of Congress, and Tuskegee trustees for Howard University. The proposed cut was restored to the appropriations bill.

101. W. P. Thirkield's address of Nov. 15, 1907, entitled "The Meaning and Mission of Education."

102. Washington to Thirkield, Aug. 15, 1909, *BTW Papers*, 10:156–57.

103. Quoted in Harlan, *Booker T. Washington: The Wizard of Tuskegee*, p. 179.

104. Washington to James G. Merrill, March 14, 1905, *BTW Papers*, 8:216–17, and to Margaret Washington, p. 216. Washington secured financial grants from Carnegie for black and white schools, including libraries and other assistance for more than thirty colleges. He also helped such cities as Atlanta,

Louisville, Montgomery, Jacksonville, New Orleans, Birmingham, Houston, Little Rock, and Mound Bayou to secure Carnegie libraries.

105. Quoted in Harlan, *Booker T. Washington: The Wizard of Tuskegee*, p. 182.

106. See Richardson, *History of Fisk University*, pp. 68–100; Harlan, *Booker T. Washington: The Wizard of Tuskegee*, p. 185; and various letters and articles by Washington concerning Fisk and other colleges in his papers.

107. Charles D. McIver, "Disfranchisement and Education," *Southern Workman* 30 (Feb. 1901), pp. 89–90.

108. Harlan, *Booker T. Washington: The Wizard of Tuskegee*, pp. 189–90.

109. Washington's letter to Baldwin, Sept. 9, 1903, quoted in Harlan, *Booker T. Washington: The Wizard of Tuskegee*, p. 190. See also Baldwin's letter to Washington, Sept. 11, 1903, *BTW Papers*, 7:282–83.

110. Quoted in Harlan, *Booker T. Washington: The Wizard of Tuskegee*, pp. 193–94. See also Buttrick to Washington, June 18, 1910, *BTW Papers*, 10:340.

111. Washington to Frissell, Nov. 1, 1901, *BTW Papers*, 6:283–84. See also Washington to Frissell, Aug. 19, 1901, *BTW Papers*, 6:187.

112. Washington to Frissell, July 18, 1906, *BTW Papers*, 9:43, and Harlan, *Booker T. Washington: The Wizard of Tuskegee*, p. 192.

113. See B. T. Washington file in Hampton University Archives.

114. Jeanes to Washington, Feb. 25, 1905, *BTW Papers*, 8:201–2.

115. Jeanes to Washington, March 25, 1905, *BTW Papers*, 8:243, and Washington to Buttrick, April 11, 1905, *BTW Papers*, 8:255–57.

116. Harlan, *Booker T. Washington: The Wizard of Tuskegee*, p. 195.

117. Ibid., pp. 196–97; *The Jeanes Story: A Chapter in the History of American Education*. This book gives good background on Anna Jeanes (pp. 8–12), her bequest to Washington and Frissell (pp. 96–98), and early workers.

118. See Washington to George A. Myers, Feb. 17, 1911, *BTW Papers*, 10:589–91. Rosenwald gave $25,000 to each city that raised $75,000 for building YMCAs and also aided universities and hospitals. He also offered new ideas and encouragement for many social improvements.

119. Harlan, *Booker T. Washington: The Wizard of Tuskegee*, pp. 197–98; F. B. Dresslar, *Rosenwald School Buildings;* Robert Moton gave the introduction, stating that Rosenwald gave $140,000 a year for schools in eleven southern states. In four years, 720 schools were built under the direction of Clinton J. Calloway of Tuskegee.

120. Washington to Rosenwald, March 17, 1915, quoted in Harlan, *Booker T. Washington: The Wizard of Tuskegee*, p. 198.

121. Washington to Rosenwald, Oct. 15, 1915, quoted in ibid., pp. 198–99.

122. Ibid., pp. 199–201.

123. Ibid., p. 199.

124. Undated and unpublished paper by Willie J. Ellison, "Booker T. Washington's Influence on Africa, 1900–1910."

125. Louis R. Harlan, "Booker T. Washington and the White Man's Burden," pp. 455–56. When he succeeded Roosevelt, Taft wanted Washington to advise him on southern and black problems; Scott, therefore, went to Africa in Washington's place.

126. Ibid., pp. 448–58. See also Booker T. Washington, "Cruelty in the Congo Country," pp. 375–77, *BTW Papers*, 8:85–90; Booker T. Washington, "Industrial Education in Africa," also in *BTW Papers*, 8:548–52. From 1907 on, the papers reflect extensive attention to African problems, with a variety of correspondence to government officials in the United States and other countries.

127. To the editor of the *Liberian Register*, Jan. 5, 1911, *BTW Papers*, 10:531.

128. *BTW Papers*, 5:633–36 and 639–42, reflect the initial plans between German company and Washington for the project. See 6:26–27 for description of colony; see pp. 98–99, 110–12, 126–29, 142–43, 285–86, 455–56, 480–81, 488–89, 494 for more details. See 7:404, 425, 8:184–85 for Washington's recommendations for Africa based on this project. See also James N. Calloway (who headed the project), "Tuskegee Cotton-Planters in Africa"; Harlan, "Booker T. Washington and The White Man's Burden," pp. 442–48.

129. *Tuskegee Student* 18 (April 1906).

130. Blackwell, "A Black Institution Pioneering Adult Education," p. 63; Harlan, *Booker T. Washington: The Wizard of Tuskegee*, pp. 273–74, and "Booker T. Washington and the White Man's Burden," p. 459, n. 73. See also *BTW Papers*, 12:349 regarding James L. Sibley (1883–1929) who prepared a system of textbooks for Liberian schools, introduced the Jeanes system of supervising teachers in Liberia, and founded the Booker T. Washington Institute in Liberia.

131. Harlan, "Booker T. Washington and the White Man's Burden," pp. 459–60 and *Booker T. Washington: The Wizard of Tuskegee*, p. 273.

132. Harlan, *Booker T. Washington: The Wizard of Tuskegee*, pp. 274–75.

133. Blackwell, "A Black Institution Pioneering Adult Education," pp. 63–64.

134. *BTW Papers*, 4:450, Garrison to Washington, July 18, 1898; 5:120–21, Sturge to Washington, May 24, 1899.

135. Wesley Warren Jefferson to Washington, Dec. 6, 1899 (from Montserrat, West Indies), *BTW Papers*, 5:286–88; Jefferson to Washington, July 10, 1900.

136. Ibid., 5:129–30. Jefferson went on to Howard University's dental school and became a successful dentist in Norfolk, Virginia.

137. George A. Gates to Washington, Dec. 4, 1911, and Washington to Gates, ibid., 11:288–89 and 400–401.

138. Harlan, *Booker T. Washington: The Wizard of Tuskegee*, p. 277.

139. Tuskegee *Southern Letter* 29 (Oct. 1913), p. 2, and Harlan, *Booker T.*

Washington: The Wizard of Tuskegee, p. 277; Washington to Nasichi Masaoka, Dec. 5, 1912.

140. Harlan, *Booker T. Washington: The Wizard of Tuskegee,* pp. 277–78.

141. *New York Herald,* May 10, 1903, p. 33, quoted in ibid., p. 279.

142. Ibid., pp. 278–79.

143. Anagarika H. Dharmapala to Washington, June 20, 1903, Washington's papers in Tuskegee archives.

144. Dharmapala to Washington, Dec. 26, 1903; Washington to Dharmapala, Dec. 31, 1903. See also *BTW Papers,* 13:507–8.

145. H. G. Wells, *The Future in America: A Search after Realities,* especially the chapter, "The Tragedy of Colour," pp. 259–81. See also Wells to Washington, March 10, 1906, *BTW Papers,* 8:545–46, asking Washington to meet him in the North because Tuskegee was too far away. Washington (March 24, 1906) expressed regret that Wells could not see the Negro in the South, "where the whole problem of his future is to be worked out."

146. Robert E. Park (1864–1944), a white journalist and sociologist, worked with Washington from 1905 to 1914. Educated at the University of Michigan and Harvard University, Park also had a doctorate from the University of Heidelberg, Germany. Splitting his time between Tuskegee and his home near Boston, Park helped Washington with speeches, articles, letters, and books. He made large contributions to *The Story of the Negro* (1909), *My Larger Education* (1911), and *The Man Farthest Down* (1912). Washington and Park had a close collaboration and friendship. Park said later, "I think I probably learned more about human nature and society, in the South under Booker Washington, than I had learned elsewhere in all my previous studies" (Robert E. Park, *Race and Culture: Essays in the Sociology of Contemporary Man,* p. vii).

147. *BTW Papers,* 10:368–76, from Washington's pocket notebook, Aug. 28–Oct. 7, 1910; Booker T. Washington and Robert E. Park, *The Man Farthest Down: A Record of Observations and Study in Europe.* See also *BTW Papers,* 11: 131–40, 240–47, 259, 397.

148. See Washington to Laurence Abbott (from Vienna), Sept. 10, 1910, *BTW Papers,* 10:384, and to Scott, Sept. 2, 1910, 10:382; report from the *New York Evening Post,* Oct. 3, 1910, regarding dinner with Danish royal family, 10:391–92; Harlan, *Booker T. Washington: The Wizard of Tuskegee,* pp. 291–93; and *Tuskegee Student* 22 (Sept. 10, 1910).

149. Quoted from a 1942 interview with Robert E. Park on Washington in Fred H. Matthews, *Quest for an American Sociology: Robert E. Park and the Chicago School,* p. 66.

150. Washington and Park, *The Man Farthest Down,* p. 19.

151. Washington to Park, Aug. 5, 1914, quoted in Harlan, *Booker T. Washington: The Wizard of Tuskegee,* p. 294.

152. *BTW Papers,* 8:548–52.

153. Ibid., 10:588, Feb. 15, 1911.

154. Harlan, *Booker T. Washington: The Wizard of Tuskegee*, pp. 275–76; Maurice S. Evans, "International Conference on the Negro." Washington also contributed his leadership to an international Sunday School Convention in June 1914 in Chicago, *BTW Papers*, 13:75.

CHAPTER 7

1. Burton W. Kreitlow et al., *Examining Controversies in Adult Education*.

2. Gordon G. Darkenwald and Sharan B. Merriam, *Adult Education, Foundations of Practice*, p. 58.

3. Paulo Freire, *Education for Critical Consciousness* and *Pedagogy of the Oppressed*.

4. Freire, *Education for Critical Consciousness*, pp. 17–19. See also Eduard C. Lindeman, *The Meaning of Adult Education*. Lindeman believed that revolution was necessary when "faith in intelligence breaks down."

5. August Meier, "Toward a Reinterpretation of Booker T. Washington," p. 220.

6. See Louis R. Harlan, "Booker T. Washington in Biographical Perspective" and "The Secret Life of Booker T. Washington."

7. Meier, "Toward a Reinterpretation," pp. 220–21.

8. Matthews' discussion of Park in *Quest for an American Sociology*, p. 71, contends that Park's records suggest "that even Washington's moderate position went beyond the limits that "responsible" northern whites would sanction. Even "tactful exposure of racial injustice" was edited out of Washington's frequent reference to it before publication.

9. Meier, "Toward a Reinterpretation," pp. 222–25; see *BTW Papers* from 1900 to 1912 for the most accurate view of Washington's political motivations and actions, often at variance with revisionistic interpretations of them.

10. See Harlan, *Booker T. Washington: The Making of a Black Leader*, pp. 304–24; below, n. 52, Park.

11. *BTW Papers*, 9:118, Theodore Roosevelt's letter to Washington, Nov. 5, 1906. See also pp. 113, 153–54 for other examples of Washington's attention to the Brownsville soldiers and Tinsley, "Roosevelt, Foraker, and the Brownsville Affray."

12. Ibid., 9:147–48, Nov. 26, 1906, from Washington to Roosevelt.

13. Ibid., 9:686, Roosevelt to Washington, Nov. 5, 1908.

14. Ibid.

15. Harlan, *Booker T. Washington: The Wizard of Tuskegee*, p. 323.

16. Meier, "Toward a Reinterpretation," pp. 221–22. In Maryland, Washington also worked through Catholic leaders and a Catholic lawyer, F. L. McGhee, to oppose disfranchisement in 1904. Similar efforts were exerted in Virginia and Kentucky from 1901 to 1904.

17. Washington to Walter L. Cohen, chairman of the Republican state central committee of Louisiana, Oct. 5, 1905, *BTW Papers*, 8:396–97; vol. 9, Washington to Villard, Sept. 7, 1908, p. 618.

18. Meier, "Toward a Reinterpretation," p. 225; *BTW Papers*, 7:423, Washington to Wilford Smith, Feb. 2, 1904; Smith to Washington, pp. 461–62, March 7, 1904.

19. Meier, "Toward a Reinterpretation," pp. 225–26; the Washington papers address this peonage case over a number of years.

20. *BTW Papers*, 7:447–48, "A Protest against Lynching," Feb. 22, 1904, in Birmingham *Age-Herald; BTW Papers*, 13:208, "The Lynching Record for 1914," and p. 227, editorial of Jan. 16, 1915, in *New York World* on lynching. Tuskegee archives maintains a comprehensive historical file on lynching.

21. Meier, "Toward a Reinterpretation," p. 226; *BTW Papers*, 7:323, 324, 326, Washington to John Gant, Nov. 2, 1903, to Napier, Nov. 2, 1903, and to Du Bois, Dec. 14, 1903; William H. Baldwin, Jr. to Washington, Jan. 7, 1904, 7:387–88; Washington to Robert Todd Lincoln, 7:3, Jan. 2, 1903, and Oct. 28, 1903, pp. 312–13. Through his secretary, Lincoln said that he had received a number of letters, that he was fully aware of black opinions about the Pullman car matters, and that a conference with blacks would do more harm than good; he did not meet with them.

22. Meier, "Toward a Reinterpretation," p. 226, *BTW Papers*, 9:12, 13, 24–25, 27, Kelly Miller to Washington, May 22, 1906, Grimké to Washington, May 25, 1906, Washington to Grimké, June 2, 1906, and Scott to R. J. Thompson, June 5, 1906.

23. C. Vann Woodward, *Origins of the New South, 1877–1913*, p. 367.

24. Meier, "Toward a Reinterpretation," pp. 226–27.

25. Dewayne Wickham, " 'Quiet Riots' Segregate USA Today," in the Hattiesburg, Miss., *American*, March 13, 1988.

26. Charles W. Chesnutt in the *Saturday Evening Post*, quoted in Thrasher, *Tuskegee*, pp. 197–98.

27. Washington, *Up from Slavery*, p. 220.

28. Ibid., p. 204.

29. Franklin, *From Slavery to Freedom*, p. 274.

30. Bond, *Negro Education in Alabama*, p. 224.

31. Ibid., p. 225.

32. Ibid., p. 256. Bond noted that "illiteracy of Negroes over ten years of age had been reduced spectacularly during the past forty years."

33. Ibid., p. 222.

34. Ibid., p. 221; Charles S. Johnson, *Shadow of the Plantation*. Johnson compared families of Macon County, Alabama, with Gibson County, Tennessee, an area of poor small farms with no tradition of the plantation, an unfair comparison (pp. 94–95).

35. Bond, *Negro Education*, pp. 234–35.

36. Ibid., p. 236.

37. Johnson, *Shadow of the Plantation*, pp. 144–45. In spite of Johnson's gloom, passed on to Bond, Johnson's chart, which compared scores on physical housing between Macon County subjects and Gibson County (p. 95), reflected that Macon rated more than twenty points higher than Gibson. In 1925 in Macon County, according to Johnson (p. 104), 277 black farmers and 248 white farmers owned their farms; there was, however, a larger number of black tenant farmers because of the larger black population. Johnson provided no statistics for the period prior to 1881 for comparison.

38. Ibid., pp. 143–45. See also Charles S. Johnson et al., *Into the Main Stream*.

39. Bond, *Negro Education*, p. 221.

40. Ibid., p. 223.

41. Ibid., p. 224.

42. Louis R. Harlan, *Separate and Unequal: Public School Campaigns and Racism in the Southern Seaboard States, 1901–1915*, p. 43. There is a general unevenness among earlier and later writings of Harlan. In his 1966 article, "Booker T. Washington and The White Man's Burden," for instance, Harlan states that Washington advocated industrial education for Africa (p. 449), proposing "the same accommodation, economic and cultural subordination, and incentives to individual self-help that characterized his racial philosophy in the United States" (pp. 448–49). By contrast, in *Booker T. Washington: The Wizard of Tuskegee* (1983), Harlan argues against Jones's conclusion that black Africans were best suited for industrial education, a position Washington never endorsed, according to Harlan (p. 201). Within Harlan's two-volume biography (1972 and 1983), there is further evidence of contradictory positions and tones. See, for example, chapter 13, "The Brownsville Ghouls" (pp. 323–37) and chapter 8, "Other People's Schools" (pp. 174–201) in *Booker T. Washington: The Wizard of Tuskegee*.

43. Harlan, *Booker T. Washington: The Wizard of Tuskegee*, p. 4. See also Louis R. Harlan, *The Negro in American History*.

44. Harlan, *Booker T. Washington: The Wizard of Tuskegee*, p. xi.

45. Ibid., p. x. It should be noted that Washington made little effort to "win over" the "Talented Tenth."

46. Harlan, *Booker T. Washington: The Making of a Black Leader*, pp. ix–x.

47. Stephen R. Fox, *The Guardian of Boston*, p. 32.

48. Ibid., pp. 91–92.

49. Ibid., p. 145.

50. Ibid., p. 272.

51. Washington to Oswald G. Villard, Dec. 11, 1910, *BTW Papers*, 10:503.

52. See Washington to T. Thomas Fortune, Jan. 20, 1911, ibid., 10:555–56: "There are some curious things going on," Washington wrote. "It seems to me

that our friends Villard and John E. Milholland are attempting to run and control the destinies of the Negro race through Du Bois." See also Matthews, *Quest for an American Sociology*, pp. 76–78, for Park's observations on the subject. Park called Villard a "meddling intellectual reformer whose zeal blinded him to the 'realities' of Southern life." Writing later about Villard's nasty letters, Park thought Villard tried to control Washington because the former had helped Tuskegee. "These benevolent people seem to have got the idea that they were God's chosen people and seemed to feel the Negro belonged to them" (p. 77). Park maintained that the "personal qualities of the 'radicals'' doomed them to failure in practical affairs," because they were not politicians and lacked the ability to deal with human beings. Washington, Park felt, "attained political influence because he realized that politics was the art of the possible" (p. 77). According to Park, Washington "looked at the Negro situation realistically" and "could be relied upon to take a common-sense view" (pp. 77–78). Following the Washington doctrine on racial matters the rest of his life, Park had other observations on his leadership, as summarized by Matthews (p. 78): "The confidence of Theodore Roosevelt was founded in the president's faith that Booker T. Washington would not embarrass him by recommending unsound men for federal office. Further, Washington refused to succumb to bitterness and thus discourage his clientele of Negro artisans and peasants in the South. He gave them present activity to keep away despair, and the hope of gradual improvement at the end of tasks which began immediately and involved them personally. Washington 'was never frustrated as Du Bois always was and he did have the faith in the common man that Du Bois never seems to have had.' "

53. *BTW Papers*, 13:237–38, Feb. 9, 13, 1915, entries in R. S. Baker's notebook; *BTW Papers*, 10:342, Baker's letter of June 20, 1910. Baker had declined a committee position, "thinking it better not to appear to support a cause with which I find myself in disagreement at so many points." On May 13, 1910, Baker wrote to Washington, "The more I see of this whole matter, the more I feel sure that you are on the right track—that it is only by patient development and growth that the evils can be met." *BTW Papers*, 10:334; Harlan, *Booker T. Washington: The Wizard of Tuskegee*, p. 367.

54. Moton to Washington, Dec. 2, 1910, *BTW Papers*, 10:498. Moton said that the circular letter distributed in Europe had been written by Du Bois and that Villard's and Du Bois's contention that the national organization (the National Negro Committee, later changed to the NAACP) was "not responsible for the action of its members is all moonshine." A letter to Moton from Allen W. Washington, Moton's assistant commandant at Hampton, Aug. 9, 1909, Hampton Archives, stated another opinion of Du Bois: "If Dr. Washington needs anyone to help him kick Du Bois tell him to call on me and I shall be right at his elbow. Du Bois is hard to suit and very unruly."

Ralph Waldo Tyler, a black journalist and politician, wrote Emmett Scott of the growing impact of the national organization, also expressing doubts about its leadership: "We cannot afford to openly oppose the N.A.A.C.P. for the reason that its fundamental principles are precisely what we all desire to see in force. With its present leaders, we cannot afford to go over to it in a body." *BTW Papers*, 12:401–2, Jan. 4, 1914.

55. Moton to Oswald Garrison Villard, March 5, 1914, *BTW Papers*, 12:469.

56. Washington to Ray S. Baker, May 24, 1910, *BTW Papers*, 10:333–34. "No individual in America realizes more keenly than I do the injustices put upon our race," Washington added, "but at the same time I realize fully that we cannot change conditions by merely demanding that they should be changed."

57. This letter was headed, "An Open Letter to the People of Great Britain and Europe" by W. E. B. Du Bois and others, dated Oct. 26, 1910, and written on stationery of the Headquarters National Negro Committee. It was circulated in Europe in response to speeches Washington gave at the end of his European tour on October 6, 1910, in London to the Anti-Slavery Protection Society and the National Liberal Club. See Du Bois circular letter, *BTW Papers*, 10:422–25, and earlier John E. Milholland circular letter of Oct. 6, 1910, pp. 394–400. See also *London Times* report on speeches, Oct. 7, 1910, *BTW Papers*, 10:401–4, and *Manchester Guardian* report on Oct. 8, 1910, pp. 404–5. Washington did not deny that blacks had been wronged; he did, as was his philosophy, emphasize the progress his race had made. The prime minister sent Washington greetings, thanking him for his educational work for American blacks and for his leadership with many "difficulties in many parts of the Empire" which had been "helped towards solution" by the results of his work, 10:402. On the evening of this speech, Washington addressed the National Liberal Club on "The Economic Progress of the Negro in America."

58. Washington to J. R. Barlow, March 1, 1911, *BTW Papers*, 10:608–9. Washington noted that Du Bois stirred up strife between the whites and blacks, which would not be so bad if, after doing so, "he would live in the South and be brave enough to face conditions which his unwise course has helped to bring about." Instead, "he flees to the North and leaves the rank and file of colored people in the South no better off because of the unwise course which he and others like him have pursued."

59. Fox, *Guardian of Boston*, p. 143.

60. W. E. B. Du Bois, *Dusk at Dawn*, pp. 309–10. Du Bois left the NAACP in 1934, but he was offered a job in the organization ten years later and returned. See *Autobiography of W. E. B. Du Bois*, pp. 326–39. Du Bois was dismissed from this position for "refusing to cooperate," he said, p. 335, not "because of my radical thought," p. 336.

61. *Autobiography of W. E. B. Du Bois*, p. 440. See also pp. 431–37 for selected bibliography of Du Bois's prolific writings; August Meier, *Negro Thought in America*, chap. 11, "The Paradox of W. E. B. Du Bois," pp.

190–206, and chap. 12, "Booker T. Washington and the 'Talented Tenth,' " pp. 207–47.

62. See James McPherson, "Reconstruction Reconsidered," for more insight into the "ripple of revisionism" beginning in the 1950s that "became a tidal wave that capsized the traditional view of Reconstruction" (p. 75).

63. Harlan, *Booker T. Washington: The Wizard of Tuskegee*, pp. 202–3.

64. Ibid., p. 202.

65. Ibid., p. x.

66. Gunnar Myrdal, "Foreword," in *The Negro in America*, ed. Arnold Rose (New York: Harper and Row, 1964), pp. xiii–xiv. See also Myrdal's preface to *American Dilemma*, 1:ix–xx; David M. Kennedy, "The Making of a Classic," *Atlantic Monthly* 259 (May 1987), pp. 86–89; David W. Southern, *Gunnar Myrdal and Black-White Relations: The Use and Abuse of an American Dilemma, 1944–1969;* and Matthews, *Quest for an American Sociology*, pp. 184–85, 189. Matthews compared Park, Washington's collaborator and an influential sociologist, with Myrdal, calling them both "prophets of change" (p. 189). Park had encouraged Myrdal to study the Negro as the "focus for studying a changing America" (p. 185). Park differed from Myrdal in believing that the mechanism for change would be through the "struggle and transformation of the peoples concerned," rather than through social engineering, according to Matthews— lingering shades of the Washington philosophy.

67. Myrdal, "Foreword," to Rose, *Negro in America*, pp. xiv–xv.

68. Myrdal, *American Dilemma*, 1:63.

69. "Booker T. Washington: The Rise of a Black Man." *Intellectual Digest* (February 1973), pp. 25–32.

70. Myrdal, *American Dilemma*. All further references to this work in these conclusions will appear in the text.

71. The relationship between Washington and Park is another unexplored example of interracial mentoring. Matthews contended in *Quest for an American Sociology* that Washington had a significant impact on the ideology of Park, who later directed the "Chicago School" of sociology and taught such racial scholars as Charles S. Johnson, E. Franklin Frazier, Donald Pierson, Edgar T. Thompson, and Louis Wirth (p. 176).

72. The subject of putting humans back into history was explored recently by Gilbert T. Sewall, "American Textbooks: Where Do We Go from Here?," *Kappan* 69 (April 1988), pp. 553–58. Sewall lamented: "Figure and event make the scene. But individuals in textbooks are curiously disembodied, without flair, personality, or distinction" (p. 556).

73. In many respects a simple man, Washington loved nothing better than digging in his garden or riding with his children through the woods. Acquainted with glory, he was also well acquainted with personal grief, public defamation, and indignities of bodily injury. See Willard B. Gatewood, "Booker T. Washington and the Ulrich Affair"; Rayford W. Logan, *The Negro in the United*

States: A History to 1945; From Slavery to Second-Class Citizenship (New York: Van Nostrand Rheinhold, 1970), 1:69–70.

74. Thomas Fortune, quoted in Thrasher, *Tuskegee*, p. 196.

CHAPTER 8

1. Myrdal, *American Dilemma*, 2:997, 1024.

2. "The American Creed," *Americana* (New York: Americana Corp., 1964), 1:567b–68.

3. Kallen, *Philosophical Issues*, p. 56.

4. Ibid., p. 9. See also Henry Adams, *The Education of Henry Adams* (Boston: Houghton Mifflin, 1918) and Robert Peers, *Adult Education in Practice.*

5. Kallen, *Philosophical Issues*, p. 50.

6. Ibid., p. 52.

7. Ibid., p. 53.

8. Ibid., p. 54.

9. Summarized from Knowles' division of periods I–III, depicting the maturation of America. Malcolm S. Knowles, *The Adult Education Movement in the United States.*

10. See Scott and Stowe, *Booker T. Washington: Builder of a Civilization.*

11. Malcolm S. Knowles, "Adult Education," *Americana*, 1:157.

12. Ibid., p. 157.

13. Rubin, *Teach the Freeman*, 1:xv–xvi.

14. Ibid., 1:xiv–xx.

15. Ibid., 1:xxi–xxiv; Atticus G. Haygood, *Our Brother in Black*, pp. 17, 42, 80–81, 133.

16. Rubin, *Teach the Freeman*, 1:xxvi–xxvii.

17. Ibid., 1:xxviii.

18. Bond, *Negro Education in Alabama*, pp. 198–203.

19. Rubin, *Teach the Freeman*, 1:xxxvii–xxxviii.

20. Discussion of adult education philosophy was briefly summarized from John L. Elias and Sharan B. Merriam, *Philosophical Foundations of Adult Education*, and Robert Ulich, *History of Educational Thought*. See also Lindeman, *Meaning of Adult Education.*

21. Gordon G. Darkenwald and Sharan B. Merriam, *Adult Education*, pp. 41–70.

22. K. Patricia Cross, *Adults as Learners*, pp. 222–28; Knowles, *Modern Practice of Adult Education;* Virginia L. Denton, "Do Grades Sabotage Self-Direction in Adult Learning?"

23. Cross, *Adults*, pp. 228–29; J. R. Kidd, *How Adults Learn;* Allen Tough, *The Adult's Learning Projects* (Ontario: Institute for Studies in Education, 1971).

24. Cross, *Adults*, pp. 229–32; Havighurst, *Developmental Tasks and Education.*

25. Cross, *Adults*, pp. 232–34.

26. Quoted in Matthews, *Quest for an American Sociology*, p. 62.

27. Kallen, *Philosophical Issues*, pp. 68–69. Kallen sounded very much like Washington here: "From the standpoint of the American Idea the important thing is that communication shall liberate, that education shall use whatever can serve as an instrument of liberation without prejudice, and use it with the consent and cooperation of the adult as he is, where he is, as a heart and head, when he comes questing to school" (p. 67).

28. Ulich, *History of Educational Thought*, pp. 337–39.

29. Ibid., pp. 345–50c.

30. Ibid., p. 346.

31. *BTW Papers*, 3:234–35.

32. James Truslow Adams, *The Epic of America* (New York: Little, Brown and Co., 1931), p. v.

33. Lindeman, *Meaning of Adult Education*, pp. 104–5.

SELECTED BIBLIOGRAPHY

MANUSCRIPTS AND DOCUMENTS

Annual Reports of the Principal to the Board of Trustees, 1868–1915. Huntington Collins Library Archives, Hampton University, Hampton, Virginia.

Annual Reports of the Principal to the Board of Trustees, 1881–1915. Hollis Burke Frissell Library Archives, Tuskegee University, Tuskegee, Alabama.

The Samuel Chapman Armstrong Collection. Hampton Archives, Hampton, Virginia.

James Burroughs Estate Inventory. Franklin County Courthouse, Rocky Mount, Virginia.

George Washington Carver Papers. Tuskegee Archives, Tuskegee, Alabama.

Hollis Burke Frissell Papers. Hampton Archives, Hampton, Virginia.

Lynching Files, 1881–1966. Tuskegee Archives, Tuskegee, Alabama.

James F. B. Marshall Correspondence. Hampton Archives, Hampton, Virginia.

Robert R. Moton Papers. Tuskegee Archives, Tuskegee, Alabama.

Emmett J. Scott Correspondence. Hampton Archives, Hampton, Virginia; Tuskegee Archives, Tuskegee, Alabama.

The Booker T. Washington Collection. 35 boxes. Hampton Archives, Hampton, Virginia.

The Booker T. Washington Collection. 133 boxes. Tuskegee Archives, Tuskegee, Alabama.

The Booker T. Washington Papers. 13 vols. L. R. Harlan et al., eds. Urbana: University of Illinois Press, 1972–84.

PRIMARY PUBLICATIONS, JOURNALS, AND NEWSPAPERS

Hampton Student. Hampton Institute, March 15, 1909–December 15, 1924.
Journal of Ethnic Studies. Hampton Institute.
Montgomery Advertiser. Montgomery, Alabama.
The Negro Farmer. Tuskegee Institute, 1911–1914.
Roanoke Times. Roanoke, Virginia.
Sage Journal for Black Women. Hampton Institute.
Southern Letter. Tuskegee Institute, 1900–1910.
Southern Workman. Hampton Institute, January 1872–July 1939.
Tuskegee Alumni Bulletin. Tuskegee Institute.
Tuskegee Messenger. Tuskegee Institute.
Tuskegee News. Tuskegee, Alabama.
Tuskegee Student. Tuskegee Institute, 1890–1919.

BOOKS AND ARTICLES

Alexander, Fred M. *Education for the Needs of the Negro in Virginia.* Washington, D.C.: The Southern Education Foundation for the John F. Slater Fund Studies in Education of Negroes, no. 2, 1943.
Ambler, Charles H. *A History of Education in West Virginia from Early Colonial Times to 1949.* Huntington, W. Va.: Gentry Bros., 1951.
———. *Sectionalism in Virginia from 1776 to 1861.* Chicago: University of Chicago Press, 1910.
Aptheker, Herbert. *Nat Turner's Slave Rebellion.* 1966: Reprint. New York: Grove Press, 1968.
———. "Negro Casualties in the Civil War." *Journal of Negro History* 32 (January 1947): 10–80.
———. "The Quaker and Negro Slavery." *Journal of Negro History* 25 (1940): 331–62.
Armstrong, M. F., and Helen W. Ludlow. *Hampton and Its Students.* 1874: Reprint. Chicago: Afro-Am Press, 1969.
Armstrong, Samuel Chapman. *Armstrong's Ideas on Education for Life.* n.d.: Reprint. Hampton, Va.: Hampton Institute Press, 1940.
———. "Lessons from the Hawaiian Islands." *Journal of Christian Philosophy* (January 1884). Reprint in Hampton Archives.
———. *Twenty-Two Years' Work at Hampton Normal and Agricultural Institute.* Hampton, Va.: Hampton Normal School Press, 1893.
Atkinson, George W. *History of Kanawha County, from Its Organization in 1789 until the Present Time.* Charleston, W.Va.: 1876.
Bacote, Clarence A. *The Story of Atlanta University.* Atlanta: Atlanta University Press, 1969.

Beard, Augustus Field. *A Crusade for Brotherhood: A History of the American Missionary Association.* Boston: Pilgrim Press, 1909.

————. Special report to Booker T. Washington on the history of the American Missionary Association work in Alabama from 1865 to 1892. 1893. Tuskegee Archives, box 1, folder 9.

Bergevin, Paul. *A Philosophy for Adult Education.* New York: Seabury Press, 1967.

Birney, James G. *The American Churches, the Bulwarks of American Slavery, by an American.* Newburyport, 1842.

Blackiston, Harry S. "Lincoln's Emancipation Plan." *Journal of Negro History* 7 (July 1922): 257–77.

Blackwell, Velma L. "A Black Institution Pioneering Adult Education: Tuskegee Institute Past and Present, 1881–1973." Ph.D. diss., Florida State University, 1973.

Blanchard, F. Q. "A Quarter Century in the American Missionary Association." *Journal of Negro Education* 6 (April 1937): 152–56.

Blassingame, John W. *Black New Orleans, 1860–1880.* Chicago: University of Chicago Press, 1973.

————. *The Slave Community: Plantation Life in the Antebellum South.* New York: Oxford University Press, 1972.

Bond, Horace M. *The Education of the Negro in the American Social Order.* New York: Prentice Hall, 1934.

————. *Negro Education in Alabama: A Study in Cotton and Steel.* Washington, D.C.: Associated Publishers, 1939.

"Booker T. Washington: The Rise of a Black Man." *Intellectual Digest* (February 1973): 25–32.

"Booker T. Washington Visits Old Home." *Roanoke Times,* Roanoke, Virginia, September 27, 1908.

"Booker T. Washington Visits Roanoke." *Roanoke Times,* Roanoke, Virginia, September 26, 1908.

Botume, Elizabeth Hyde. *First Days Amongst the Contrabands.* Boston, 1893.

Brownlee, Frederick L. *American Missionary Association, 1935, Annual Report: A Review of the American Missionary's Eighty-Ninth Year.* Tuskegee Archives.

————. *Heritage of Freedom: A Centenary Story of Ten Schools Offering Education in Freedom.* Philadelphia: United Church Press, 1963.

————. *A New Day Ascending.* Boston: Pilgrim Press, 1946.

Bruce, Roscoe C. "Tuskegee Institute." In *From Servitude to Service.* 1905: Reprint. New York: Negro Universities Press, 1969.

Bullock, Henry Allen. *A History of Negro Education in the South from 1619 to the Present.* 1967: Reprint. New York: Praeger Publishers, 1970.

Butchart, Ronald E. *Northern Schools, Southern Blacks, and Reconstruction.* Westport, Conn.: Greenwood Press, 1980.

Butler, Addie L. J. *The Distinctive Black College: Talladega, Tuskegee, and Morehouse*. Metuchen, N.J.: Scarecrow Press, 1977.

Calloway, James N. "Tuskegee Cotton-Planters in Africa." *Outlook* 70 (March 29, 1902): 772–76.

Campbell, Thomas Monroe. *The Movable School Goes to the Negro Farmer*. Tuskegee: Tuskegee Institute Press, 1936.

Carson [Lowitt], Suzanne. "Samuel Chapman Armstrong: Missionary to the South." Ph.D. diss., Johns Hopkins University, 1952.

Carter, Franklin. *General Armstrong's Life and Work: Founder's Day Address, 1902*. Hampton, Va.: Hampton Institute Press, 1917.

Carver, George Washington. "Twelve Ways to Meet the New Economic Conditions of the South." *Experiment Station Bulletin*, no. 33 (1917).

Citro, Joseph F. "Booker T. Washington's Tuskegee Institute: Black School-Community, 1900–1915." Ph.D. diss., University of Rochester, 1972.

Cooke, Edward F. *A Detailed Analysis of the Constitution*. 1958: Reprint. Totowa, N.J.: Littlefield, Adams and Co., 1977.

Couch, W. T., ed. *Culture of the South*. Chapel Hill: University of North Carolina Press, 1934.

Cross, K. Patricia. *Adults As Learners*. San Francisco: Jossey-Bass, 1983.

Current, Richard N. "The Friend of Freedom." In *Reconstruction*, edited by Kenneth M. Stampp and Leon F. Litwack, 25–47. Baton Rouge: Louisiana State University Press, 1969.

———. *The Lincoln Nobody Knows*. New York: McGraw Hill, 1958.

Curry, J. L. M. *The Negro since 1860*. John F. Slater Fund for Education of Freedmen, Occasional Papers, no. 3. Baltimore, Md., 1891.

Curti, Merle. *The Social Ideas of American Educators*. Totowa, N.J.: Littlefield, Adams, and Co., 1966.

Darkenwald, Gordon G., and Sharan B. Merriam. *Adult Education: Foundations of Practice*. New York: Harper and Row, 1982.

Delaney, William H. *Learn By Doing: A Projected Educational Philosophy in the Thought of Booker T. Washington*. New York: Vantage Press, 1974.

Denton, Virginia L. "Do Grades Sabotage Self-Direction in Adult Learning?" *Lifelong Learning* (May 1986): 19–22, 28.

Donald, Henderson H. *The Negro Freedman*. New York: Henry Schuman, 1952.

Dorsey, Carolyn A. "Olivia Davidson Washington's Story." *Sage Journal for Black Women* 2 (Fall 1985): 69–72.

Douglass, Frederick. "A Defense of the Negro Race." Address delivered at the annual meeting of the American Missionary Association in New York. Undated copy in Tuskegee Archives.

Drake, Thomas E. *Quakers and Slavery in America*. New Haven: Yale Univ. Press, 1950.

Dresslar, F. B. *Rosenwald School Buildings*. Report Bulletin no. 1. Nashville, Tenn.: Julius Rosenwald Fund, 1920.

Drinker, Frederick E. *Booker T. Washington: The Master Mind of a Child of Slavery*. 1915: Reprint. New York: Negro Universities Press, 1970.

Du Bois, W. E. B. *The Autobiography of W. E. B. Du Bois*. n.p.: International Publishers, 1968.

———. *Dusk at Dawn: An Essay Toward an Autobiography of a Race Concept*. New York: Harcourt Brace, 1940.

———. *The Education of Black People: Ten Critiques, 1906–1960*. Edited by Herbert Aptheker. Amherst: University of Massachusetts Press, 1973.

———. *The Negro Church*. Atlanta: Atlanta University Press, 1903.

———. *The Philadelphia Negro*. Philadelphia: University of Pennsylvania, 1896.

———. *The Souls of Black Folk: Essays and Sketches*. Chicago: A. C. McClurg, 1903.

———. *The Suppression of the African Slave Trade*. 1896: Reprint. Baton Rouge: Louisiana State University Press, 1969.

Eggleston, G. K. "The Work of Relief Societies during the Civil War." *Journal of Negro History* 14 (July 1929): 272–99.

Elias, John L., and Sharan B. Merriam. *Philosophical Foundations of Adult Education*. Huntington, N.Y.: Robert E. Krieger, 1980.

Ellison, Willie J. "Booker T. Washington's Influence on Africa, 1900–1910." Undated manuscript in Tuskegee Archives.

Engs, Robert F. *Freedom's First Generation: Black Hampton, Virginia, 1861–1890*. Philadelphia: University of Pennsylvania Press, 1979.

Evans, Maurice S. "International Conference on the Negro." *Journal of the African Society* 11 (July 1912): 416–29.

Fleming, John E. *The Lengthening Shadow of Slavery*. Washington, D.C.: Howard University Press, 1976.

Fox, Stephen R. *The Guardian of Boston: William Monroe Trotter*. New York: Atheneum, 1970.

Franklin, John Hope. *The Emancipation Proclamation*. New York: Doubleday, 1963.

———. *From Slavery to Freedom*. 5th ed. New York: Alfred A. Knopf, 1980.

Frazier, E. Franklin. *The Negro in the United States*. New York: Macmillan Co., 1949.

Freire, Paulo. *Education for Critical Consciousness*. New York: Seabury Press, 1973.

———. *Pedagogy of the Oppressed*. New York: Seabury Press, 1970.

French, Mrs. A. M. *Slavery in South Carolina and the Ex-Slaves or the Port Royal Mission*. New York: Winchell M. French, 1862.

Gannett, William Channing, and Edward Everett Hale. "The Education of the Freedmen." *North American Review* 101 (Oct. 1865): 528–49.

Gardner, Booker T. "The Educational Contributions of Booker T. Washington." *Journal of Negro History* 14 (Fall 1975): 502–18.

Garland, William. "Common Everyday Black Life in Hampton, Virginia: 1870–1910." *College of William and Mary Update* 4 (Fall 1987): 6–7.

Gatewood, Willard B. "Booker T. Washington and the Ulrich Affair." *Journal of Negro History* 55 (1970): 29–44.

Gerteis, Louis S. *From Contraband to Freedman: Federal Policy toward Southern Blacks, 1861–1865.* Westport, Conn.: Greenwood Press, 1973.

Gesell, Arnold, and Frances Ilg. *The Child from Five to Ten.* New York: Harper and Brothers, 1946.

Gibson, John H. *The Colored America from Slavery to Honorable Citizenship.* Naperville, Ill.: J. L. Nichols and Co., 1902.

Gottschalk, Jane. "The Rhetorical Strategy of Booker T. Washington." *Phylon* 27 (Spring 1966): 388–95.

Graham, Shirley. *Booker T. Washington: Educator of Hand, Head, and Heart.* New York: Messner, 1955.

Grant, Joanne, ed. *Black Protest: History, Documents, and Analyses, 1619 to the Present.* New York: Fawcett, 1968.

Gray, Lewis C. *History of Agriculture in the Southern United States to 1860.* 1933: Reprint. Clifton, N.J.: A. M. Kelley, 1973.

Green, Fletcher M. "Northern Missionary Activities in the South, 1846–1861." *Journal of Southern History* 21 (May 1955): 147–72.

Gutman, Herbert G. *The Black Family in Slavery and Freedom, 1750–1925.* New York: Pantheon, 1976.

Guzman, Jessie P. "Olivia A. Davidson: Educator and Co-Founder of Tuskegee Institute." Undated copy in Tuskegee Archives.

Hampton-Tuskegee Results: A Story Every American Should Know. New York: Hampton-Tuskegee Joint Commission, 1925. Tuskegee Archives.

Harlan, Louis R. "Booker T. Washington in Biographical Perspective." *American Historical Review* 75 (October 1970): 1581–99.

———. *Booker T. Washington: The Making of a Black Leader, 1856–1901.* New York: Oxford University Press, 1972.

———. "Booker T. Washington and the National Negro Business League." In *Seven on Black: Reflections on the Negro Experience in America,* 73–91, Philadelphia: J. B. Lippincott Co., 1969.

———. "Booker T. Washington and the White Man's Burden." *American Historical Review* 71 (January 1966): 441–67.

———. *Booker T. Washington: The Wizard of Tuskegee, 1901–1915.* New York: Oxford University Press, 1983.

———. *The Negro in American History.* Washington, D.C.: American Historical Association, 1965.

———. "The Secret Life of Booker T. Washington." *Journal of Southern History* 37 (August 1971): 393–416.

246 BOOKER T. WASHINGTON AND THE ADULT EDUCATION MOVEMENT

––––––. *Separate and Unequal: Public School Campaigns and Racism in the Southern Seaboard States, 1901–1915.* Chapel Hill: University of North Carolina Press, 1958.

Havighurst, Robert J. *Developmental Tasks and Education.* 1948: Reprint. New York: Longmans, Green and Co., 1953.

Hawkins, Hugh, ed. *Booker T. Washington and His Critics: The Problem of Negro Leadership.* Lexington, Mass.: D. C. Heath and Co., 1962.

Haygood, Atticus G. *Our Brother in Black.* New York, 1881.

Herbert, Hilary A. "The Conditions of the Reconstruction Problem." *Atlantic Monthly* 87 (Feb. 1901): 145–57.

Hesslink, George K. *Black Neighbors: Negroes in a Northern Rural Community.* 2d ed. New York: Bobbs-Merrill Co., 1974.

History of the American Missionary Association with Facts and Anecdotes Illustrating Its Work in the South. 2d ed. New York: American Missionary Association, 1874.

Hollender, A. N. J. Dan. "The Tradition of the 'Poor White'." In *Culture in the South,* edited by W. T. Couch, 403–31. Chapel Hill: University of North Carolina Press, 1934.

Houle, Cyril O. "Continuing Education at Tuskegee," Report to Luther H. Foster. Tuskegee Institute, Tuskegee, Alabama, 1967.

––––––. *The Design of Education.* San Francisco: Jossey-Bass, 1973.

Howard, Oliver Otis. "Hampton and General Armstrong." *Southern Workman* 18 (June 1889): 6, 75–76.

Howells, William Dean. "An Exemplary Citizen." *North American Review* 173 (Aug. 1901): 280–88.

Hughes, W. H., and F. D. Patterson, eds. *Robert Russa Moton of Hampton and Tuskegee.* Chapel Hill: University of North Carolina Press, 1956.

Hunter, Wilma King. "Three Women at Tuskegee, 1882–1925: The Wives of Booker T. Washington." *Journal of Ethnic Studies* 3 (Sept. 1976): 76–89.

Illich, Ivan. *Deschooling Society.* New York: Harper and Row, 1970.

Jackson, Luther P. "The Origin of Hampton Institute." *Journal of Negro History* 10 (April 1925): 131–50.

James, Jacqueline. "Uncle Tom? Not Booker T." *American Heritage* 19 (Aug. 1968): 50–63.

The Jeanes Story: A Chapter in the History of American Education, 1908–1968. NASC Interim History Writing Committee of the Southern Education Foundation. Atlanta: NASC, 1979.

Jenifer, George D. "A Day at Tuskegee." *Education* (Oct. 1905). Tuskegee Archives.

Johnson, Charles S. "The Rise of Negro Magazines." *Journal of Negro History* 13 (January 1928): 7–21.

––––––. *Shadow of the Plantation.* Chicago: University of Chicago Press, 1934.

Johnson, Charles S., et al. *Into the Main Stream: A Survey of Best Practices in*

Race Relations in the South. Chapel Hill: University of North Carolina Press, 1947.

Johnson, Clifton. "Tuskegee: A Typical Alabama Town." *Outlook* 72 (Nov. 1, 1902): 519–26.

Jones, Jacqueline. *Soldiers of Light and Love: Northern Teachers and Georgia Blacks, 1865–1873.* Chapel Hill: University of North Carolina Press, 1980.

Jones, Lee A. "The Influence of Tuskegee on Education of Negroes in Macon County, 1881–1946." Master's thesis, Tuskegee Institute, 1947.

Kallen, Horace M. *Philosophical Issues in Adult Education.* Springfield, Ill.: Charles C. Thomas, 1962.

Katz, William Loren. *Educating the Negro in Virginia.* Hampton Institute Press, 1940: Reprint. New York: Arno Press and *New York Times,* 1969.

———, ed. *History of Schools for the Colored Population.* New York: Arno Press, 1969.

Kidd, J. R. *How Adults Learn.* New York: Association Press, 1973.

Knowles, Malcolm S. *The Adult Education Movement in the United States.* New York: Holt, Rinehart and Winston, 1962.

———. *The Modern Practice of Adult Education: From Pedagogy to Andragogy.* New York: Cambridge, 1980.

———. "Philosophical Issues that Confront Adult Educators." *Adult Education* 7 (1957): 234–40.

Kreitlow, Burton W., et al. *Examining Controversies in Adult Education.* San Francisco: Jossey-Bass, 1981.

Lindeman, Eduard C. *The Meaning of Adult Education.* 1926: Reprint. Montreal: Harvest House, 1961.

Litwack, Leon. *Been in the Storm So Long: The Aftermath of Slavery.* New York: Alfred A. Knopf, 1979.

Ludlow, Helen W., ed. *Ten Years Work for the Indians.* Hampton, Va.: Institute Press, 1888.

McGee, Leo. "Booker T. Washington and George Washington Carver: A Tandem of Adult Educators at Tuskegee." *Lifelong Learning* (October 1984): 16–18, 31.

———. "Decline of Black Owned Rural Land: Implications for Adult Education." *Adult Leadership* 35 (March 1977): 207–9.

McKenzie, Leon. *Adult Education and the Burden of the Future.* Washington, D.C.: University Press of America, 1978.

Mackintosh, Barry. *Agriculture on the Burroughs Plantation, 1856–1865.* Washington, D.C.: National Park Service, Dec. 13, 1968.

———. *Booker T. Washington: An Appreciation of the Man and His Times.* Washington, D.C.: National Park Service, Government Printing Office, 1972.

———. *Booker T. Washington National Monument: An Administrative History.* Washington, D.C.: National Park Service, 1969.

———. *General Background Studies: The Burroughs Plantation, 1856–1865, Part A*. Washington, D.C.: National Park Service, Dec. 20, 1968.

———. *The Hale's Ford Community, 1856–1865, Part B*. Washington, D.C.: National Park Service, Nov. 13, 1968.

McMurry, Linda O. *George Washington Carver: Scientist and Symbol, 1864–1943*. New York: Oxford University Press, 1981.

McPherson, James. "Reconstruction Reconsidered." *Atlantic Monthly* 261 (April 1988): 75–77.

Maslow, Abraham H. *Motivation and Personality*. New York: Harper and Row, 1954.

Mathews, Basil. *Booker T. Washington: Educator and Interracial Interpreter*. 1948: Reprint. College Park, Md.: McGrath, 1969.

Matthews, Fred H. *Quest for an American Sociology: Robert E. Park and the Chicago School*. Montreal: McGill-Queen's University Press, 1977.

Mayo, A. D. *Southern Women in the Recent Educational Movement in the South*. 1892: Reprint. Baton Rouge: Louisiana State University Press, 1978.

Meier, August. "Booker T. Washington and the Negro Press." *Journal of Negro History* 38 (1953): 67–90.

———. "Booker T. Washington and the Town of Mound Bayou." *Phylon* 15 (Winter 1954): 396–401.

———. *Negro Thought in America, 1880–1915: Racial Ideologies in the Age of Booker T. Washington*. 1963: Reprint. Ann Arbor: University of Michigan Press, 1966.

———. "Toward a Reinterpretation of Booker T. Washington." *Journal of Southern History* 23 (1957): 220–27.

Meier, August, and Elliott M. Rudwick. "Come to the Fair?" *Crisis* 72 (March 1965): 146–47.

Merriam, Sharan. "Mentors and Proteges: A Critical Review of the Literature." *Adult Education Quarterly* 33 (Spring 1983): 161–73.

Mitchell, George S. *The Industrial Revolution in the South*. Baltimore: Johns Hopkins Press, 1930.

"A Model Negro Village." In *An Education Center for Colored People*. Undated pamphlet in Tuskegee Archives.

Morris, Robert C. *Reading, 'Riting, and Reconstruction: The Education of Freedmen in the South, 1861–1870*. Chicago: University of Chicago Press, 1981.

Moton, Robert R. "The Aim and Scope of Tuskegee Institute." *Journal of Educational Sociology* 7 (Nov. 1933): 151–52.

———. *Finding a Way Out*. New York: Doubleday and Page Co., 1921.

———. *What the Negro Thinks*. New York: Doubleday and Page Co., 1930.

Myrdal, Gunnar. *An American Dilemma: The Negro Problem and Modern Democracy*. 2 vols. 6th ed. New York: Harper and Brothers, 1944.

Newby, I. A. *The South: A History*. New York: Holt, Rinehart and Winston, 1978.

Oates, Stephen B. *The Fires of Jubilee: Nat Turner's Fierce Rebellion.* 1975: Reprint. New York: New American Library, 1976.

Oubre, Claude F. *Forty Acres and a Mule: The Freedmen's Bureau and Black Ownership.* Baton Rouge: Louisiana State University Press, 1978.

Page, Walter H. "Booker T. Washington." *Everybody's Magazine* 6 (April 1902): 392–98.

Park, Robert E. *Race and Culture: Essays in the Sociology of Contemporary Man.* Glenco, Ill.: University of Chicago Press, 1950.

———. "Tuskegee's Principal at His Own Home." *Tuskegee Student* 20 (Oct. 3, 1908): 2.

Parton, J. *General Butler in New Orleans.* New York, 1864.

Paterson, R. W. K. *Values, Education, and the Adult.* London: Routledge and Kegan Paul, 1979.

Peabody, Francis Greenwood. *Education for Life: The Story of Hampton Institute.* New York: Doubleday, Page and Co., 1926.

Peers, Robert. *Adult Education in Practice.* London: Macmillan, 1934.

Peirce, Paul Skeels. *The Freedmen's Bureau: A Chapter in the History of Reconstruction.* Iowa City: University of Iowa, 1904.

Pierce, Edward L. "The Contrabands at Fortress Monroe." *Atlantic Monthly* 8 (Nov. 1861): 624–40.

———. "The Freedmen at Port Royal." *Atlantic Monthly* 12 (Sept. 1863): 291–315.

Population Census of Franklin County, Virginia: Free and Slave Schedule. National Archives, Washington, D.C.

Posey, Thomas E. *The Negro Citizen of West Virginia.* Institute, W.Va., 1934.

Products of Agriculture, Franklin County, Virginia. Virginia State Library, Richmond.

"Proposed Scheme for Hilton Head Settlement." Undated typescript in Washington's papers.

Quarles, Benjamin. *The Negro in the Civil War.* 1953: Reprint. Boston: Russel and Russel, 1968.

Rachal, John R. "Gideonites and Freedmen: Adult Literacy Education at Port Royal, 1862–1865." *Journal of Negro Education* 55 (Fall 1986): 453–69.

Ramsey, Harold W. *Franklin County Public Schools: A Century of Progress.* Franklin Co., Va.: School Board, 1975.

Rice, Otis K. *The Allegheny Frontier: West Virginia Beginnings, 1730–1830.* Lexington: University of Kentucky Press, 1970.

Richardson, Joe M. *Christian Reconstruction: The American Missionary Association and Southern Blacks, 1861–1890.* Athens: University of Georgia Press, 1986.

Robinson, William H. "Indian Education at Hampton Institute." In *Stoney the Road: Chapters in the History of Hampton Institute,* edited by Keith L. Schall, 1–33. Charlottesville: University of Virginia Press, 1977.

Rose, Willie Lee. "The Old Allegiance." In *Reconstruction,* edited by Kenneth M. Stampp and Leon F. Litwack, 175–92. Baton Rouge: Louisiana State University Press, 1969.

———. *Rehearsal for Reconstruction: The Port Royal Experiment.* Indianapolis: Bobbs-Merrill, 1964.

Rubin, Louis D., ed. *Teach the Freeman: The Correspondence of Rutherford B. Hayes and the Slater Fund for Negro Education, 1881–1887.* 2 vols. Baton Rouge: Louisiana State University Press, 1959.

Schall, Keith L., ed. *Stoney the Road: Chapters in the History of Hampton Institute.* Charlottesville: University of Virginia Press, 1977.

Schweningen, Loren. "The American Missionary Association and Northern Philanthropy in Reconstruction Alabama." *Alabama Historical Quarterly* 32 (Fall and Winter 1970): 126–56.

Scott, Emmett J. "Mrs. Booker T. Washington's Part in Her Husband's Work." *Ladies Home Journal* (May 1907): 42.

Scott, Emmett J., and Lyman B. Stowe. *Booker T. Washington: Builder of a Civilization.* Garden City, N.Y.: Doubleday, Page and Co., 1918.

Shields, Adella R. "Influence of Tuskegee on Health, Economy, and Political Aspects of Negro Population of Macon County." Master's thesis, Tuskegee Institute, 1951.

Smith, Lillian. *Killers of the Dream.* 1949: Reprint. New York: W. W. Norton, 1978.

Southern, David W. *Gunnar Myrdal and Black-White Relations: The Use and Abuse of an American Dilemma, 1944–1969.* Baton Rouge: Louisiana State University Press, 1987.

Spencer, Samuel R., Jr. *Booker T. Washington and the Negro's Place in American Life.* Boston: Little, Brown and Co., 1955.

Spivey, Donald. *Schooling for the New Slavery.* Westport, Conn.: Greenwood Press, 1978.

Stampp, Kenneth M. "Abraham Lincoln: The Politics of a Practical Whig." In *The Era of Reconstruction, 1865–1877.* New York: Vantage Books, 1965, pp. 24–49.

———. *The Era of Reconstruction, 1865–1877.* New York: Vantage Books, 1965.

Stampp, Kenneth M., and Leon F. Litwack, eds. *Reconstruction.* Baton Rouge: Louisiana State University Press, 1969.

Stewart, Ruth Ann. *Portia: The Life of Portia Washington Pittman, the Daughter of Booker T. Washington.* New York: Doubleday and Co., 1977.

Stokes, Anson Phelps. *A Brief Biography of Booker T. Washington.* Hampton, Va.: Hampton Institute Press, 1936.

———. *Tuskegee Institute: The First Fifty Years.* Tuskegee: Tuskegee Institute Press, 1931.

Swint, Henry Lee. *The Northern Teacher in the South, 1862–1870.* Nashville: Vanderbilt University Press, 1941.

Talbot, Edith Armstrong. *Samuel Chapman Armstrong, A Biographical Study.* New York: Doubleday, Page, and Co., 1904.

Thornbrough, Emma Lou. "The Brownsville Episode and the Negro Vote." *Mississippi Valley Historical Review* 44 (December 1957): 469–83.

————. *T. Thomas Fortune: Militant Journalist.* Chicago: Univ. of Chicago Press, 1972.

Thrasher, Max Bennett. "How Life in a Country Town Was Made Social." *Chautauquan* 30 (Jan. 1900): 360–63.

————. *Tuskegee: Its Story and Its Work.* 1901; Reprint. New York: Negro Universities Press, 1969.

————. "Tuskegee Negro Conference." *Chautauquan* 31 (Aug. 1900): 504–7.

Tinsley, J. A. "Roosevelt, Foraker and the Brownsville Affray." *Journal of Negro History* 41 (January 1956): 43–65.

Tuskegee Normal and Industrial Institute: Its Methods, Its Spirit, Its Ideals. American Association of School Administration Report. 1905. Tuskegee Archives.

Ulich, Robert. *History of Educational Thought.* New York: American Book Co., 1950.

U. S. Bureau of the Census. *Negro Population, 1790–1915.* Washington, D.C.: Government Printing Office, 1918.

Vincent, Charles. "Booker T. Washington's Tour of Louisiana, April, 1915." *Louisiana History* 22 (Spring 1981): 189–98.

Wadsworth, Erwing W. "A Historical Perspective of Education in Macon County, Alabama: 1836–1967." Ph.D. diss., Auburn University, 1968.

Walker, Anne K. *Tuskegee and the Black Belt: A Portrait of a Race.* Richmond: Dietz Press, 1944.

Walton, John C. *Hampton Normal and Agricultural Institute: Its Evolution and Contribution to Education as a Land Grant College.* Bureau of Education, U.S. Department of Interior, Bulletin no. 27. Washington, D.C.: Government Printing Office, 1923.

Washington, Booker T. "Aims of Tuskegee Institute." *Southern Letter* 28 (Dec. 1912): 48–49.

————. *Character Building.* New York: Doubleday, Page and Co., 1902.

————. "Christmas Days in Old Virginia." *Suburban Life.* 5 (1907): 336–37.

————. "Cruelty in the Congo Country." *Outlook* 78 (Oct. 1904): 375–77.

————. *Frederick Douglass.* Philadelphia and London: G. W. Jacobs and Co., 1907.

————. "Fundamental Needs for the Progress of the Race." 1904. Tuskegee Archives.

————. *The Future of the American Negro.* Boston: Small, Maynard, 1899.

————. "Industrial Education in Africa." *Independent,* 60 (March 15, 1906): 616–19.

————. "Is the Negro Having a Fair Chance?" *Century* 85 (Nov. 1912): 50–55.

————. *My Larger Education*. New York: Doubleday, Page and Co., 1911.

————. "My Life Work at Tuskegee, Alabama." *New York Teacher's Magazine* 2 (June 1899): 36–38.

————. "My Views of Segregation Laws." *New Republic* 5 (Dec. 1915): 112–15.

————. *The Negro in Business*. Boston and Chicago: Hertel, Jenkins and Co., 1907.

————. "The Negroes' Life in Slavery." *Outlook* 93 (Sept. 11, 1909): 71–78.

————. "The Privilege of Service." *Southern Workman* 36 (Dec. 1907): 684–88.

————. *Putting the Most into Life*. New York: T. Y. Crowell and Co., 1906.

————. "Returning Home to Roanoke, Virginia." Speech of Sept. 25, 1908. Tuskegee Archives, Box 117.

————. *Some Results of the Armstrong Idea*. Hampton, Va.: Hampton Institute Press, 1909.

————. *Sowing and Reaping*. Boston: L. C. Page and Co., 1900.

————. *The Story of My Life and Work*. Naperville, Ill.: J. L. Nichols, 1900.

————. *The Story of the Negro: The Rise of the Race from Slavery*. 2 vols. New York: Doubleday, Page and Co., 1909.

————. *Tuskegee and Its People*. New York: D. Appleton and Co., 1905.

————. "Two Generations Under Freedom." *Outlook* 73 (Feb. 7, 1903): 293–305.

————. "A University Education for Negroes." *Independent* 68 (March 1910): 613–18.

————. *Up from Slavery*. New York: Doubleday, Page and Co., 1901.

————. "What I Am Trying to Do." *World's Work* 27 (Nov. 1913): 102–6.

————. *Working with the Hands*. New York: Doubleday, Page and Co., 1904.

Washington, Booker T., and Robert E. Park. *The Man Farthest Down: A Record of Observations and Study in Europe*. New York: Doubleday, Page and Co., 1912.

Washington, E. Davidson, ed. *Selected Speeches of Booker T. Washington*. Garden City, N.Y.: Doubleday, Doran and Co., 1932.

Weeks, Stephen B. *Southern Quakers and Slavery: A Study in Institutional History*. Baltimore: Johns Hopkins Press, 1896.

Wells, H. G. *The Future in America: A Search after Realities*. London, 1906.

Wesley, Charles H. "Lincoln's Plan for Colonizing the Emancipated Negro." *Journal of American History* 4 (January 1919).

West, Richard S. *Lincoln's Scapegoat General: A Life of Benjamin F. Butler, 1818–1893*. Boston: University Press, 1965.

Wiley, Bell Irvin. *Southern Negroes, 1861–1865*. 1938: Reprint. Baton Rouge: Louisiana State University Press, 1974.

Williamson, Joel. *After Slavery: The Negro in South Carolina During Reconstruction, 1861–1877*. Chapel Hill: University of North Carolina Press, 1965.

————. "The Meaning of Freedom." In *Reconstruction*, edited by Kenneth M.

Stampp and Leon F. Litwack, 193–219. Baton Rouge: Louisiana State University Press, 1969.

Wingfield, Marshall. *Franklin County, Virginia: A History*. Berryville, Va.: Chesapeake Book Co., 1964.

Wise, John S. *The End of an Era*. Boston: Houghton, Mifflin, and Co., 1899.

Woodson, Carter G. *Early Negro Education in West Virginia*. Institute, W.Va., 1934.

————. *The Education of the Negro Prior to 1861*. 2d ed. 1919: Reprint. New York: Arno Press, 1968.

————. *The History of the Negro Church*. Washington, D.C.: Associated Publishers, 1921.

Woodward, C. Vann. *Origins of the New South, 1877–1913*. Baton Rouge: Louisiana State University Press, 1951.

————. *The Strange Career of Jim Crow*. New York: Oxford University Press, 1957.

Work, Monroe E. "Tuskegee Institute More than an Educational Institute." *Journal of Educational Sociology* 7 (November 1933): 197–205.

Wright, Stephen J. "The Development of the Hampton-Tuskegee Pattern of Higher Education." *Phylon* 10 (Fall 1949): 335–42.

INDEX

Library of Congress Cataloging-in-Publication Data

Denton, Virginia Lantz.
    Booker T. Washington and the adult education movement / Virginia
Lantz Denton.
        p.   cm.
    Includes bibliographical references and index.
    ISBN 0–8130–1182–5
    1. Adult education—United States—History.   2. Washington, Booker
T., 1856–1915—Contributions in adult education.   I. Title.
LC5251.D46   1993   92–27094
374′.973—dc20   CIP